Aunt Bee's
DELIGHTFUL
DESSERTS

Aunt Bee's
DELIGHTFUL
DESSERTS

KEN BECK and JIM CLARK

RUTLEDGE HILL PRESS

Nashville, Tennessee

Dedicated to the cast,
production crew, and writers of
The Andy Griffith Show.

The Andy Griffith Show and all related elements TM & © 1996 Mayberry Enterprises, Inc. All Rights Reserved.

Recipes, additional material, and compilation copyright © 1996 Ken Beck and Jim Clark.

Published in Nashville, Tennessee, by Rutledge Hill Press, Inc.
211 Seventh Avenue North, Nashville, Tennessee 37219

Distributed in Canada by H. B. Fenn & Company, Ltd.,
1090 Lorimar Drive, Mississauga, Ontario L5S 1R7

Typography by Roger A. DeLiso
Design by Harriette Bateman

Library of Congress Cataloging-in-Publication Data

Beck, Ken, 1951–
    Aunt Bee's delightful desserts / Ken Beck and Jim Clark.
      p.   cm.
    Consists of dessert recipes, plus photographs and dialogue from the Andy Griffith
television show.
    Includes index.
    ISBN 1-55853-402-4 (pbk.)
    1. Desserts. 2. Andy Griffith show (Television program).
I. Clark, Jim, 1960– .   II. Andy Griffith show (Television program).
III. Title.
TX773.B415 1996   96-13202
641.8'6—dc20   CIP

Printed in the United States of America

1 2 3 4 5 6 7 8 9— 99 98 97 96

Contents

A Mayberry Grace

Give us, Lord, a bit o' sun,
A bit o' work, and a bit o' fun.
Give us all in the struggle and splutter,
Our daily bread and a bit o' butter.

Origin unknown, submitted by Margie Mode
Clarksville, Indiana

A Favorite Recipe
Good for All Souls

Take a cup of kindness,
And mix it well with love.
Add a lot of patience,
And faith in God above.
Sprinkle very generously with
Joy and thanks and cheer.
And you'll have lots of angel food
To feast on all the year!

Submitted by Wanda C. Fields from her church cookbook
Reidsville, North Carolina

Aunt Bee

Acknowledgments

First and foremost, we salute the actors, writers, and production crew who worked on *The Andy Griffith Show* and built the place called Mayberry that has been enjoyed and loved by generations—a place that continues to warm our hearts today. Without the fruits of their talents and efforts, we wouldn't be able to offer pies or any of the other treats that have that very special flavor of Mayberry.

Many of those same people have shared recipes for this book and allowed us to use photographs that capture their Mayberry roles—all of which has helped this book be an even more meaningful tribute to Mayberry. We're most grateful for their participation.

We also thank everyone across the country who provided us with their favorite recipes. Recipes are the heart of any cookbook. (And we have the stomachs to prove it!) Attribution for each contributor accompanies the recipes, and we extend our heart-felt and stomachfelt gratitude to you all.

We likewise appreciate the assistance of several friends who helped us round up recipes from other folks. They are Kenneth Junkin, Neal Brower, David Fernandes, Dale Robinson, Nancy Clark, Harriet Patterson, Rebecca Barnes, John Faulkner, Katherine Clark, Albert Culbreath, Jim Ballance, John Lock, Randy Bash, Sherwin Bash, Carolyn Moore, Jon Snyder, Joel Rasmussen, Gary Cannon, Bruce Fisher, Alex Mebane, Janice Starnes, Ren Hood, Bert Phifer, Jan McNees, Peggy Myres, and Roland White.

In addition, we thank folks who made contributions beyond the recipes themselves. For assistance with photographs, we thank *The Tennessean* and Frank Sutherland; David Turner and Mitch Powers at Small World Productions; Dennis Hasty; Jackie Joseph; Arlene Golonka; Bob Wagner; Don Pitt; and Albert Cooper. For invaluable help both with photographs and in rounding up recipes, we give particular recognition to Jim Schwenke and Steve Cox.

We have special thanks for producer Aaron Ruben for introducing us to the tremendous work done by the National Court Appointed Special Advocate Association (CASA), and to Mercedes Lawry at National CASA for providing further information about the organization's efforts.

Our primary expertise with food is eating. As Goober once summed up our sentiments, "Three hours is a long time to go without eating." Ken has always cleaned his plate and saved room for dessert when eating the cooking of Grandma Beck, Grandma Rogers, and Hazel (Mama) Beck, and today he shares wife Wendy's good desserts with daughter Kylie and son Cole.

The clock in Jim's stomach first began ticking while eating desserts from the kitchen of Tonya (Gramma) Hamel and Nancy (Mom) Clark. And you'd better watch out for his hearty eatin' around wife Mary's cooking. Even after he's given battered beaters a licking, his stomach keeps on ticking.

Finally, we thank Viacom for entrusting this cookbook with us, and Larry Stone at Rutledge Hill Press for again believing in Mayberry and this project. Editor Amy Lyles Wilson, recipe editor Laurin Stamm, Charla Honea, Mike Towle, Jennifer B. Greenstein, Bryan Curtis, Kath Hansen, Kirsten Hansen, and many other fine folks at Rutledge Hill all helped this Mayberry dream become a reality.

Thank you all for your help. We appreciate it!

—Ken Beck and Jim Clark

Introduction

Aunt Bee is known far and wide for her cooking of all kinds, but if you were to ask Andy and Opie and Barney and Goober where Aunt Bee really shines, they'd most certainly agree it's her desserts. Of course, you might get that answer in part because desserts happen to be their favorite part of the meal. But either way, Aunt Bee's desserts win blue ribbons every time.

And so, following the warm response to our original *Aunt Bee's Mayberry Cookbook* (Rutledge Hill Press, 1991), a complete cookbook of everything from appetizers through desserts, we thought it would be fitting to devote a new cookbook to the sweetness of Mayberry.

Once again we have gathered recipes from folks who share both a fondness for Mayberry and a knack for cooking. Within these pages, you'll find more than 350 recipes from some of the country's best cooks and most devoted Mayberry fans. Many of these recipes—all of which are different from those in *Aunt Bee's Mayberry Cookbook*—have been family favorites for generations.

We've selected recipes that are representative of the kinds of down-home desserts you'd expect to find Aunt Bee making. But you'll also find quite a few that can be mastered by Opie and Goober, and even Ernest T. Bass. And we've blended in recipes that we learned about in neighboring Mt. Pilot and down the road in Raleigh, so you'll discover an occasional "big city" taste that we think you'll really enjoy.

This cookbook is meant to be a tribute (through recipes) to all of the talented people who helped make Mayberry such an appealing place. For that reason, we're especially pleased to be able to include recipes from more than forty of the show's actors, writers, production crew members, and their families. They've submitted some of their personal favorites, as well as ones that they think might be appropriate for their part in Mayberry.

Beyond the outstanding recipes, we've also tried to make this cookbook one that'll be as inviting just to sit down and read as it is to use for cooking. We've included more than a hundred photos (many rarely before seen) and lots of dialogue about food, eating, and cooking, plus trivia and other reading that we hope you'll find interesting and fun. There's even a checklist of episode summaries to help you maintain a balanced diet of *Andy Griffith Show* reruns.

And just as desserts are the crowning glory of a good meal, this book has a happy ending in that a portion of the proceeds will support the efforts of the National Court Appointed Special Advocate Association (CASA), which assists children in need (read more about the program and its ties to Mayberry in the back of this book).

We appreciate your coming to Mayberry for a visit, and we hope you'll come back often. But eating speaks louder than words, so let's see what mouthwatering desserts and happy memories Aunt Bee and friends have in store for us in the friendly town of Mayberry.

—Ken Beck and Jim Clark

The Andy Griffith Show

Cast

Andy Griffith—Andy Taylor
Don Knotts—Barney Fife
Ron Howard—Opie Taylor
Frances Bavier—Aunt Bee Taylor
Howard McNear—Floyd Lawson
Hal Smith—Otis Campbell
Betty Lynn—Thelma Lou
Aneta Corsaut—Helen Crump
Jim Nabors—Gomer Pyle
George Lindsey—Goober Pyle
Jack Dodson—Howard Sprague
Paul Hartman—Emmett Clark
Jack Burns—Warren Ferguson
Hope Summers—Clara Edwards Johnson
Denver Pyle—Briscoe Darling
Maggie Ann Peterson—Charlene Darling
The Dillards (Doug Dillard, Rodney Dillard, Mitch Jayne, and Dean Webb)—
    The Darling Boys
Howard Morris—Ernest T. Bass
Elinor Donahue—Ellie Walker
Jack Prince—Rafe Hollister
Dick Elliot—Mayor Pike
Parley Baer—Mayor Roy Stoner
Ken Berry—Sam Jones
Arlene Golonka—Millie Hutchins
Buddy Foster—Mike Jones
Joyce Jameson—Fun Girl Skippy
Jean Carson—Fun Girl Daphne and escaped convict Naomi
Dennis Rush—Howie Pruitt/Williams
Sheldon Golomb—Arnold Bailey
Richard Keith (Keith Thibodeaux)—Johnny Paul Jason
Bernard Fox—Malcolm Merriweather
James Best—Jim Lindsey
Hoke Howell—Dud Wash
Joanna Moore—Peggy McMillan
Cheerio Meredith—Emma (Watson) Brand
Clint Howard—Leon
Rance Howard—Various characters

Guest Stars

Jackie Joseph—Ramona Ankrum
Frank Sutton—Sgt. Carter
Charles P. Thompson—Asa Breeney
Enid Markey—Mrs. Mendelbright
Will Wright, Tol Avery, and Jason Johnson—Ben Weaver
Olan Soule—John Masters
Josie Lloyd—Lydia Crosswaith

Barbara Perry—Flossie, Mary Lee, Lavinia, and Doris Williams
Norman Leavitt, Trevor Bardette, and Cliff Norton—Wally
Jane Dulo—Escaped convict Sally
Barbara Eden—Ellen Brown
Mary Grace Canfield—Mary Grace Gossage
Joyce Van Patten—Laura Hollander
Robert Cornthwaite—Inspector Somerset
Alan Oppenheimer—Mr. Ruskin, the Interpreter
R.G. Armstrong—Farmer Flint
Elaine Joyce—Mavis Neff
The Country Boys (Roland White, LeRoy McNees, Clarence White,
    Eric White, and Billy Ray Latham)—Local musicians
Joel Redlin—Ferdie
Alvy Moore—Kitchenwares salesman
Dave Ketchum—Fred Michaels, Harry Walker
George Spence—Frank the fiancé
Brad (Joe Bolleter) Olson—Esquire Club member John Danby

Production Crew

Danny Thomas Productions—Production company
Sheldon Leonard—Executive producer
Richard O. Linke—Associate producer
Aaron Ruben—Producer and director
Bob Ross—Producer and director
Bob Sweeney—Director
Earle Hagen—Music director
Lee Greenway—Makeup
Frank E. Myers—Production manager
Ronald Jacobs—Assistant to producer
Sid Hickox—Director of photography
Ruth Burch—Casting
Rosemary Dorsey—Script continuity

Core Writers

Arthur Stander
David Adler
Jim Fritzell and Everett Greenbaum
Harvey Bullock and Ray Saffian Allen
Jack Elinson and Charles Stewart
Sam Bobrick and Bill Idelson
Fred S. Fox
Fred Freeman and Lawrence Cohen
Ben Joelson and Art Baer
Ben Gershman and Leo Solomon
Dick Bensfield and Perry Grant
Joe Bonaduce
Michael Morris and Seamon Jacobs
Aaron Ruben
Bob Ross

Aunt Bee's
DELIGHTFUL
DESSERTS

Sipping with both barrels

Beverages

Regal Order Root Beer Ice Cream Fluff

Here's to good fellowship.

2 cups root beer   2 cups vanilla ice cream

Pour ice cold, root beer into a large bowl set in a pan of crushed ice. Add ice cream and beat with a beater until smooth and fluffy. Serve immediately.

Makes 4 servings.

Alice Schwenke—Houston, Texas

Floyd's Punch in the Mouth

Not in the nose this time.

2 quarts water   1 large can pineapple juice
2 cups sugar   2 packages Kool-Aid, any flavor
Juice of 2 lemons   1 large bottle ginger ale

Mix all ingredients, except ginger ale, and chill. Add chilled ginger ale when ready to serve.

Makes 40 punch cups.

Judy B. Coleman—Asheboro, North Carolina

Barney's about to float out of the drugstore:

BARNEY: Another root beer float.

ELLIE: Barney, don't you think you've had enough?

BARNEY: Ellie, you let me worry about that.

ELLIE: But Barney, four inside of fifteen minutes! Putting all that ice cream and soda in your stomach—

BARNEY: Ellie, if you won't sell them to me, I'll just buy it somewheres else.

Wally's Bottle of Pop Float

A favorite of Opie's cool aunt.

Here's an easy recipe that's a real hit with my kids. After a fresh snowfall, scoop up a big glass of fresh snow. Pour in about a half glass of Coca-Cola (cream soda's good also). Stir and eat with a spoon. If you're feeling really exotic, give it a squirt of chocolate syrup.

Serves 1.

Bob Scheib, Wally's Service—Bradford, Ohio

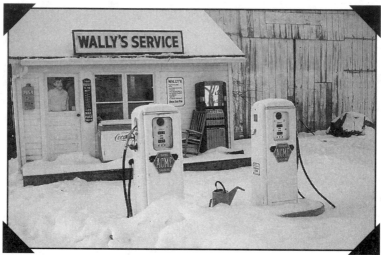

CHECK YOUR ANTI-FREEZE?—*Bob Scheib's replica of Wally's Service Station is covered from a snowfall that's perfect for making Wally's Bottle of Pop Float. The Mayberry Squad Car Rendezvous is held at this Bradford, Ohio, site each summer.* COURTESY OF ALBERT COOPER

Fill 'er up at Wally's:

FLOYD: You got the best pop in town.

WALLY: Yeah.

FLOYD: You've got more variety than they've got at the drugstore. Oh, they've got cherry and orange. You've got just about ever . . . Say, I noticed a new one in there for Huckleberry Smash. I would've tried it, but I already had the cap off of this Nectarine Crush.

WALLY: Another I've got you oughta try—high octane ethyl.

FLOYD: Oh, that's a new one, that high octane ethyl?

Elinor's Eggnog

A Mayberry holiday tradition.

6 eggs
1 cup milk
⅔ cup sugar
1 teaspoon nutmeg

¼ teaspoon salt
1 teaspoon vanilla extract
1 cup heavy whipping cream
Rum or brandy, optional

Separate eggs. Put whites in a bowl and refrigerate. In a glass bowl, beat egg yolks; then add milk, sugar, nutmeg, and salt. Mix well and microwave on high power for 3 minutes, stirring well after each minute. Chill mixture for several hours. Beat egg whites until fluffy and then gently stir them into chilled egg-milk mixture. Stir in vanilla. Whip cream until thick; then add to the rest. (When Barney's not looking, Otis likes to add a little rum or brandy.) Serve very cold. If using a punch bowl, chill bowl in freezer beforehand.

Makes 1 quart.

Cindee and Paul Mulik—Joplin, Missouri

It's beginning to taste a lot like Christmas:

ANDY: Oh, looky at the eggnog!
ELLIE: Try some right now.
ANDY: All right. I'll try a bite of that. Golly, that's good eggnog!

CHRISTMAS SPIRITS—*Even Scrooge couldn't resist Ellie's Eggnog during Christmastime in Mayberry.*

So how does Aunt Bee's lemonade rate with somebody who's been watching Andy replace shingles on a hot roof all day?:

MR. WHEELER: Mmm, mmm, mmm! Just hits the spot!

Mayberry Hospitality Lemonade

The friendly tonic.

1¼ cups sugar
½ cup boiling water

1½ cups fresh lemon juice
4½ cups water

Pour sugar into boiling water, stirring until sugar dissolves. Add lemon juice and cold water. Mix well. Serve over ice.

Makes 7 cups.

Alma Venable—Mount Airy, North Carolina

A sucker for a snowcone:

BARNEY: Boy, if I knew then what I know now. She used to do one thing that really used to burn me up.

ANDY: What was that?

BARNEY: You know how I like snowcones.

ANDY: Raspberry.

BARNEY: Right. Well, there wasn't a day went by that I didn't offer that girl a bite of my snowcone. You know what she used to do every single time?

ANDY: What?

BARNEY: She used to bite off the end, sip out all the syrup, and leave me with nothing but the ice.

ANDY: The ice?

BARNEY: Yeah, the ice.

ANDY: That's terrible. Today you'd know different.

BARNEY: Ha, are you kidding?! Listen, if I had a date with Vicky Harmes today and I got myself all shaved and I went over to her house with my snowcone, you know what I'd do?

ANDY: What?

BARNEY: The minute she opened that door I'd bite off the end of the cone, sip out the syrup, and hand her the cone. What do you think of that?

ANDY: Well, I'll tell you the truth, Barn. If I was Vicky Harmes and a 35-year-old man come up to my house with a snowcone in his hands, I wouldn't even answer the door.

4

Tweeky's Class Reunion Punch

Unforgettable.

1 large can pineapple juice
1 quart cranberry juice
1 2-liter bottle pale dry ginger ale

2 12-ounce cans frozen orange juice
concentrate

Freeze pineapple juice in ring. When frozen, put in bowl with remaining ingredients.

Makes about 30 punch cups.

Diane and Steve McCarty—New Freedom, Pennsylvania

Barney
"Tweeky" Fife

NEED GLASSES?—Andy and Barney strain to recognize faces while manning the punch bowl at their high-school class reunion.

5

Russian Diplomat Tea

A flow-through breakthrough.

4 small tea bags
½ gallon water
1 teaspoon whole cloves
1 stick cinnamon

2 cups sugar
1 cup orange juice
½ cup lemon juice
8 cups water

Put tea bags in water. Add remaining ingredients and let come to a boil but do not boil. Simmer for 30 minutes. Very good reheated.

Makes about ¾ gallon.

Toni and Neal Brower—Lewisville, North Carolina

Hot Plate Hot Chocolate

Folks will come knocking on your door for it.

1 8-quart box nonfat dry milk
1 pound confectioners' sugar
11 ounces coffee creamer

2 pounds Nestle's Quick
2 teaspoons cinnamon, optional

Mix all ingredients. Use ¼ cup mixture to 1 serving cup hot water. Stir.

Gary Wedemeyer—Fall Branch, Tennessee

Lady Shoplifter's Chocolate Nonfat Milkshake

Keeps you light on your feet.

1 pint chocolate nonfat yogurt or ice cream
4 cups nonfat milk (3 if you like it thick)
8 heaping tablespoons chocolate Ovaltine

Blend ingredients until you can drink mixture through a straw. If you can't drink it all, put it in a plastic cup and freeze it. It tastes good that way, too. Serves 4 to 6.

Sam Bobrick—Writer

Down the stretch

GREAT MOMENTS

Among the most popular episodes written by Sam Bobrick and partner Bill Idelson are "The Shoplifters" (Episode #117), "A Deal Is a Deal" (Episode #122), "Barney and Thelma Lou, Phfft!" (Episode #126), "Barney's Bloodhound" (Episode #128), "Barney Fife, Realtor" (Episode #143), and "Goober Takes a Car Apart" (Episode #144).

Myers Lake

It's the spot.

½ cup sugar
2 cups water
½ teaspoon cinnamon

2 to 3 cups orange juice, no pulp
1 cup pineapple juice
6 cups apple juice or cider

Boil water and sugar together until sugar melts, stirring often. Mix cinnamon in well; add juices. Refrigerate overnight or several hours to meld flavors. Decorate punch bowl with cinnamon sticks, orange and/or lemon slices studded with whole cloves, and frozen cider ice molds.

Makes 25 punch cups.

Janine Johnson—Orlando, Florida

"Now, take down your fishin' pole and meet me at the fishin' hole."

Howard's Bachelor Pad Punch

Bubbly, boys.

1 packet cherry Kool-Aid
1 packet strawberry Kool-Aid
2 cups sugar
2 quarts cold water

1 6-ounce can frozen orange juice
1 6-ounce can frozen lemonade
1 quart ginger ale

Dissolve Kool-Aid and sugar in water. Add juices. Pour into punch bowl and slowly add ginger ale.
Makes 1 gallon.

Janine Johnson—Orlando, Florida

Great shakes at Opie's new soda fountain job:

HOWARD (to Andy): He's a pro at that counter, all right. I especially like the way he makes the malteds. You know, he gets the ice cream mixed in thoroughly.

Later:

HOWARD: Hey, Ope. That malted you made for me at lunch—par excellence.

Without his bow tie, Howard could be Mayberry's swingingest bachelor.

BOY, OH, BOYSINGER'S!—Millie and Sam may be sweet on each other, but young Mike sticks to the pastries.

Breads

Mrs. Lesch's Lemon Bread

Right on the money.

1 cup sugar
5 tablespoons melted butter
2 eggs, beaten
½ cup milk
1½ cups all-purpose flour

½ teaspoon salt
1 lemon rind, grated
Juice of 1 lemon
⅓ cup sugar

Cream sugar, butter, and eggs. Add milk and dry ingredients alternately. Add lemon rind. Pour into a 9x5-inch (or two smaller pans) greased bread pans. Pull knife through batter to eliminate air bubbles. Bake at 350° for 1 hour.

For topping, mix lemon juice and sugar; pour over hot bread. Let bread sit overnight. Can refrigerate up to 3 weeks. Can freeze.

Makes 1 or 2 loaves.

Karen Mol—Grand Rapids, Michigan

Things get sweeter at the bakery when Millie arrives:

GOOBER: Hey, look. She's going into Boysinger's Bakery.

ANDY: Oh, yeah. I bet she's gonna work there. Mr. Boysinger said he had a new girl coming in from Mt. Pilot.

HOWARD: Hey, Andy. When's the last time you had a cream bun?

ANDY: Ohhh.

HOWARD: Me too, you know. And I got a real craving for a cream bun right now. How 'bout you?

ANDY: A little close to lunch, Howard.

HOWARD: Oh, it's my treat.

ANDY: Oh, I don't know.

HOWARD: Oh, come on, Andy. It's my treat, my treat.

ANDY: Okay. I wouldn't stand in between you and a cream bun.

HOWARD: Well, good. How about you, Goober?

GOOBER: I have to go to work, but you owe me one.

Mayberry Molasses Bread
It's slow good.

1 cup whole-wheat flour
1 cup all-purpose flour
1 teaspoon baking soda
1 teaspoon salt

½ cup sugar
½ cup dark molasses
1½ cups milk (do not use skim)

Preheat the oven to 325°. Spray a 9x4-inch loaf pan with cooking spray. Sift together dry ingredients. Mix liquid ingredients; then add to dry mixture. Mix well with electric mixer. Pour into greased loaf pan. Bake for 1½ hours. Cool for 10 minutes in pan; then turn out and allow to cool completely. Delicious with cream cheese.
     Freezes well.
     Makes 1 loaf.

Annette Davis—Greensboro, North Carolina

Jimmy's Chew Bread
It's dynamite!

2 sticks butter
1 box light brown sugar
2 eggs, beaten
1½ cups all-purpose flour

½ cup self-rising flour
1 cup chocolate chips
1 cup nuts

Melt butter; mix in remaining ingredients. Put in a greased 13x9-inch cake pan. Bake for 45 minutes at 350°.
     Makes 12 servings.

Rhonda Brewington—Lebanon, Tennessee

Goober Beanie Zucchini Bread
It's got you covered.

3 eggs
2¼ cups sugar
3 teaspoons vanilla extract
1 cup vegetable oil

3 teaspoons cinnamon
3 cups all-purpose flour
2 cups grated zucchini
Walnuts or pecans, optional

Use a large bowl to cream eggs and sugar. Add vanilla and oil. Sift remaining dry ingredients. Alternate adding dry ingredients and zucchini to bowl with oil, sugar, and eggs. Add nuts to taste. Bake in large loaf pans for 1 hour at 350°.

Makes 1½ large loaves.

Teri Cannon—Old Hickory, Tennessee

Barney's Judo Gingerbread

It's a snap.

½ cup butter
½ cup sugar
½ cup sorghum
½ cup sour milk
1 egg

¼ teaspoon soda
1 teaspoon ginger
1 teaspoon cinnamon
1 cup all-purpose flour

Mix all ingredients and bake in an 8x8-inch pan at 350° until sides pull away from pan, about 25 minutes.

Makes 8 servings.

Beverly Stump—Lebanon, Indiana

PASSING THE TIME—Let's hope this is nothing like the clock in Barney's stomach!

13

THREE'S COMPANY—And four's a crowd on this bench.

Depression Pancake
Provides deep-down goodness.

1. Take 1 egg (my mother wouldn't just take it; she'd borrow it from the neighbor).
2. Separate the white and the yolk.
3. Stir the yolk until smooth. Whip the white until fluffy.
4. Mix the yolk into the white and pour the mixture into a lightly greased frying pan.
5. Cook on both sides until golden brown.
6. Remove from pan and coat with sugar or jelly.
7. Serve and apologize.
   Serves 1 well.

Art Baer—Writer

Mr. Goss's Golden Puffs

No complaints here.

2 cups sifted flour
¼ cup sugar
3 tablespoons double-action
   baking powder
¾ teaspoon salt

1 teaspoon nutmeg
¼ cup oil
¾ cup milk
1 egg
Cinnamon sugar or confectioners' sugar

Sift dry ingredients together. Add oil, milk, and egg. Stir with a fork until thoroughly mixed. Drop by teaspoonful into deep, hot oil at 375°. (Note: Oil is 375° when a 1-inch bread cube browns in 40 seconds. If too many puffs are cooked at the same time, they will be soaked in grease. Puffs that are too large will not cook through.) Fry until golden brown, about 3 minutes. Drain on absorbent paper towels. Roll warm puffs in cinnamon sugar or glaze puffs by dipping into confectioners' sugar.

Makes about 2½ dozen.

Mary Ellis—Albuquerque, New Mexico

Cranston's Cranberry Apple Loaf

Let your taste buds be the judge!

1¼ cups sugar
½ cup shortening
2 eggs
½ cup sour cream
½ cup orange juice

3 cups self-rising flour
2 cups coarsely chopped fresh cranberries
1 cup shredded, peeled, cored apple
1 cup chopped nuts

Preheat the oven to 350°. Grease and flour bottom and ½ inch up sides of a 9-inch loaf pan. Cream sugar and shortening. Add eggs, sour cream, and orange juice; mix. Stir in flour just until moistened. Fold in cranberries, apples, and nuts and pour into prepared pan. Bake for 50 to 60 minutes. Cool for 10 minutes. Wrap tightly and refrigerate.

Makes 1 loaf.

Whitney Laird—Anniston, Alabama

THE ART OF WRITING

The first episode written by Art Baer and partner Ben Joelson was "Opie's Fortune" (Episode #136), and they went on to write others, such as "TV or Not TV" (Episode #150) and "Aunt Bee's Invisible Beau" (Episode #154), as well as the food-oriented "Eat Your Heart Out" (Episode #182) and George Lindsey's personal all-time favorite: "A Man's Best Friend" (Episode #170).

Country Girl's Banana-Carrot-Ginger Bread

Favored by the Country Boys.

2 ripe bananas, mashed
2 large or 3 medium carrots, grated
2 extra large eggs or ¾ cup
   egg substitute
⅓ cup canola oil
¼ cup orange blossom honey
1 teaspoon finely grated fresh ginger

Juice of ½ lemon
1⅔ cups whole-wheat flour
⅓ cup plain cornmeal (not self-rising)
¼ teaspoon salt
1 teaspoon baking soda
¼ teaspoon allspice
1½ cups chopped fresh walnuts

Preheat the oven to 350°. Grease (with margarine) and flour a loaf pan. Mix bananas, carrots, eggs, oil, honey, ginger, and lemon juice, either by hand or with electric mixer on low speed. Stir flour, cornmeal, salt, baking soda, and allspice in a separate bowl. Stir flour mixture and then walnuts into wet mixture, being careful not to overmix. Pour into loaf pan and bake for 1 hour, or until a wooden toothpick inserted in center comes out clean. Remove from pan and cool on a rack. (You can grate ginger with a cheese grater and put it in the lemon juice while you prepare the rest of the mixture. Then strain the lemon juice and add it to the batter. That way you won't have pieces of ginger in the bread and the ginger flavor won't be too strong.)
   Makes 1 loaf.

Diane Bouska—Nashville, Tennessee

Main Street Monkey Bread

Snappy breakfast dessert.

3 cans buttermilk biscuits
   (10-biscuit size)
1 cup granulated sugar
1 teaspoon cinnamon or other flavoring

1 cup chopped pecans, optional
1 cup brown sugar
1 stick margarine

Cut each biscuit into fourths with kitchen shears. Shake biscuits in a plastic bag with granulated sugar and cinnamon. (A few at a time works best.) Put layers of biscuits into a greased tube pan. Sprinkle chopped nuts between layers, if desired. Melt brown sugar and margarine. Let boil for 1 minute; then pour over biscuits. Bake at 350° for 35 minutes. Let stand for 10 minutes before removing from pan. To serve, just pinch off and eat with your fingers. Monkey see, monkey do!
   Makes about 40 pinches.

Mary and Charles Dowell, Snappy Lunch
Mount Airy, North Carolina

Fife the Fierce

Untapped Source of Lifetime Happiness Blueberry Muffins

Even better than being a civil servant.

1 egg, beaten
¼ cup oil, optional
½ to 1 cup honey
1¾ cups milk or water
1 to 2 cups blueberries (thaw and drain if using frozen; can use apples, bananas, etc.)

2 cups whole-wheat flour
2 teaspoons baking powder
½ teaspoon salt

Preheat oven to 375°. Mix wet ingredients, except blueberries; add to flour, baking powder, and salt, combining ingredients until flour is just moistened. Stir in fruit. Pour into oiled muffin pans or muffin papers. Bake for about 25 minutes.

Makes approximately 30 two-inch muffins.

Margaret Adams—Rockford, Illinois

Banana Nutsy Bread

Arresting flavor.

½ cup butter
1 cup sugar
2 eggs
1 cup crushed bananas

2 cups flour
1 teaspoon soda
½ cup nuts
¼ teaspoon salt

Mix butter and sugar. Add remaining ingredients and pour into a loaf pan. Bake for 40 to 50 minutes at 350°.

Makes 1 loaf.

Cindy and Andy Kinder—St. Peters, Missouri

Another party at Mrs. Wiley's?

Romeena's Creamed Corn Sticks Surprise!

Perfect for leftovers of Sweet Romeena's Creamed Corn on page 158 of Aunt Bee's Mayberry Cookbook.

2 cups cornbread stuffing mix
  in the canister
1 cup flour
¼ cup sugar
4 teaspoons baking powder
1 8-ounce serving cream-style corn
  (use a can, if necessary)

½ cup milk
¼ cup margarine or butter, melted
1 egg, slightly beaten
Your choice of rum, bourbon, maple
  syrup, sour cream, brown sugar,
  or confectioners' sugar
Fruit

Preheat the oven to 450°. Grease a cast-iron corn stick mold. Place prepared mold in oven; heat for 10 minutes prior to spooning in batter.

For batter, mix stuffing, flour, sugar, and baking powder in large bowl. Stir in corn, milk, margarine, and egg. Spoon ¼ cup batter into each indentation of mold. Bake for 12 minutes, or until golden brown. After creamed corn sticks are baked, at your discretion, drizzle a tad of syrup or "spirits" over sticks, or serve with a dollop of sour cream topped with brown or confectioners' sugar. Be a free spirit and try both kinds of sugar! Serve with favorite fruit in season.

Makes about 2 dozen.

Jackie Joseph—Cast member

FAIR LADY OF MAYBERRY

In her one appearace as Ramona Ankrum, Jackie Joseph won the heart of Ernest T. Bass and fans in "My Fair Ernest T. Bass" (Episode #113).

And after we walked all the way over here just for cream buns:

MILLIE: Well, what can I do for you?

HOWARD: Andy here has a real craving for a cream bun. Right, Andy?

ANDY: Yes, I do.

MILLIE: Oh, I'm sorry. Mr. Boysinger didn't bake the cream buns yet. What about a lemon roll or a ladyfinger. I know. What about a nice rum cake, sheriff?

ANDY: Oh, I don't know. It's a little early in the day for that.

HOWARD: Actually, the alcoholic content of rum cake is very negligible, Andy.

ANDY: Well, Howard, if you want to take your chances with rum cake, you're on your own. I have to go to work. Hey, Howard, when you come out of here you better be able to walk a chalk line.

Mama Morelli's Modern Panettone

You'll knead a machine.

Dough:
½ cup milk
2 eggs
5 tablespoons margarine or butter
½ teaspoon salt
3¼ cups flour
3 tablespoons sugar

1 package yeast
½ cup liquid from cherries (see below)
Goodies:
1 cup chocolate chips
⅔ cup slivered almonds
1 10-ounce jar pitted, stemless
  maraschino cherries

Drain cherries and reserve liquid. Allow "dough" ingredients to come to room temperature; then put in pan in order recommended by bread machine manufacturer. If there's less than ½ cup of liquid from cherries, add a little milk to make ½ cup.

Select "Fruit and Nut" cycle, set crust to the lightest possible setting, and press Start. When the machine beeps, add the "goodies." If your machine doesn't have a beep signal, you'll have to watch the time and add these ingredients about 5 minutes before the end of the last kneading cycle. Some machines may have difficulty mixing all of the ingredients; it may be necessary to stir dough further with a wooden spoon.

Makes 1 loaf.

Cindee and Paul Mulik—Joplin, Missouri

20

Shoplifter's Sticky Buns

They'll give you sticky fingers.

2 tablespoons maple syrup
3 tablespoons brown sugar
Chopped pecans
1 can refrigerated biscuits (10-biscuit size)

1 stick melted butter
Mixture of 1 cup white sugar
    and cinnamon

Preheat the oven to 375°. Using an 8x8-inch cake pan, pour syrup on bottom of pan. Sprinkle brown sugar over syrup and then nuts on top of sugar. Dip biscuits in butter and roll in sugar-cinnamon mixture and place in prepared pan (will hold only 9 biscuits).

Bake for 20 to 25 minutes or until quite brown. Place aluminum foil on a cake rack and turn up sides of foil. Turn rolls out on foil. Serve hot.

Serves 6 to 8.

Ann Clark—Charlotte, North Carolina

Dummy and dummier

21

Stranger in Town Strawberry Bread

This'll make you feel right at home in Mayberry.

3 cups all-purpose flour
1 teaspoon soda
1 teaspoon salt
1 tablespoon cinnamon
2 cups sugar

4 eggs, beaten
2 10-ounce packages sliced frozen
   strawberries, thawed
¾ cup chopped pecans
1¼ cups vegetable oil

Preheat the oven to 350°. Combine all ingredients in a bowl; mix well. Pour into 2 greased 9x5-inch loaf pans. Bake for 1 hour. Remove to a wire rack. Cut into thin slices.

   Makes 1 loaf.

Alma Venable, Mayberry Motor Inn—Mount Airy, North Carolina

Wally's Super Pumpkin-Nut Bread

Acme performance.

1 cup vegetable oil
⅔ cup water
4 eggs
3 cups sugar
1 can (15 to 16 ounces) cooked,
   mashed pumpkin
2½ cups unbleached flour
1 cup whole-wheat flour

2 teaspoons baking soda
1½ teaspoons salt
2 teaspoons cinnamon
1 teaspoon nutmeg
1 teaspoon ginger
1½ to 2 cups chopped walnuts
1 cup raisins, optional

Preheat the oven to 350°. Lightly grease 2 loaf pans, bottoms only, with flour. In a large bowl combine oil, water, eggs, sugar, and pumpkin. Blend until well creamed. In a large mixing bowl, combine all dry ingredients, except nuts and raisins. Add mixture by thirds until dry ingredients are moist (don't overmix). Add nuts and raisins. Pour into loaf pans and bake

---

ANDY'S MEAL SERVICE QUIZ

1. Who serves Andy the three spaghetti dinners he eats in one evening?
   Answer: Goober, Howard Sprague and his mother, and Helen and her Uncle Edward
2. What is the "secret" ingredient of each spaghetti sauce?
   Answer: Oregano
3. What do Juanita Beasley, Olive, and Flora Malherbe have in common?
   Answer: They're all waitresses in Mayberry.

---

for 1 hour to 1 hour and 15 minutes. If tops appear to brown too quickly, reduce oven temperature to 300° after 30 minutes. Tops should be peaked and cracked for traditional looking loaves. Allow to cool for 30 minutes to 1 hour before removing to a rack for cooling. Double wrap to store. Freezes well.

Makes two 5x9-inch loaves or 4 small loaves.

LuAnne and Bill Dugan—Wynne, Arkansas

Keeper of the Door Monkey Bread

Just say "Geronimo" and you're in for a treat!

4 cans refrigerated biscuits
  (10-biscuit size)
2 tablespoons cinnamon
¾ cup sugar

1 cup brown sugar
1½ sticks margarine
1 cup chopped nuts

Quarter biscuits and shake in a large bowl with cinnamon and sugar. (Let this sit while dissolving other ingredients; then shake again.)

Dissolve brown sugar and margarine. When dissolved, add nuts. Grease a bundt pan; then place ½ biscuits in pan. Pour ½ dissolved mixture over them; then add remaining biscuits and mixture. Bake at 350° for 30 minutes.

Serves 10.

Wanda C. Fields—Reidsville, North Carolina

"Enter in the name of good fellowship."

Ellie and Andy

Cakes

Aunt Edna's Cake
Sugar and spice and everything nice.

1 cup oil
1½ cups sugar
3 eggs
1 cup buttermilk
1 teaspoon vanilla extract
2 cups flour
1 teaspoon salt
1 teaspoon soda
1 teaspoon nutmeg
1 teaspoon cinnamon
1 teaspoon allspice, optional

1 small jar baby food purée with tapioca
  (any flavor)
Topping:
1 cup sugar
½ cup buttermilk
½ teaspoon soda
⅛ teaspoon salt
4 tablespoons oleo
1 tablespoon light corn syrup
½ teaspoon vanilla extract
Pecans, chopped

Mix oil, sugar, eggs, buttermilk, and vanilla. Add flour with salt, soda, nutmeg, cinnamon, and allspice to oil mixture. Stir in baby food. Bake in a 13x9x2-inch pan for 1 hour at 300°. Cool. Stick toothpick in top of cake to let topping run through.

For topping, mix first 6 ingredients and cook over low heat until soft ball forms in cold water; add vanilla. Pour over cake. Cover with chopped pecans.

Serves 10 to 12.

Diana and Bob Scheib, Wally's Service—Bradford, Ohio

A fruitcake is missing:

BARNEY: Andy, I don't like to say this, but—
  ANDY: You don't have to.
BARNEY: If it was anybody else, I'd say she was tiddly.
  ANDY: If it was anybody else, you'd be right, but she won't even allow fruitcake in the house—account of a brother she had.
BARNEY: Well, where there's smoke, there's firewater.

Helen's Homemade Five-Pound Fruit Cake

Makes the grade.

1 quart chopped pecans
1 4-ounce can flaked coconut
½ pound candied pineapple, cut into chips
½ pound candied cherries, cut into chips
1 1-pound box white raisins
1½ cups plain flour

1½ cups sugar
2 sticks butter
¼ cup shortening
½ cup whiskey
1½ cups self-rising flour

In a large bowl, mix pecans, coconut, and fruits with plain flour. Let sit for 3 to 4 hours or overnight.

To make batter, combine sugar, butter, shortening, whiskey, and self-rising flour. Mix with fruit and nuts. Line bottom of a tube pan with greased and floured brown paper. Pack mixture in pan. Start in a cold oven and bake at 300° for approximately 1½ hours.

Serves 10 to 12.

Helen Phifer—Marshville, North Carolina

Charlie Varney's Vanilla Wafer Cake

A great deal is in the cards.

Cake:
2 cups sugar
1 cup butter or margarine
6 eggs
1 12-ounce box vanilla wafers, crushed
½ cup milk
¼ cup oil
1 7-ounce package grated coconut
1 cup chopped nuts (or less)

1 teaspoon vanilla extract
Sauce:
⅓ cup milk
⅓ cup sugar
Frosting:
8 ounces cream cheese
½ cup butter
1 pound confectioners' sugar
1 teaspoon vanilla extract

Cream sugar, butter, and eggs. Add vanilla wafers and milk alternately.

Mix oil, coconut, nuts, and vanilla. Bake at 350° for 35 to 45 minutes. Test with a toothpick. Makes 3 layers.

For sauce, combine ⅓ cup milk and ⅓ cup sugar, bring to boil, and pour over layers while warm.

For frosting, cream cream cheese and butter. Add confectioners' sugar and vanilla. Frost cake. Freezes well.

Serves 10 to 12.

Kevin Snead—Tuscaloosa, Alabama

Shopping pals

Summer's Day Dessert
Refreshing!

1 9-ounce box golden cake mix
1 can crushed pineapple, drained
2 packages instant vanilla pudding

3 cups milk
Nondairy whipped topping, optional
Chopped nuts, optional

Prepare cake according to package directions. Bake in a 13x9-inch pan. Spread drained pineapple evenly over cooled cake. Mix pudding with milk. Pour over cake. If desired, cover with whipped topping and sprinkle with chopped nuts.

Serves 12.

Terry Quinsey—Fort Erie, Ontario

Hearty Eatin' Heavenly Hash Cake

More power to ya!

3 sticks margarine, divided
8 tablespoons cocoa, divided
2 cups sugar
1½ cups flour
2 eggs

1 cup pecans
Miniature marshmallows
1 box confectioners' sugar
4 tablespoons evaporated milk (or more)

Combine 2 sticks margarine, 4 tablespoons cocoa, sugar, flour, eggs, and pecans and mix well. Pour into a greased and floured 13x9x2-inch cake pan. Bake at 350° for 25 minutes. When done, cover with miniature marshmallows and return to oven. Let marshmallows melt. Remove and cool in pan.

For frosting, mix 4 tablespoons cocoa, 1 stick margarine, confectioners' sugar, and evaporated milk until creamy. Spread on cooled cake in pan. Serves 12.

Linda Snead—Tuscaloosa, Alabama

Strawberry Festival Cake

Raleigh good.

1 box white cake mix
1 3-ounce package strawberry gelatin
¾ cup Crisco oil
¾ cup milk
4 eggs

1 cup shredded coconut
1 cup chopped pecans
1 10-ounce package frozen strawberries
1 stick margarine
1 pound confectioners' sugar

Blend white cake mix with gelatin. Add oil and milk. Add eggs, 1 at a time, beating well after each addition. Fold in ½ of the coconut, ½ of the nuts, and ½ of the thawed strawberries and juice. Pour into 3 greased 8-inch layer pans and bake at 350° until done.

For frosting, whip margarine with confectioners' sugar until light and fluffy. Whip in remainder of strawberries, using enough juice to give proper spreading consistency. Fold in remaining nuts and coconut. Serves 10 to 12.

Linda Snead—Tuscaloosa, Alabama

Good one, Goob:

GOOBER: Hey, Mill. How's the sweetest thing in the bakery?

28

BAKERY SWEETNESS—Millie Hutchins

Millie's Chocolate Chip Chocolate Cake

Direct from Boysinger's Bakery.

½ pound pitted dates, quartered
1 teaspoon baking soda
¼ pound butter
1 cup sugar
2 tablespoons unsweetened cocoa

2 eggs
½ cup sifted flour
Chocolate chips
Chopped nuts
Confectioners' sugar

Put dates in boiling water; let soak and cool. Add baking soda. Cream butter; then add sugar, cocoa, and eggs. Beat for a long time. Add date mixture and flour. Pour into a 13x9-inch greased pan. Sprinkle top with chocolate chips and nuts. Bake at 350° for 30 to 35 minutes. Dust with confectioners' sugar.

Serves 10 to 12.

Arlene Golonka—Cast member

Boysinger's Bakery Cocoa Cupcakes

Nice and sweet.

1¼ cups sugar
¾ cup shortening
2 eggs
2 cups sifted flour
1 tablespoon cocoa
1 teaspoon salt

1 teaspoon vanilla extract
1 cup cold water mixed with 1 teaspoon
   baking soda
1 cup miniature chocolate chips
Chopped nuts, optional

Mix sugar, shortening, and eggs. Add other ingredients. Add chopped nuts, if desired. Pour into baking cups and bake for 20 minutes in a 350° oven.

Makes about 2 dozen.

Heidi Krueger—Cokato, Minnesota

NIP IT IN THE BUD!—
Barney knows that Mayberry's Main Street is not Park Place.

Deputy Fife's Dusty Gun Streusel Coffee Cake

Don't cut it with a rusty knife!

1½ cups self-rising flour
¾ cup sugar
¼ cup butter
1 egg
½ cup milk
1 teaspoon vanilla extract

½ cup brown sugar
2 tablespoons plain flour
1½ teaspoons cinnamon
2 tablespoons melted butter
½ cup chopped pecans

Sift together flour and sugar. Cut in ¼ cup butter. Blend egg and milk and add to flour mixture. Add vanilla and mix to make batter.

For topping, mix remaining ingredients.

Place half of the batter in an 8x8-inch or 9x9-inch baking dish; add half of the topping mixture. Then add remaining batter. Finish with topping. Bake at 375° for 30 minutes.

Serves 8.

Julia, Tim, and Hayley Dale—Glen Alpine, North Carolina

Roger Hanover's Cheesecake

If you don't like it, just "hang it on the wall."

Crust:
1½ cups graham cracker crumbs
¼ cup sugar
1 stick margarine, softened
Filling:
24 ounces cream cheese, softened
1½ cups sugar
⅛ teaspoon salt

4 eggs
1 teaspoon vanilla extract
Topping:
1 cup sour cream
¼ cup sugar
1 teaspoon vanilla extract
Fruit, optional

Mix first 3 ingredients to form crust. Press over bottom of a greased 9-inch springform pan. Chill.

Beat softened cream cheese; blend in sugar and salt. Beat until fluffy. Add eggs 1 at a time, beating well after each addition. Add vanilla. Pour into crust. Bake at 350° for 50 minutes or until firm in center (cake browns on top and splits along the edges). Remove from the oven and let sit for 15 minutes. Warm the oven to 450°.

For topping, mix sour cream, sugar, and vanilla. Pour over cheesecake and return to the oven for 10 minutes. Cool for a few minutes and remove side of pan. Chill. May be served plain or topped with fruit of your choice.

Makes 12 servings.

Susie Luguire—Tuscaloosa, Alabama

Bottle of Pop Cake
Fabulous fizz.

2 cups all-purpose flour
2 cups sugar
2 sticks butter or margarine
1 cup Coca-Cola
3 tablespoons cocoa powder
½ cup buttermilk
1 teaspoon baking soda
2 eggs
1 teaspoon vanilla extract

1½ cups miniature marshmallows
Frosting:
1 stick butter
3 tablespoons cocoa powder
6 tablespoons Coca-Cola
1 pound confectioners' sugar, sifted
1 cup chopped pecans
1 teaspoon vanilla extract

Preheat the oven to 350°. Grease a 9x12-inch pan. Stir flour and sugar in a large mixing bowl. Melt butter; add Coca-Cola, cocoa, and buttermilk to butter in a saucepan and bring to a boil (or melt in the microwave and mix well). Pour butter-Coca-Cola mixture over flour mixture; add baking soda, eggs, vanilla, and marshmallows and mix well. Pour batter into prepared pan and bake for about 45 minutes, or until it tests done. Let cake cool for 10 to 15 minutes.

For frosting, combine butter, cocoa, and Coca-Cola in a pan and bring to a boil (or heat in the microwave). Remove from heat; mix in confectioners' sugar, pecans, and vanilla. Spread over warm cake.

Mary Alice Holt—Elizabethtown, Kentucky

Front porch topic:
    ANDY: You know what'd be a good idea?
BARNEY: What?
    ANDY: We all went up town and got us a bottle of pop.
BARNEY: Yeah, that's a good idea—we all went up town and got a bottle of pop.
    ANDY: You think Mr. Tucker'd like to go?
BARNEY: Why don't we ask him if he'd like to go up town and get a bottle of pop.
    ANDY: (leaning over) Mr. Tucker?
(No response from Mr. Tucker, who has nodded off into peaceful sleep.)
    ANDY: (to Barney) Wanna let's me and you go?
BARNEY: Where?
    ANDY: Up town and get a bottle of pop?
(Barney nods.)

One false move and blooey!

Loaded Goat Blueberry Cheesecake
Bluey.

Crumb Mixture:
1 box yellow cake mix
⅓ cup soft butter
Filling:
3 large eggs
¾ cup sugar
16 ounces cream cheese, softened

2 teaspoons vanilla extract
Topping:
2 cups sour cream
¼ cup sugar
1 tablespoon vanilla extract
1 can blueberry pie filling

For crumb mixture, mix cake mix, butter, and 1 egg until crumbly. Press lightly into a 9x13x2-inch baking dish.

For filling, beat 2 eggs, ¾ cup sugar, cream cheese, and 2 teaspoons vanilla until smooth. Pour over crumb mixture. Bake at 350° for 25 minutes or until set.

For topping, mix sour cream, ¼ cup sugar, and 1 tablespoon vanilla. Spread over cheese. Cool. Spread blueberry pie filling on top. Refrigerate overnight.

Serves 12.

Deloris Cummings—Tuscaloosa, Alabama

Mrs. Hawkin's Chocolate Cake

All eyes are on this one.

2 cups flour
2 cups sugar
1 stick butter
½ cup shortening
1 cup cold water
4 tablespoons cocoa
½ cup buttermilk or
   1½ teaspoons vinegar with ½ cup milk
1 teaspoon baking soda
1 teaspoon cinnamon

1 teaspoon vanilla extract
¼ teaspoon salt
2 eggs
Frosting:
1 stick butter
4 tablespoons cocoa
5 tablespoons milk
1 teaspoon vanilla extract
1 box powdered sugar
½ cup chopped nuts

Mix flour and sugar. Boil butter, shortening, water, and cocoa. Pour over flour and sugar mixture and beat. Add buttermilk and milk. Add cinnamon, soda, vanilla, and salt; then add 2 eggs. Mix well and bake in a greased 13x9-inch pan at 400° for 20 minutes.

For frosting, boil butter, cocoa, and milk. Add vanilla, powdered sugar, and nuts.

Suzanne and Jay Lipscomb—Dallas, Texas

Mayberry smiles

Mrs. Wiley's Wine Cake

Favored in the Back Bay.

½ cup chopped pecans
1 box yellow cake mix
1 3-ounce box instant vanilla pudding
2 teaspoons cinnamon
¼ cup brown sugar
¼ cup white sugar
¾ cup water
¾ cup oil

¼ cup wine (Riunite soft semi-dry)
4 eggs
Confectioners' sugar
Glaze:
1 stick margarine
1 cup sugar
¼ cup water
¼ cup wine

Sprinkle pecans in bottom of a greased bundt pan. Mix remaining ingredients. Pour into the prepared pan. Bake at 325° for 1 hour. Check after 40 minutes. Sprinkle top of cake with confectioners' sugar.

For glaze, boil margarine, sugar, and water for 2 or 3 minutes. Remove from heat; add wine. Beat for 1 minute. Spoon ½ over hot cake in pan. Turn cake out on plate and spoon remaining glaze over cake. Freezes well. Serves 10 to 12.

Judy Cannon—Mt. Juliet, Tennessee

Irma Bishop's Miss Congeniality Cake

A real beauty.

¾ cup warm water
3 heaping tablespoons cocoa
1 teaspoon baking soda
2½ cups sugar
½ pound butter
3 eggs
1 cup buttermilk

3 cups plain flour
1 teaspoon vanilla extract
Filling:
2½ cups sugar
1 cup Pet milk
½ pound butter
1 teaspoon vanilla extract

Mix and dissolve warm water, cocoa, and soda. Cream sugar and butter. Add remaining ingredients to sugar and butter mixture. Add cocoa and baking soda mixture to batter and beat. Spray 4 layer pans with nonstick cooking spray. Bake at 350° for 30 minutes, or until a toothpick comes out clean.

For filling, mix sugar, milk, and butter well. Place over medium heat. Stir constantly until it boils. Cook at low to medium boil for 35 minutes. Add vanilla and beat until cool. Spread filling on top of each layer and over entire cake. Serves 10 to 12.

Jeanne Swanner Robertson—Burlington, North Carolina

Name Ain't Clem Applesauce Cake
It's d'Andy!

2 teaspoons baking soda dissolved in
  ½ cup boiling water, cooled
½ cup shortening
2 cups sugar
1 egg
1½ cups applesauce
2½ cups flour

½ teaspoon salt
½ teaspoon cinnamon
½ teaspoon nutmeg
½ teaspoon cloves
½ cup nuts, floured
1 cup raisins, floured
1 can caramel icing

Mix all ingredients and pour into a 9x13-inch pan. Bake at 350° for 45 minutes. Ice with storebought caramel icing.
    Serves 12.

Beverly Stump—Lebanon, Indiana

Wally's 7-Up Pound Cake
You'll never tire of this.

2 sticks margarine
½ cup shortening
3 cups sugar
5 eggs
1½ teaspoons lemon extract

1½ teaspoons vanilla extract
3 cups all-purpose flour, measured
  before sifting
8 ounces 7-Up

Cream margarine, shortening, and sugar. Add eggs 1 at a time, beating after each addition. Add lemon and vanilla extracts and beat. Add flour and 7-Up, beating after each addition. Finish with 7-Up. Spray a 10-inch tube pan with nonstick cooking spray. Cook at 300° for 1½ hours or until cake tests done. Let sit out for 30 minutes before placing on a plate.
    Serves 10 to 12.

Jeanne Swanner Robertson—Burlington, North Carolina

Beast of the Fourth Floor Banana Split Cake
Passes the test.

2 sleeves graham crackers
1 cup margarine, melted and divided
1 box confectioners' sugar
3 to 4 bananas, sliced

1 large can crushed pineapple, drained
1 12-ounce carton nondairy whipped
  topping
1 pint strawberries or cherries

36

Make crust with graham crackers mixed with ½ cup melted margarine. Press into bottom of a 13x9-inch cake pan. Whip confectioners' sugar and ½ cup melted margarine until fluffy. Spread on top of crust. Layer sliced bananas and crushed pineapple. Top with whipped topping, followed by strawberries or cherries. Refrigerate.

Serves 12.

Cindy and Andy Kinder—St. Peters, Missouri

Whistling team

Happy couple

Ernest T.'s Mother Figure
Fig Preserves Loaf Cake

Make this fig yours.

1 cup buttermilk
3 eggs, beaten
1 cup canola or safflower oil
1½ cups sugar
1 teaspoon vanilla flavoring
½ teaspoon butter flavoring
1 teaspoon orange extract
2 cups all-purpose flour

1 teaspoon cinnamon
1 teaspoon allspice
1 teaspoon baking soda
½ teaspoon salt
1 cup chopped pecans, rolled in flour
1 cup fig preserves (whirl in blender to
    remove large chunks)

Mix buttermilk, eggs, canola oil, sugar, vanilla and butter flavorings, and orange extract. Sift together flour, cinnamon, allspice, soda, and salt; add to buttermilk mixture. Fold in pecans and fig preserves. Bake in a loaf pan at 300° for approximately 1 hour. This moist cake keeps well in the refrigerator.

Makes 1 loaf.

Linda Stewart—Dallas, Texas

Big Orange Slice Fruit Cake
What it is, is delicious!

1 cup butter or butter-flavored shortening
2 cups sugar
4 eggs, beaten
2 teaspoons grated orange rind
   (fresh is best)
1 cup buttermilk
3½ cups all-purpose flour
1 teaspoon baking soda
8 ounces dates, finely chopped

1 pound candy orange slices, cut up
   with scissors
1 can flaked coconut
2 cups chopped pecans
Glaze:
1½ cups confectioners' sugar
½ cup orange juice
1 tablespoon grated fresh orange rind

Blend butter with sugar. Add and mix thoroughly eggs, orange rind, and buttermilk. Add flour and baking soda and mix. Fold in dates, orange slices, coconut, and pecans. Bake at 300° in a greased and floured bundt pan for 1 hour 45 minutes. Cool for 5 minutes and leave in pan.

For glaze, mix all ingredients. Pour over cake in pan.

Serves 10 to 12.

Linda Stewart—Dallas, Texas

Hubcaps Lesch's Lucky Lemon Sour Cream Pound Cake
A sweet deal.

1 cup margarine
½ cup shortening
3 cups sugar
6 eggs
8 ounces sour cream

¼ cup milk
3 cups all-purpose flour
½ teaspoon baking powder
1 teaspoon lemon extract
1 teaspoon vanilla extract

Preheat oven to 325°. Mix butter, shortening, sugar, and eggs. Combine sour cream and milk. Stir until smooth. Add flour and baking powder. Mix until blended. Stir in lemon and vanilla extracts. Bake in a greased 10-inch tube pan for 1½ hours or until done.

Serves 10 to 12.

Whitney Laird—Anniston, Alabama

Mt. Pilot Pig Pickin' Cake

For picky eaters.

1 box butter cake mix, prepare according
   to package directions
½ cup oil
4 eggs
1 11-ounce can mandarin oranges
   with juice

Icing:
1 3-ounce package vanilla instant pudding
9 ounces nondairy whipped topping
1 large can crushed pineapple with juice

Mix first 4 ingredients and bake in 4 layers. Bake at 325° for about 15 minutes.
   For icing, mix ingredients and spread on cake layers.
   Serves 10 to 12.

Lorraine Gilley—Pilot Mountain, North Carolina

Siler City Cake

Mighty neighborly.

6 egg yolks, well beaten
1 cup sugar
⅓ cup butter
1 cup pecans, finely chopped
½ cup dates, finely chopped

½ cup raisins, finely chopped
1 cup coconut, finely chopped
¼ teaspoon salt
½ cup condensed milk
3 layers yellow cake, mix or scratch

Mix all ingredients, except cake, in top of a double boiler. Cook until melted and thick. Put mixture between cake layers and on outside of cake. Let cake sit for 24 hours.
   Serves 10 to 12.

Vickie and Larry Russell
(current owners of Frances Bavier's last residence)
Siler City, North Carolina

Mr. McBeevee's Apple Torte

Tree-mendous!

⅔ cup flour
3 teaspoons baking powder
1 teaspoon salt
2 eggs
1½ cups sugar

3 teaspoons vanilla extract
2 cups diced apples
1 cup chopped nuts
Whipped cream

Sift together flour, baking powder, and salt. Beat eggs well and add sugar and vanilla. Beat well. Sift in dry ingredients and beat well. Fold in diced apples and nuts. Pour into a greased 8x12-inch pan. Bake at 350° for 45 minutes. Top with whipped cream.

Serves 8 to 10.

Peggy Seil—Scottsdale, Arizona

HAPPY BEGINNING—*Aunt Bee agrees to stay with Andy and Opie.*

Runaway Opie has been eating apples all day, but:

AUNT BEE: (to Opie) Now I'm going to fix you some supper before you go to bed. You must be starved, and wait 'til you see what I've fixed special for you—your favorite—apple pie!

Dessert time

Opie's Apple Cake

It sure beats planting spinach.

2 cups sugar
3 cups plain flour
1 teaspoon salt
¾ cup grated coconut
1 teaspoon baking soda
1½ cups oil
1½ teaspoons cinnamon
2 cups chopped nuts

3 eggs
3 cups chopped apples
Topping:
½ cup buttermilk
¼ cup butter
½ teaspoon baking soda
1 teaspoon white corn syrup
1 cup sugar

Blend ingredients thoroughly. Bake at 375° for 1 hour and 15 minutes in a tube pan.

For topping, boil ingredients, but do not overcook. Pour over cake while in the pan, and let cool before removing.

Serves 10 to 12.

Vickie and Larry Russell
(current owners of Frances Bavier's last residence)
Siler City, North Carolina

A great combination:
AUNT BEE: Well, I'll get the cake, if you'll pour the coffee.
HELEN: Fine.

Cave Rescue Coffee Cake
You'll be a hero with this one.

1 cup margarine, softened
1¼ cups sugar
2 eggs
1 cup sour cream
1 teaspoon vanilla extract
2 cups plain flour
1 teaspoon baking powder

½ teaspoon baking soda
Topping:
¾ cup brown sugar
1 teaspoon cinnamon
2 tablespoons flour
2 tablespoons margarine
½ cup nuts

Cream margarine, sugar, and eggs. Add sour cream and vanilla and mix well. Add flour, baking powder, and soda. Mix well and pour into a greased 9x13-inch glass baking dish.

For topping, mix brown sugar, cinnamon, flour, margarine, and nuts. Sprinkle over cake mixture. Bake for 30 minutes at 325°.

Serves 12.

Sara Brower—Asheboro, North Carolina

Lazy Days Oatmeal Cake
Popular every day in Mayberry.

1¼ cups boiling water
1 cup oatmeal
½ cup margarine, softened
1 cup sugar
1 cup brown sugar
1 teaspoon vanilla extract
2 eggs
1½ cups self-rising flour

¼ teaspoon cinnamon
¼ teaspoon nutmeg
Frosting:
¼ cup margarine, melted
½ cup brown sugar
3 tablespoons half-and-half
⅓ cup chopped pecans
¾ cup grated coconut

Pour boiling water over oatmeal and let stand for 20 minutes. Beat margarine until creamy. Gradually add sugars and beat until fluffy. Blend in vanilla and eggs. Add oats mixture and flour and spices. Bake in a 9-inch square pan at 350° for 50 to 55 minutes.

For frosting, leave cake in pan. Mix frosting ingredients and spread evenly over cake. Broil until frosting becomes bubbly. Serve warm or cold.

Serves 9.

Phyllis Rollins—Greensboro, North Carolina

Evie-Joy's Baby Food Cake

Hold on to this one.

1 cup vegetable oil
2 cups sugar
3 eggs
1 small jar baby food prunes
1 small jar baby food apricots
1 teaspoon nutmeg
1 teaspoon cinnamon
1 teaspoon baking soda

2 cups flour, sifted
¼ teaspoon salt
¾ cup chopped pecans
Frosting:
1 cup confectioners' sugar
3 tablespoons butter or oleo, softened
3 tablespoons milk
1 teaspoon vanilla extract

Combine oil and sugar. Add eggs 1 at a time, beating well after each addition. Add prunes and apricots. Sift flour, measure; then sift together flour, nutmeg, cinnamon, soda, and salt. Add to first mixture. Add chopped pecans. Bake in a greased and floured tube pan for 1 hour at 350°.

For frosting, mix ingredients and frost cake while it is slightly warm. Serves 10 to 12.

Alice Schwenke—Houston, Texas

Mayberry's first family

County Fair Cranberry Cake with Hot Butter Sauce

Takes the blue ribbon every time.

2 tablespoons butter
1 cup sugar
1 teaspoon vanilla extract
2 cups sifted flour
3 teaspoons baking powder
½ teaspoon salt

1 cup milk
2 cups raw cranberries
Hot Butter Sauce:
½ cup butter
1 cup sugar
½ cup coffee cream

Cream butter and sugar. Beat in vanilla. Sift flour, baking powder, and salt together. Add alternately with milk into creamed mixture. Fold in cranberries. Pour into a greased 8- or 9-inch square pan. Bake at 400° for 35 minutes, or until done. Serve with sauce.

For Hot Butter Sauce, melt butter in a saucepan; blend in sugar and stir in cream. Simmer for 3 to 4 minutes, stirring occasionally. Can be refrigerated and warmed in microwave before serving, if made ahead.

Serves 9.

Sue and Jack Fellenzer—Cedar Falls, Iowa

Mother's Black Walnut Cake

Mmm, mmm.

1 cup shortening
2 cups sugar
4 eggs
3 cups self-rising flour
1 cup sweet milk
1 tablespoon vanilla extract

Icing:
2 cups sugar
1 cup water
Dash of salt
1 cup black walnuts
1 tablespoon butter
1 teaspoon vanilla extract

Cream shortening and sugar. Add eggs, beating after each addition. Add flour and milk alternately. Add flavoring; beat well and bake in 3 layers at 325° for about 25 minutes.

For icing, mix sugar, water, and salt in a heavy pan. Bring to a boil; add walnuts and cook to soft-ball stage. Add butter and vanilla. Spread on cake.

Serves 10 to 12.

Autice Culbreath—Union Grove, Alabama

Sally's Red Velvet Cake

Makes your taste buds dance with conviction.

1 cup butter or margarine
2 cups sugar
2 eggs
1 tablespoon vinegar
1 tablespoon cocoa
½ teaspoon salt
2½ cups cake flour
1½ teaspoons baking soda
1 cup buttermilk

1 teaspoon vanilla extract
2 ounces red food coloring
Frosting:
8 ounces cream cheese
1 stick butter or margarine
1 box confectioners' sugar
2 teaspoons vanilla extract
1 cup chopped nuts

Cream butter and sugar. Add eggs and beat until fluffy. Make paste of vinegar and cocoa. Add to creamed mixture. Sift salt, flour, and soda together. Add flour mixture to creamed mixture alternately with buttermilk. Blend well. Stir in vanilla and food coloring. Pour into a greased 9x13-inch pan or 3 cake pans. Bake for 30 minutes at 350° and frost.

For frosting, whip cream cheese and butter until fluffy. Add sugar and vanilla. Stir in nuts.

Serves 12.

Sally and Jim Lord—Seattle, Washington

Happy Motoring Cheesecake

Take a taste drive.

1¾ cups graham cracker crumbs
⅓ cup margarine
¼ cup sugar
16 ounces cream cheese
3 eggs

⅔ cup sugar
⅛ teaspoon almond extract
2 cups sour cream
3 tablespoons sugar
1 teaspoon vanilla extract

To make crust, blend first 3 ingredients. Press firmly against bottom and sides of a greased 9-inch pan. Let cheese become room temperature; then beat until light and creamy. Add eggs and portions of sugar alternately, beating after each addition. Add extract and beat for 5 minutes. Pour into crust. Bake at 325° for 50 minutes. Cool for 20 minutes while preparing sour cream.

Beat sour cream, sugar, and vanilla. Spoon over top of cheesecake. Return to the oven and bake for 15 minutes. Cool to room temperature. Delicious topped with fruit pie filling.

Serves 8.

Ellen Booth—Tempe, Arizona

Andrew Jackson Taylor: High-school valedictorian

Andy's Nut Cake
Nuttin' better.

1¼ pounds vanilla wafers
2 cans sweetened condensed milk
2 pounds pecans

2 pounds English walnuts
1 box raisins
1 regular can grated coconut

Grease a bundt pan. Crumble vanilla wafers in a large pan. Pour milk over crumbs. Let stand for 5 minutes. Add remaining ingredients and mix well. Pack in the pan and refrigerate overnight.

Serves 10 to 12.

Carolyn and Sterling White—Florence, Alabama

Mayberry on Record
Cherry Upside-Down Cake

The flip side has the best cuts.

1¼ cups sifted flour
1¼ teaspoons baking powder
¼ teaspoon salt
1¼ cups sugar, divided
1¾ cups pitted and drained red cherries,
    fresh or canned

8 tablespoons butter, divided
1 egg, well beaten
½ cup milk
1 teaspoon vanilla extract

Sift flour once; measure. Add baking powder, salt, and sugar and sift 3 times. Cream 4 tablespoons butter. Add dry ingredients, egg, milk, and vanilla and stir until all flour is dampened. Then beat vigorously for 1 minute. Melt 4 tablespoons butter over low heat in an 8x8x2-inch pan or an 8-inch skillet. Add ½ cup sugar and stir until thoroughly mixed. Arrange cherries atop this mixture. Pour batter over cherries. Bake at 350° for 50 minutes, or until done. Loosen cake from sides of pan. Turn upside down on a dish.

Serves 8 to 10.

Anna Mode Wolfe—Mar Vista Hills, California

Barney doesn't like it when Andy gets "purposely obtuse."

48

Grandma's Orange Cake

Have a great big piece.

1 yellow cake
4 to 6 oranges

1 cup sugar

Use your favorite yellow cake recipe. Peel oranges and cut into very small pieces. Remove seeds. Pour sugar over oranges and let stand. When cake is removed from pan, pour juice from oranges on cake, allowing it to soak in. Top with small orange pieces.
Serves 10 to 12.

Autice Culbreath—Union Grove, Alabama

Jelly Jail Cake

A cell-abration!

½ cup jelly, any flavor
1 stick butter
1¼ cups brown sugar

2 teaspoons cinnamon
2 cans refrigerated biscuits
 (10-biscuit size)

Spray a bundt pan with nonstick cooking spray. Put jelly in bottom of pan. Melt butter and mix with brown sugar and cinnamon. Dip biscuits in mixture and place on jelly. Bake at 350° for 30 minutes.
Serves 10 to 12.

Gary Wedemeyer—Fall Branch, Tennessee

Beautiful, Delicate Women's Pecan Cake

It's a Darling!

2 cups butter or margarine
2⅓ cups sugar
6 eggs
4 cups flour
1 2-ounce bottle or 4 tablespoons lemon
 extract (use pure extract)

½ teaspoon salt
¼ pound white raisins
¼ pound candied cherries
¼ pound candied pineapple
1 quart shelled pecans

Cream butter or margarine and sugar. Add eggs 1 at a time and beat well. Add flour. Add lemon extract and salt. Add chopped fruits and nuts, which have been dredged in flour. Bake in 2 tube or loaf pans at 300° for 1 to 1½ hours. Freezes well.
Makes 2 loaves.

Mary Barnes—Tuscaloosa, Alabama

Hazel's Pound Cake

Receives a chorus of praises every time.

3 sticks margarine
1 heaping wooden spoonful shortening
3 cups sugar
6 large eggs

1 cup whole milk or canned milk
3 cups all-purpose flour
½ teaspoon baking powder
1 teaspoon vanilla or lemon flavoring

Mix margarine, shortening, and sugar thoroughly. Add eggs 2 at a time, beating after each addition. Add milk and beat well. Add flour and baking powder and beat well. Add vanilla or lemon extract and beat well. Pour into a greased tube pan lined with waxed paper going 1 inch up sides of the pan. Shake down to settle. Bake at 300° for 1 hour and 15 minutes. Take out and let cool for about 10 minutes. Loosen around edges with a knife. Turn out on a folded towel covered with waxed paper. After cooking, cover while still warm.
    Serves 10 to 12.

Hazel T. Laxton—Lenoir, North Carolina

Alma's Buttermilk Pound Cake

Save room for this one.

3 cups sugar
2 sticks margarine
½ cup shortening
6 eggs
3 cups plain flour, sifted 3 times
1 cup buttermilk

¼ teaspoon baking soda
½ teaspoon lemon flavoring
1 teaspoon vanilla flavoring
½ teaspoon rum flavoring
¼ teaspoon coconut flavoring
¼ teaspoon mace

Cream sugar, margarine, and shortening. Add eggs, 1 at a time, blending after each addition. Alternately add flour and buttermilk mixed with baking soda to mixture; add flavorings. Pour into a greased tube pan and bake at 325° for 90 minutes.
    Serves 10 to 12.

Alma Venable, Mayberry Motor Inn—Mount Airy, North Carolina

AL BE DARNED

Revered comedienne Jane Dulo is loved in Mayberry for her role as lady convict Sally in "Convicts at Large" (Episode #74), even if she did think Barney was her old boyfriend, Al. Among Jane's many other television roles was that as Agent 99's mother in *Get Smart*.

Sally's Favorite Fruit Bundt Cake

*Jane used to visit us once or twice a year in Kansas City,
but only if I promised to make my Fruit Bundt Cake; she'd have
it for breakfast with coffee and as dessert with dinner. She just loved it.*

8 ounces dried prunes
8 ounces dried peaches or apricots
1 cup boiling water
Cinnamon and sugar, mixed together
1 box yellow cake mix

1 small box instant vanilla pudding mix
½ cup vegetable oil
4 eggs
1 cup water

Preheat the oven to 350°. Pit and cut up dried prunes, peaches, and/or apricots. Pour boiling water over dried fruit, soak until soft, and drain. Grease a bundt cake pan. Sprinkle pan with cinnamon and sugar mixture. Mix cake mix, pudding, oil, eggs, and water according to directions on package. Pour into prepared pan. Drop dried soft fruit evenly over top of batter. Bake for 45 to 55 minutes.

Serves 12 to 16.

Shirley D. Gordon—Sister of cast member Jane Dulo

WANTED: Escaped convict #1000, known as Sally. Last seen in the vicinity of Chuck O'Malley's cabin near Mayberry. Known accomplices: Big Maude Tyler (alias Clarice Tyler, Maude Clarice Tyler, Annabelle Tyler, and Ralph Henderson), Jelene Naomi Conners, and Al. Known Hangout: Cascade Club in Toledo. Reputed member of Girl Campers of America.

CABIN FEVER—Big Maude comforts convict Naomi as Floyd worries.

Floyd's Cabin Fever Banana Cake

Forget about the hamburgers, Al!

3 sticks butter, divided
2 cups graham cracker crumbs
2 eggs
2 cups confectioners' sugar
5 ripe bananas

1 can crushed pineapple
1 large container whipped topping
1 small package chopped pecans
1 small bottle maraschino cherries

Mix 1 stick butter with graham cracker crumbs and spread over bottom of a 13x9x2-inch pan. Take 2 sticks butter and mix with eggs and confectioners' sugar for 15 minutes with a mixer. Spread over crumbs in pan and cover with sliced bananas (cut round or long). Add pineapple, top with whipped topping, and sprinkle chopped pecans and cherries on top. Refrigerate overnight.

Dennis Hasty—Lockland, Ohio

Strawberry Fields Short Cake

An Oscar-winning performance.

1 box white cake mix
1 quart strawberries, fresh or frozen

1 cup sugar
8 ounces nondairy whipped topping

Prepare 2 cake layers according to package directions. Cool layers. Mash strawberries. Add sugar and mix well. Put half of mixture on top and sides of first layer of cake and cover with whipped topping. Repeat with second layer of cake, remaining mixture, and whipped topping. Decorate cake with strawberries.

Serves 10 to 12.

Marie Fields—Summerfield, North Carolina

Barney's First Cake
Take it for a spin and see how it tastes.

1 small box lemon gelatin
1 cup boiling water
½ cup cooking oil
4 eggs
1 box yellow cake mix

1 teaspoon lemon flavoring
Topping:
1 fresh lemon
1 to 1½ cups confectioners' sugar

Add gelatin to boiling water. Combine all ingredients, adding 1 egg at a time. Pour into a greased tube or bundt pan. Bake at 350° for 25 to 30 minutes, or until golden brown. Set aside and allow to cool.

For topping, squeeze juice and add to sugar. Mix until smooth. Top cake.
Serves 10 to 12.

Gary Wedemeyer—Fall Branch, Tennessee

Harriet's Rich Strawberry Cake
You can take this one to the bank.

2 sticks butter
2 cups sugar
2½ cups all-purpose flour or cake flour
   (sift before measuring)
½ teaspoon salt
1 teaspoon baking powder

5 eggs
1 cup milk
1 teaspoon vanilla extract
2 tablespoons confectioners' sugar
4 pints whipped cream
2 quarts sliced strawberries

Cream butter and sugar. Combine flour, salt, and baking powder and add to batter. Add eggs, milk, and vanilla. Pour into two 8- or 9-inch greased and floured pans. Bake at 350° for 45 to 50 minutes. Cool and slice each layer in half to make 4 layers.

Add confectioners' sugar to whipping cream and beat until stiff but spreadable. Put some whipped cream on a layer and then generously cover with sliced strawberries. Repeat for each layer. Put whipped cream on top and sides and cover top with remaining sliced strawberries.

Serves 10 to 12.

Harriet Patterson—Greensboro, North Carolina

Strongbow's Strawberry Pecan Cake

A Tuckahoosie winner from Tuscaloosa.

1 box white cake mix
1 3-ounce box strawberry gelatin
1 cup vegetable oil
½ cup milk
4 eggs
1 cup frozen strawberries
1 cup grated coconut
1 cup chopped pecans

Filling:
1 stick margarine
1 box confectioners' sugar
½ cup frozen strawberries, drained
½ cup grated coconut
1 cup pecans, chopped
8 ounces cream cheese

Mix cake mix and gelatin. Add next 6 ingredients. Pour into three 9-inch greased pans and bake at 350° for 20 to 25 minutes.

For filling, mix remaining ingredients. Spread between layers and on top of cake.

Serves 10 to 12.

Deloris Cummings—Tuscaloosa, Alabama

Leon's Peanut Butter Fudge Cake

Eatin' speaks louder than words.

1 cup butter or margarine
¼ cup cocoa
1 cup water
½ cup buttermilk
2 eggs, well beaten
2 cups sugar
2 cups unsifted all-purpose flour
1 teaspoon baking soda
1 teaspoon vanilla extract

Icing:
1½ cups creamy peanut butter
1½ tablespoons peanut oil
½ cup butter or margarine
¼ cup cocoa
6 tablespoons buttermilk
1 pound confectioners' sugar
1 teaspoon vanilla extract

In a saucepan, combine butter, cocoa, water, buttermilk, and eggs. Stir constantly over low heat until mixture boils. In a large bowl, mix sugar, flour, and soda. Stir hot mixture into dry ingredients. Beat until smooth. Stir in vanilla. Spread into a greased 13x9x2-inch pan. Bake at 350° for 25 to 30 minutes. Cool cake in pan.

For icing, combine peanut butter and oil until smooth. Spread evenly over cooled cake.

In a saucepan, heat butter, cocoa, and buttermilk until bubbly. Place sugar in a mixing bowl. Beat in hot mixture until smooth. Stir in vanilla. Spread over cake.

Serves 12.

Deloris Cummings—Tuscaloosa, Alabama

"There's my darling person."

Charlene's Sad Cake

Needless to say, this one makes her cry.

3 eggs, beaten
1 pound brown sugar
2 cups baking mix, such as Bisquick

1 cup chopped pecans
Whipped cream

Mix all ingredients, except whipped cream, and bake in a greased iron skillet at 350° for 30 to 40 minutes. Serve with whipped cream.
Serves 8 to 10.

Maggie Peterson—Cast member

Pounded Cake à la Morelli

Wave reviews!

½ pound butter
3 cups sugar
5 eggs
1½ teaspoons baking powder

½ teaspoon salt
3 cups cake flour
1 cup milk
1 teaspoon vanilla or lemon flavoring

Cream butter and sugar; add eggs 1 at a time. Mix well. Add baking powder and salt to flour. Add half of flour; beat well. Add milk; then add remaining flour. Add flavoring. Bake in a tube pan at 350° for 1 hour and 10 minutes.
Serves 10 to 12.

Harriet Patterson—Greensboro, North Carolina

STRONG LINKE TO MAYBERRY

In addition to his role as associate producer for *The Andy Griffith Show*, Richard O. Linke was Andy Griffith's longtime personal manager. Others with a Mayberry connection that he has managed are Jim Nabors, Maggie Peterson, Ken Berry, Jerry Van Dyke, and Ronnie Schell.

Associate Producer Richard O. Linke

Linke Family Luchen Kugel
Produces a winner.

1 pound broad noodles, cooked	1 pint sour cream
1 cup sugar	¼ pound melted butter
1 pound cottage cheese	Topping:
1½ teaspoons vanilla extract	1 cup frosted corn flakes, crushed
1 cup white raisins	1 tablespoon cinnamon
7 eggs	1 tablespoon sugar
2 cups milk	Butter

Mix all ingredients in large bowl. Pour into a large baking pan and refrigerate for 3 hours or overnight.

For topping, mix corn flakes, cinnamon, and sugar and sprinkle over noodle mixture.

Dot with butter. Bake at 350° for 1 to 1½ hours or until golden brown. Serves 10 to 12.

Bettina and Richard O. Linke —Associate producer

Angel Cake Ange

Earns its star.

1½ cups sugar, divided
1 cup sifted cake flour
2 cups egg whites
¾ teaspoon salt

2 teaspoons cream of tartar
1 teaspoon vanilla flavoring
1 teaspoon almond flavoring
Frosting of choice

Sift sugar once; add ½ cup sugar to flour and sift together 3 times. Beat egg whites until stiff enough to hold their shape. Add remaining sugar gradually, beating thoroughly after each addition. Fold in flour with whip beater, folding in about ¼ at a time. When all flour is in, add flavorings and fold a few additional times. Pour into a large angel food cake pan. Place in a cold oven. Bake for 1 hour at 350°. Don't overbake. Frost as desired.
Serves 8 to 10.

Charlotte Womack—Greensboro, North Carolina

Sheriff's Chocolate Cookie Sheet Cake

They'll badger you for this one.

2 sticks margarine
4 tablespoons cocoa
1 cup water
2 cups all-purpose flour
½ teaspoon salt
2 cups sugar
1 teaspoon baking soda
½ cup buttermilk
2 eggs

1 teaspoon vanilla extract
Frosting:
1 stick margarine
4 tablespoons cocoa
6 tablespoons buttermilk
1 pound confectioners' sugar
1 teaspoon vanilla extract
1 cup nuts

Melt margarine and add cocoa and water. Bring to a boil. Mix dry ingredients and pour boiled mixture over it. Add buttermilk, eggs, and vanilla. Mix well. Bake on a greased cookie sheet at 350° for 15 to 20 minutes.
For frosting, melt margarine. Mix margarine, cocoa, and buttermilk. Bring to a boil. Add remaining ingredients. Mix. Spread on cake while hot.
Serves 12 to 15.

Kym Stone—Greensboro, North Carolina

Two Plus Two Strawberry Cake

Sum treat four you.

2 cups all-purpose flour
½ teaspoon salt
½ teaspoon baking soda
3 eggs
1 cup vegetable oil
1 cup sugar
1 3-ounce package strawberry gelatin

½ cup buttermilk
1 10-ounce package frozen strawberries, thawed
Strawberry Icing:
¼ cup butter or margarine, softened
1 pound confectioners' sugar
⅓ to ½ cup strawberry juice

Preheat the oven to 350°. Grease and flour two 8-inch round cake pans. Combine flour, salt, and soda; set aside. Beat eggs in a large mixing bowl. Add oil, sugar, gelatin, and buttermilk; stir vigorously until well blended. Add flour mixture and blend well. Drain ½ cup juice from strawberries; reserve for strawberry icing. Fold berries into batter. Pour batter into prepared pans. Bake for 25 to 30 minutes, or until golden brown. Remove from the oven. Cool for 5 minutes, turn out of pan onto rack, and cool completely. Frost.

For icing, combine butter or margarine and sugar. Add juice until desired consistency. Beat until creamy and spread on cake.

Serves 10 to 12.

Susan Cloninger—Greensboro, North Carolina

Old Family Recipe Eggless Fruitcake

This is a family recipe that's more than two hundred years old.

1 cup butter
2 cups sugar
4 cups sifted flour
1 teaspoon baking powder
1 teaspoon baking soda
Pinch of salt
1 cup buttermilk
1 cup cold coffee

1 teaspoon nutmeg
1 teaspoon cloves
1 teaspoon allspice
1 teaspoon cinnamon
1 cup raisins, ground
½ cup currants
1 cup apples, peeled, cored, and ground
1 cup chopped nuts

Mix butter and sugar until creamy. Sift flour, baking powder, soda, and salt together 4 times. Set ½ cup of this mixture aside. Combine butter and sugar with flour mixture. Stir buttermilk into mixture; then stir in cold coffee. Stir in nutmeg, cloves, allspice, and cinnamon. Take ½ cup flour mixture and mix with raisins, currants, apples, and nuts; then stir this mixture in last. Pour the mixture into a 12-inch angel food cake or square pan. Bake at 350° for 1 hour.

Serves 10 to 12.

Jean and Rance Howard—Parents of cast members Ron and Clint Howard

Nana's Pound Cake

Everybody wants Nana's seconds, so it goes fast.

3 sticks butter, softened
3 cups sugar
1 teaspoon vanilla extract
1 teaspoon lemon extract
6 eggs

3 cups sifted plain flour
½ teaspoon baking powder
Pinch of salt
1 cup sweet milk

Cream butter and sugar until light and fluffy. Add vanilla and lemon extracts and blend well. Add eggs, 1 at a time, beating after each addition. Sift flour, baking powder, and salt together and add alternately to creamed mixture with milk. Pour into a greased and floured tube pan. Bake at 325° for 1½ hours.

Serves 10 to 12.

Dot Harper—Greensboro, North Carolina

A FAMILIAR FACE IN THE CROWD—
This Mayberry regular (Rance Howard) does everything
from driving the governor's car and Cousin Virgil's bus to
working for the Treasury Department ("T-man")
to hanging out at surprise parties.

Daydreaming about Aunt Bee's good desserts?

Gomer's Fill 'er Up Chocolate Cupcakes
Your tummy will go from empty to full.

1½ cups cake flour
¾ cup sugar
1 teaspoon baking soda
½ teaspoon salt
1½ squares chocolate, melted
1 heaping tablespoon butter, melted

1 cup buttermilk
Whipped cream
Icing:
1 cup liquid, half milk and half cream
1½ squares chocolate
2 cups sugar

Mix ingredients in order, melting chocolate and butter together. Bake in cupcake cases at 350°. When cool, cut cap off top and save; scoop out center of cupcake to within ½ inch of bottom and sides. Fill hole in cupcake with whipped cream. Put cap back on and ice with chocolate icing.

For icing, boil milk, cream, and chocolate until thick (like pudding). Add sugar; boil slowly to soft-ball stage (about 242° on a candy thermometer). Cool; then beat with an electric mixer, adding a little cream to adjust consistency.

Makes about 20.

Dee Boquist—Minneapolis, Minnesota

Malcolm's Cupcakes

They travel well.

4 squares semisweet chocolate
2 sticks margarine
4 eggs
1¼ cups sugar

1 cup flour
1 teaspoon vanilla extract
1 cup chopped pecans or black walnuts

Melt chocolate and margarine. Beat eggs (do not use a mixer) and sugar; add flour. Combine melted mixture with egg mixture. Add vanilla and nuts. Bake in foil cups at 325° for 30 minutes.

Makes 2 dozen.

Ginger Secrest—Shelby, North Carolina

Hugo Hopfleisch's Bavarian Cream Cake

No wrong side to this one.

1 cup sugar
2 tablespoons flour
4 eggs, separated
2 cups milk
1 teaspoon vanilla extract

1 package unflavored gelatin
¼ cup cold water
1 cup heavy cream, whipped
Flaked coconut, optional

Mix sugar, flour, egg yolks, and milk. Cook over medium heat until thickened. Add vanilla. Add gelatin dissolved in ¼ cup water to hot mixture. Cool. Fold in whipped cream and 4 stiffly beaten egg whites. Pull cake apart in bite-size pieces. Spray a tube pan or 9x13-inch pan with nonstick cooking spray. Line pan with cake; add layer of custard, then cake, then custard. Layer cake and custard, ending with custard. Chill for 24 hours. May turn out of cake pan. Frost with whipped cream. Sprinkle with coconut, if desired.

Makes 18 servings.

Ginger Secrest—Shelby, North Carolina

Duck Pond Double Date Cake

Lip-smacking.

1 cup chopped dates
1 cup boiling water
1 stick butter or margarine
1 cup sugar
1 teaspoon vanilla extract
1 egg
1⅔ cups sifted flour
1 teaspoon baking soda

¼ teaspoon salt
½ cup chopped pecans
Date Frosting:
1 cup chopped dates
1 cup boiling water
1 stick butter or margarine
1 cup sugar
½ cup chopped pecans

Combine dates with boiling water. In a medium-sized heavy saucepan, put butter, sugar, and vanilla. Add dates and water and heat mixture until boiling. Lower heat and cook, stirring constantly for 10 minutes, or until slightly thickened. Remove from heat and cool. Beat eggs and stir into cooled date mixture. Sift flour with soda and salt and add gradually to date mixture, blending well. Stir in nuts. Pour batter into a 8x8x2-inch baking pan lined with greased waxed paper. Bake at 350° for 40 minutes, or until center springs back when pressed lightly. Remove from oven; spread icing on top.

For frosting, combine dates with boiling water, butter, and sugar in a heavy saucepan. Cook for about 20 minutes, stirring constantly until quite thick. Remove from heat and stir in pecans. Cool to lukewarm and spread on top of cake. Cut in small squares and top with whipped cream.

Makes 12 to 16 servings.

Tonya Hamel—Greensboro, North Carolina

Old Man Kelsey's Creek Mud Cake

Loved from coast to coast.

2 cups sugar
1 cup margarine
4 eggs
½ cup cocoa
¼ teaspoon salt
2 teaspoons vanilla extract
1½ cups flour
¾ cup chopped nuts, divided

1 large package miniature marshmallows
   or 1 large jar marshmallow crème
Frosting:
1 box confectioners' sugar
½ stick margarine
1½ teaspoons vanilla extract
½ cup milk, coffee, or coffee liqueur
⅓ cup cocoa

Beat sugar and margarine until creamy. Add eggs and cocoa. Beat until smooth. Add salt, vanilla, and flour. Beat until smooth. Fold in ½ cup nuts. Bake at 350° in a 9x13-inch pan, greased and floured, for 30 to 40 minutes. Remove from oven; turn oven temperature to low setting. Sprinkle marshmallows and return to oven to melt marshmallows (do not brown marsh-mallows). Spread and sprinkle with remaining nuts. Cool and frost.

For frosting, beat confectioners' sugar, margarine, vanilla, and coffee or coffee liqueur and cocoa. Beat until smooth and spread on cake.

Serves 12.

Tonya Hamel—Greensboro, North Carolina

Wilbur Saunders' Banana Cupcakes

Slipcovers, so to speak.

½ cup shortening	1¼ cups flour
1 cup sugar	1 teaspoon nutmeg
1 beaten egg	½ teaspoon salt
1 cup mashed bananas	1 teaspoon vanilla extract
1 teaspoon baking soda	Confectioners' sugar
1 tablespoon water	

Mix shortening and sugar. Add egg and bananas. Dissolve soda in water and add to other mixture. Mix flour, nutmeg, salt, and vanilla. Fill small greased and floured muffin tins half full and bake for 12 to 15 minutes at 350°. Remove from tins and roll in confectioners' sugar. Let cool and roll again in sugar.

Makes 6 dozen.

Ginger Secrest—Shelby, North Carolina

The eyes have it.

DREAM GIRL

After Barbara Eden made a brief stopover in Mayberry as manicurist Ellen Brown in "The Manicurist" (Episode #48), she was poured out of a magic bottle to star in *I Dream of Jeannie*.

Mommie's Pineapple Upside-Down Cake

*This is a recipe that my mother wrote out for me when I was a young bride.
If it sounds a bit simplistic and the instructions are too detailed,
it's because I didn't cook at all and she always gave me very homey and
explicit directions. I treasure this recipe and still have
"Mommie's" handwritten copy.*

1 box cake mix, any flavor
   except chocolate
1 can sliced pineapple
1 cube butter (more, not less)
1 cup brown sugar

Cherry halves
½ cup chopped nuts (or more)
Water and equal parts pineapple juice
Whipped cream, optional

Drain pineapple and save juice. In a frying pan, preferably an iron skillet, melt butter. Stir in brown sugar. Lower heat, cook, and stir until smooth. While still hot, place pineapple slices in a circle in pan. Be sure to have 1 slice in the center. Place cherry halves around pan . Sprinkle chopped nuts over all and remove from heat. Allow to set. Mix cake (I use banana nut) according to package directions, using ½ water and ½ pineapple juice for liquid. Pour batter on top of pineapple, nuts, etc. Bake at 350° for 45 min-

CUTE CUTICLE SHAPER—*Andy deserves a hand for his
handling of his nail-biting situation with manicurist Ellen Brown.*

utes, or until it tests done. Cut around edges to loosen and turn out on a cake plate with pineapple side on top. Place plate on pan. Turn pan over. If a piece should stick, replate. Serve with whipped cream with cherry juice and cherries on top, if desired.

Serves 10 to 12.

Barbara Eden—Cast member

Checkpoint Chickey Chocolate Upside-Down Cake

Slow down for this one.

1 cup flour
½ teaspoon salt
¾ cup sugar
2 teaspoons baking powder
2 tablespoons butter
1 square bitter chocolate

½ cup milk
1 teaspoon vanilla extract
½ cup nuts
4 tablespoons cocoa
½ cup white sugar
½ cup brown sugar

Combine flour, salt, sugar, and baking powder in a bowl. Melt butter and chocolate and add to dry mixture. Add milk, vanilla, and nuts. Put in a greased 9x9-inch pan. Mix cocoa and sugars and spread on top of batter. Pour 1 cup hot faucet water on top evenly; do not stir. Bake for 50 minutes at 350°. Let stand for 15 minutes. Serve warm; cut and flip over on a plate. Good with ice cream or whipped cream.

Serves 9.

Tonya Hamel—Greensboro, North Carolina

Opie's Lemonade Cake

So good you can hardly stand it.

1 box lemon cake mix
1 box lemon instant pudding
3 tablespoons flour
⅔ cup oil
4 eggs

1⅓ cups water
Confectioners' sugar
1 6-ounce can frozen lemonade
Nondairy whipped topping

Mix first 6 ingredients and bake for 40 minutes at 350°. When you take cake out of oven, punch over top of cake all the way to pan. Use a fork to pierce every inch or so. Cover with a mixture of confectioners' sugar and frozen lemonade. Pour on cake slowly until all is absorbed. Cut and top each piece with whipped topping.

Serves 10 to 12.

Jimmie La Pine—Albuquerque, New Mexico

Goober always saves room for dessert.

Call the Man Kelvinator Fruit Cake
Call the man!

½ pound graham crackers
½ cup currants
¼ teaspoon nutmeg
¼ teaspoon allspice
¼ teaspoon salt
1 cup chopped dates
2 tablespoons chopped orange peel
½ cup citron or candied pineapple,
    finely chopped

½ cup chopped raisins
2 tablespoons candied cherries, chopped
1 teaspoon cinnamon
¼ teaspoon cloves
1 cup chopped nuts
1 cup marshmallows
1 cup thick cream

Crumble crackers fine. Soften currants in hot water and drain. Add spices and salt to dry cracker crumbs and mix; then add other ingredients. Marshmallows should be cut into very small pieces, soaked in cream, and added last. Mix thoroughly until all cracker crumbs are moistened. Pack in a square tin or mold lined with waxed paper and let stand in refrigerator for 12 hours. Slice thin. Can refrigerate for several weeks.

Makes 1 two-pound loaf.

Mary Jane Houston—Springfield, Missouri

Goober Cake

Yo!

½ cup butter
1½ cups brown sugar
½ cup creamy peanut butter
1½ teaspoons vanilla extract
1 egg
1½ cups flour
⅜ teaspoon baking soda
1 teaspoon baking powder

10 tablespoons milk
Vanilla Cream Frosting:
6 tablespoons butter
1 pound confectioners' sugar
¼ cup milk
1 tablespoon vanilla extract
Pinch of salt

Cream butter, sugar, peanut butter, and vanilla. Add egg; then add dry ingredients alternately with milk. Bake in a 9-inch square pan at 350° for 25 minutes.

For frosting, cream butter until fluffy. Add sugar, milk, vanilla, and salt. Beat well until light. Spread frosting on cake.

Serves 9.

Will You Love Me When I'm Old and Ugly Persimmon Cake

Makes Andelina Darling cry for more.

1 cup butter
2 cups brown sugar
1½ cups persimmon pulp
3 eggs
2 cups self-rising flour sifted before
    measuring (reserve ½ cup for dredging)
2 cups raisins or 1 cup dates and
    1 cup raisins
½ cup candied pineapple, chopped
½ cup candied cherries, chopped

½ cup pecans, chopped
1 teaspoon cinnamon
1 teaspoon vanilla extract
1 cup sweet milk
Butter Cream Icing:
1 pound confectioners' sugar
1 stick margarine
8 ounces cream cheese
2 teaspoons vanilla extract

Cream butter and sugar. Add persimmon pulp and eggs. Dredge fruit and nuts in ½ cup flour. Add cinnamon to flour mixture. Add flour, milk, and vanilla alternately to persimmon mixture. Fold in fruit and nuts. Pour batter in three 9-inch pans lined with waxed paper. Bake at 350° for 45 minutes (check after 30 to 35 minutes.) Cool in pans for a few minutes; then turn out and remove waxed paper carefully. Ice when cool.

For icing, mix ingredients and beat until creamy. Spread between layers and on top and sides of cake.

Serves 16.

Ruby Ball—Thomasville, North Carolina

LET'S MAKE A DEAL

Multi-talented Dave Ketchum was always selling something in Mayberry. His first appearance was as real estate salesman Harry Walker in "Floyd's Barbershop" (Episode #210), and he returned a while later as petroleum salesman Fred Michaels in "Goober the Executive" (Episode #221). His ability to play multiple roles might stem from his uncanny work with disguises as Agent 13 in *Get Smart*.

Emblem Oil's Amazing Chocolate Chip Pound Cake
Super!

8 ounces cream cheese
2 sticks butter
1½ cups sugar
4 eggs
2 tablespoons sour cream
2 teaspoons vanilla extract
2¼ cups cake flour

2 teaspoons baking powder
¼ teaspoon salt
1 cup semisweet chocolate chips
  (a little more if you're greedy)
Confectioners' sugar, optional
Fudge frosting, optional

Mix cream cheese, butter, and sugar with a beater or food processor. Add eggs; then add sour cream and vanilla. Beat well. Add flour, baking powder, salt, and chocolate chips. Stir or process until mixed. Spoon into a prebuttered pan and put in a 325° oven for about an hour (or until a knife comes out clean). After cake cools, cover with confectioners' sugar or, if you're tossing caution to the wind, a layer of fudge frosting. Dangerous food, very dangerous.
    Serves 10 to 12.

Dave Ketchum—Cast member

Fresh Apple Blossom Festival Cake
Very a-peeling!

1 cup cooking oil
2 cups sugar
3 eggs, well beaten
1 tablespoon vanilla extract
2½ cups flour
1 teaspoon baking soda
2 teaspoons baking powder
1 teaspoon salt

1½ cups chopped pecans
3 cups peeled, chopped Granny Smith
  apples
Icing:
1 cup light brown sugar
½ cup butter
¼ cup evaporated milk
1 teaspoon vanilla extract

*Super salesman Fred Michaels from the
Emblem Oil Company of El Paso, Texas*

Cream oil, sugar, and eggs. Add vanilla. Sift dry ingredients together and blend into creamed mixture. Fold in pecans and apples. Pour into a well greased and floured tube pan. Bake at 350° for 50 to 60 minutes.

For icing, bring brown sugar, butter, and evaporated milk to a boil, stirring constantly. Remove from heat and stir in vanilla. Beat until icing is cooled. Dump over cake and serve warm.

Serves 10 to 12.

Lula D. Simpson—Pleasant Garden, North Carolina

Sister Ann Elizabeth's Bourbon Pound Cake
Nun better.

4 cups sifted flour or cake flour	10 eggs
½ teaspoon double action baking powder	1 teaspoon vanilla extract
1 pound butter or margarine	2 teaspoons bourbon
2⅔ cups sugar	

Sift together baking powder and flour. Cream butter and sugar until light and fluffy. Add 1 egg at a time, mixing well after each addition. Add flavorings and mix well. Add flour last. Beat with an electric mixer at medium speed for 10 minutes. Pour into a greased 10-inch tube pan and bake at 350° for 55 minutes.

Serves 12.

Mr. and Mrs. George Spence—Cast member

"THERE'S DUD"—Charlene and all the Darlings greet Dud returning from the Army.

Dud's Cracker Crummy Cheesecake

Obtained from a backwoods girl named Barb.

1¼ cups graham cracker crumbs
¼ cup melted butter
8 ounces cream cheese
½ cup sugar
1 tablespoon lemon juice
½ teaspoon vanilla extract

Dash of salt
2 eggs
Topping:
1 cup sour cream
2 tablespoons sugar
½ teaspoon vanilla extract

For crust, combine crumbs and butter. Press into a buttered 8-inch pie plate, building up sides. Beat softened cream cheese till fluffy. Gradually blend in ½ cup sugar, lemon juice, vanilla, and salt. Add eggs, 1 at a time, beating well after each. Pour filling into crust. Bake at 325° for 25 to 30 minutes, or until set.

For topping, combine sour cream, sugar, and vanilla. Spoon over top of pie. Bake for 10 minutes more. Cool; chill for several hours.

Serves 8.

Hoke Howell—Cast member

70

Dishtowel Salesman Sponge Cake

They'll clean their plates.

1 cup cake flour
6 eggs, separated
1 cup sugar
¼ cup water

½ teaspoon cream of tartar
½ teaspoon salt
1 teaspoon vanilla extract
½ teaspoon lemon extract

Sift flour; measure and resift three times. Put egg yolks in a large mixing bowl. Beat yolks on high speed for 4 to 5 minutes, or until so thick that beating slows. Gradually beat in ¼ cup sugar. Add flour and water alternately in 2 or 3 portions, beating well after each addition. Sift cream of tartar and salt over egg whites and beat until stiff; then beat in remaining ¼ cup sugar and flavorings. Cut and fold yolk mixture lightly but thoroughly into egg whites. Pour into an ungreased 10-inch tube pan. Bake at 325° for 1 hour, or until cake springs back when lightly touched. Remove from pan and invert immediately. Cool thoroughly before removing.
Serves 10 to 12.

Mary Ellis—Albuquerque, New Mexico

Mama's Cake

Mama knows best.

2 cups self-rising flour
2 cups sugar
1 stick butter
½ cup shortening
1 cup cold water
3½ tablespoons cocoa
1 teaspoon baking soda
½ cup buttermilk
2 eggs

1 tablespoon vanilla extract
Icing:
½ stick butter
3 tablespoons cocoa
⅓ cup Carnation milk
½ pound confectioners' sugar
1 cup nuts, optional
1 tablespoon vanilla extract

Sift together flour and sugar. In a saucepan, melt butter and shortening and add cold water and cocoa. Bring to a boil and pour over flour mixture (will be thin). Beat until well mixed. Mix soda, buttermilk, eggs, and vanilla. Add to other mixture and heat for 2 minutes. Bake at 350° for 30 minutes.
For icing, mix butter, cocoa, and milk. Bring to a boil in a saucepan. Add confectioners' sugar, nuts, and vanilla. Pour over warm cake.
Serves 10 to 12.

Kay Disher—Kernersville, North Carolina

71

Cousin Lillian's Pineapple Cake

A family favorite.

2 cups flour
1½ cups sugar
1 teaspoon baking soda
½ teaspoon salt
¼ cup brown sugar, packed
1 cup chopped walnuts or pecans

1 1-pound, 4-ounce can crushed pineapple
Lillian's Icing:
⅔ cup sugar
½ cup butter or margarine
¼ cup milk
½ cup shredded or flaked coconut

Combine flour, sugar, soda, salt, brown sugar, pecans, and pineapple with syrup in an ungreased 11x7-inch pan. Stir to mix well. Bake at 350° for 35 minutes.

For icing, combine sugar, butter, and milk in a saucepan. Bring to a boil and simmer for 2 minutes. Pour over warm cake and sprinkle with coconut.

Serves 10 to 12.

Elinor Donahue—Cast member

Jim Lindsey's Best Holiday Cake

A good pick.

2 cups self-rising flour
2 cups sugar
1 teaspoon cinnamon
1 teaspoon allspice
1 teaspoon nutmeg

1 cup vegetable oil
3 eggs
2 small jars baby food prunes or plums
1 cup walnuts
Confectioners' sugar

Grease and flour a 10-inch tube pan. In a large bowl, combine all ingredients, except walnuts and confectioners' sugar. Mix for 2 minutes with an electric mixer on medium speed. Fold in walnuts. Pour into prepared pan. Bake at 350° for 45 to 60 minutes. Check often; cake will be very moist. Do not overbake. Dust with confectioners' sugar.

Serves 10 to 12.

Dorothy and James Best—Cast member

PICK HIT

People often ask whether that was really James Best picking the guitar in the close-up shots of Jim Lindsey in "Guitar Player" (Episode #3) and "The Guitar Player Returns" (Episode #31). The answer is no. It was ace picker Herb Ellis.

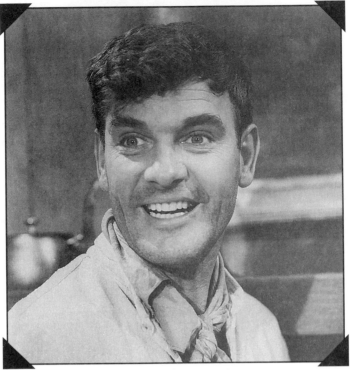

Guitar playing Jim Lindsey

Opie's Overachieving Orange Glaze Cake
A+.

1 cup sugar
1 stick butter
2 eggs, beaten
⅔ cup buttermilk
2 cups self-rising flour
1 teaspoon grated orange rind
1 package chopped dates

1 cup nuts
Icing:
1 cup sugar
½ cup orange juice
1 teaspoon grated orange rind
Whipped cream

Cream sugar and butter. Add eggs 1 at a time. Add buttermilk and then flour. (Sift flour before measuring.) Add orange rind, dates, and nuts. Pour into a greased and floured pan. Bake at 325° for 30 to 40 minutes.

For icing, combine sugar, orange juice, and rind. Frost hot cake. Cut in squares; serve with whipped cream.

Serves 10 to 12.

Charlotte Womack—Greensboro, North Carolina

RATINGS SUMMIT

The original broadcast of "Barney Hosts a Summit Meeting" (Episode #240) on January 29, 1968, earned the highest prime-time rating of any of the 249 *Andy Griffith Show* episodes. Alan Oppenheimer, who plays Mr. Ruskin the interpreter, is familiar to "Murphy Brown" fans as network boss Gene Kinsella.

Mr. Ruskin's Vienna Torte

They'll be rushin' for this.

1 cup sugar
7 eggs, separated
1 tablespoon pulverized coffee
½ pound pecans, finely chopped

⅛ teaspoon salt
¼ pound marshmallows
⅔ cup strong coffee
1 pint heavy cream, whipped

Add sugar to egg yolks. Beat until lemon colored. Mix dry coffee and nuts. Fold into egg yolks, alternating with stiffly beaten egg whites, to which salt has been added. Bake in two 10-inch layer cake pans (butter bottoms of pans) in a 350° oven for about 20 minutes. Cook marshmallows and coffee in a double boiler until blended. Chill thoroughly. Fold

SAY IT AGAIN—Interpreter Ruskin

74

into whipped cream. Spread between layers and over top of cake. (Courtesy of Aunt Irene.)

Serves 8 to 10.

Alan Oppenheimer—Cast member

Mrs. Wiley's Punch Bowl Cake

Brings out the "creaster" in you.

1 12-ounce container nondairy whipped topping, reserve some for topping
1 16½-ounce can crushed pineapple, drained
1 10-ounce package frozen strawberries
1 cup chopped pecans, reserve some for topping

1 package vanilla instant pudding (mix according to package directions, plus 1 extra cup of milk)
1 2-layer yellow cake mix, baked according to package directions

Mix pudding, pineapple, strawberries, whipped topping, and pecans. Crumble first layer of cake in bottom of a large glass bowl. Cover with half of prepared mixture. Repeat layers. End with whipped topping and nuts. Cover with foil. Refrigerate overnight.

Serves 10 to 12.

Edna Weatherly—Charlotte, North Carolina

Kitchen diplomacy:

MR. CLIFFORD: Mr. Ruskin, sit down and help yourself. You must be starved. Mr. Veseiliovich, this is what we call in America "raiding the icebox."

(Mr. Ruskin interprets.)

MR. CLIFFORD: Miss Taylor, I hope we didn't disturb you?

AUNT BEE: No, but I thought I heard somebody down here in the kitchen. Oh, you're hungry, you poor things.

MR. CLIFFORD: I hope you don't mind our helping ourselves this way.

AUNT BEE: No.

MR. VESELIOVICH: Raiding the icebox.

AUNT BEE: That's just fine. Come on over here. You sit right down. My mother said if you eat standing up, it goes right to your legs. See what we have here. Some potato salad. There you are. Some meatloaf and bread pudding.

MR. CLIFFORD: Well, this is wonderful.

Citizen's Arrest
Chocolate Cheesecake

It's so good, it's a crime.

Crust:
1½ cups graham cracker crumbs
⅓ cup sugar
⅓ cup butter or margarine
Filling:
16 ounces cream cheese, softened
1¼ cups sugar

⅓ cup Hershey cocoa
1 teaspoon vanilla extract
2 eggs
Topping:
1 cup sour cream
2 tablespoons sugar
1 teaspoon vanilla extract

Combine crumbs, sugar, and butter. Press on bottom and sides of a 9x1½-inch springform pan.

For filling, blend cream cheese with sugar, cocoa, and vanilla. Add eggs 1 at a time, beating well after each addition. Pour into crust; bake at 375° for 35 minutes. Remove from oven immediately.

For topping combine sour cream, sugar, and vanilla. Spread over top. Cool. Chill for several hours or overnight.

Serves 10 to 12.

Melanie Corgill —Raleigh, North Carolina

Aunt Bee's Toot-Toot-Tootsie
Hello Cake

Toot-Toot-Tootsie, goodbye.

½ box yellow cake mix
1 pound almonds, blanched
1 pint sweet milk
4 eggs, beaten

¼ cup sugar
2 cups muscatel wine
Whipped cream, flavored with wine

Make 1 layer of a plain cake, using half a box yellow cake mix. Cut blanched almonds in half. While cake is baking, brown almonds in oven (not too dark). In top of a double boiler, make a thick custard by warming sweet milk and adding eggs and sugar. Stir well and beat occasionally with an electric beater. Cook until very thick. When custard is cool, add wine. Split layer of cake. Pour a little custard into a glass bowl. Add half of cake. Pour half of remaining custard and half of almonds over cake. Add second layer of cake, remaining custard, and almonds. Chill. Serve with whipped cream, flavored with wine to taste.

Serves 8 to 10.

Mary Embrey Folger—Charlotte, North Carolina

Andy and Rafe Hollister sing along with Barn.

Rafe Hollister's Kahlua Cake

His best shot.

1 box yellow cake mix
1 large box instant chocolate pudding mix
1 cup vegetable oil
¾ cup water

4 large eggs
¼ cup Kahlua
¼ cup vodka
Confectioners' sugar

Put all ingredients, except confectioners' sugar, in a large bowl and mix for 5 minutes. Bake in a bundt or tube pan for 1 hour at 350°. Let cool. Sprinkle with confectioners' sugar.
    Serves 10 to 12.

Dorothy Hull —Pomona, California

Things are a little quieter at the Taylor home ever since Colonel Harvey stopped selling his elixir:

ANDY: I tell you the truth—I'm gonna kinda miss that singing. Hey, I got a idea. For supper tonight, why don't you make a nice big rum cake and get back on that piano?

AUNT BEE: Oh, Andy, please.

Blew the Scramez-vous Cherry Pineapple Nut Cake

No mix-up here.

1 20-ounce can crushed pineapple
   in heavy syrup
1 can cherry pie filling

1 2-layer yellow cake mix
1 cup chopped pecans
1 stick margarine

Preheat the oven to 350°. Grease a 9x13-inch baking dish. Spread pineapple, with its syrup, evenly in baking dish. Spread cherry pie filling over pineapple. Sprinkle dry cake mix, then pecans, over fruit. Cut margarine into thin slices and place over ingredients in pan. Bake for 50 minutes, or until golden. Serve warm.
   Serves 12.

Edna Weatherly—Charlotte, North Carolina

Troublesome Holler Cake

But really it's no trouble and they'll always holler for more.

2 cups graham cracker crumbs
1 stick butter
1 cup chopped pecans, plus extra
   for topping
8 ounces cream cheese
1 cup confectioners' sugar

4½ cups milk, divided
9 ounces nondairy whipped topping,
   divided
1 large box instant chocolate pudding
1 large box instant vanilla pudding

Mix graham crackers, butter, and pecans and press into a 9x13-inch pan. Beat cream cheese, confectioners' sugar, and 1½ cups milk. Stir in half of whipped topping and spread on crust. Let chill. Beat chocolate pudding with 1½ cups milk until thick; spread on top of cream cheese mixture. Beat vanilla pudding with 1½ cups milk and spread on top of chocolate pudding mixture. Top with remaining whipped topping and pecans.
   Serves 12.

Kim and Tim White—Blountville, Tennessee

Rodney's Gooey Butter Cake

The boys are all keyed about this one.

1 box yellow cake mix
1 stick butter, melted
3 eggs

2 cups confectioners' sugar, plus
   extra for topping
8 ounces cream cheese, softened

Combine cake mix, butter, and 1 egg in a bowl. Mix with a fork until mixture forms a paste. Use your hands to press mixture into a greased 9x13-inch pan.

In the same bowl, combine confectioners' sugar, 2 eggs, and cream cheese. Mix with an electric mixer at medium speed until creamy. Spread mixture over crust and bake at 325° for 40 minutes, or until top is firm. Cool. Sprinkle confectioners' sugar on top and cut into squares.

Serves 10 people or 2 Darlings.

Beverly and Rodney Dillard—Cast member
(Chefs of the Month at the Chat 'n' Gobble Cafe in Booger Hollow)

The Quarter of a Million Dollar Question—"Where's his bullet?"

Barney states a mouthful during dinner at the Esquire Club:

ANDY: This is good, Roger. What is it?
ROGER: It's Baked Alaska.
ANDY: I don't believe I ever heard of it.
BARNEY: Sure you have, Andy. You just forgot. That's Baked Alaska. It's that new dessert that come out since it become a state.

TAKING STOCK—
Thanks to Barney, Esquire Club member John Danby (Brad Olson) knows all about how U.S. Steel is doing.

The Esquire types

Clubmen's Baked Alaska

Perfect after a day out on the links—whether you eat it with a spoon or a fork.

1 thin sheet pound cake
1 quart brick vanilla ice cream
Meringue:
3 egg whites

3 tablespoons confectioners' sugar
¾ tablespoon lemon juice or
¼ teaspoon vanilla extract

Cover a board with white paper. Arrange cake on paper and ice cream on cake, having cake extended ½ inch beyond ice cream. (Option: Make a

80

depression in ice cream and spread with fresh sliced strawberries or raspberries in season, or preserves.)

Cover entirely with meringue. Brown quickly in a 450° oven. Slip from paper onto a platter and serve immediately.

For meringue, beat egg whites until stiff, but not dry. Beat in sugar gradually and continue beating until well blended, adding flavoring by the spoonful.

Makes 6 to 8 servings.

Renée M. Austin and the family of
Brad (Joe Bolleter) Olson—Cast member

Darling Boys Mountain Dew Cake

It sure beats their hoot owl pie.

1 box lemon cake mix
1 4½-ounce box lemon instant pudding
¾ cup vegetable oil

4 eggs
1 12-ounce can Mountain Dew

Combine first 4 ingredients; slowly add half the Mountain Dew. Mix; then slowly add remaining Mountain Dew and mix. Pour into a well-greased bundt pan. Bake at 350° (according to package directions).

Serves 10 to 12.

Kim and Tim White—Blountville, Tennessee

Hogette Winslow's Cakette

When it's gone, you won't have to ask, "Is that cake et?"
You'll already know because you et it yourself.

1 small can mandarin oranges, mashed
1 box yellow butter cake mix
4 eggs
1 stick oleo
1 cup vegetable oil

1 small box vanilla instant pudding
1 small can crushed pineapple
½ cup confectioners' sugar
9 ounces nondairy whipped topping
1 cup coconut

Mix first 5 ingredients and bake for 30 minutes at 350°. Let cool.

Mix pudding, pineapple, and confectioner's sugar and spread between layers of cooled cake.

For frosting, mix whipped topping and coconut. Spread over cake.

Serves 8 to 10.

Crystal Taylor—Biloxi, Mississippi

Clara's Nephew Ferdie's Accordion Italian Rum Cake

Otis always saves room for this treat.

2 packages anisette toast biscotti
1 large box chocolate pudding and pie
    filling mix (not instant)
1 small jar maraschino cherries,
    quartered
1 large box vanilla pudding and pie
    filling mix (not instant)

6 cups milk
4 ounces chopped walnuts
2 tablespoons rum extract (Otis adds
    2 tablespoons of real rum besides)
1 large container nondairy whipped
    topping

Slice and open anisette biscotti toasts in half lengthwise. Lay them flat in a 9x12x2-inch dish next to each other to form first layer. Cook chocolate pudding according to package directions. Pour all cooked, uncooled chocolate pudding over layered biscotti. Evenly distribute half the cherries and walnuts over pudding. Sprinkle 1 tablespoon rum extract evenly over layer. Repeat, starting with remaining cut biscotti to form second layer. Cook vanilla pudding according to package directions and pour over second layer of biscotti. Repeat distribution of cherries, walnuts, and rum extract. Cover and refrigerate for at least 2 hours. When ready to serve, spread whipped topping over top. Cut into squares.
    Serves 12.

Joel Redlin—Cast member

Bee Taylor's Deep Pink Ecstasy

Picture perfect.

1 tablespoon butter
½ cup sugar
1 cup flour
1 teaspoon baking powder
½ cup milk
½ teaspoon vanilla extract

1 can pie cherries
1 cup sugar
½ teaspoon salt
1 tablespoon lemon juice
2 tablespoons cornstarch (to thicken)
Whipped cream, optional

Cream butter with ½ cup sugar. Sift flour with baking powder and add alternately to creamed mixture with milk. Add vanilla. Place in a greased 8x8-inch pan. Mix cherries, 1 cup sugar, salt, lemon juice, and cornstarch. Pour cherry mixture on top of batter. Bake for 45 minutes at 375°. Serve plain or with whipped cream.
    Serves 8 to 10.

Dee Boquist—Minneapolis, Minnesota

ALL IN THE FAMILY—
As Clara's nephew, Ferdie just has to be a great cook!

Good Apple Kuchen
Good cookin'!

¾ cup margarine
1 box yellow cake mix
1 20-ounce can apple pie filling
¼ cup sugar

1 teaspoon cinnamon
1 cup sour cream
2 egg yolks

Preheat the oven to 350°. Cut margarine into dry cake mix until crumbly. Pat mixture into an ungreased 13x9-inch pan, building up sides slightly. Bake for 10 minutes. Arrange pie filling on warm crust. Mix sugar and cinnamon; sprinkle on apples. Blend sour cream and egg yolks; drizzle over. Bake for 25 minutes.

Serves 12 to 15.

Lexa Holder—Gordo, Alabama

ACCORDION TO FERDIE

Joel Redlin was the perfect actor to play Clara's nerdy nephew Ferdie in "A Singer in Town" (Episode #189). There aren't many people in Mayberry who can claim to play the accordion, but Clara's star nephew is one.

Barbershop trio

Howard Sprague's Island Coconut Cake
Isle be darned, it's good!

1 pound sour cream	18 ounces frozen coconut
2 cups sugar	1 box yellow butter cake mix

Mix sour cream, sugar, and coconut. Put in a covered container and refrigerate overnight. Bake cake in 2 layers, round or square, according to package directions. When cool, use a thread to split layers to make 4 layers.

Spread coconut filling between layers and on top. Always have cut layer of cake up so that filling can soak in. Wrap well in plastic wrap and refrigerate for at least 3 days before eating. Freezes well.

Serves 10 to 12.

Lois Rogers—Readyville, Tennessee

Creamy Carolina Coffee Cake

It'll put you in a good state of mind.

½ cup margarine, plus 2 tablespoons
8 ounces cream cheese
1¼ cups sugar
2 eggs
1 teaspoon vanilla extract
2 cups flour
1 teaspoon baking powder
½ teaspoon baking soda
¼ teaspoon salt
¼ cup milk
Topping:
⅓ cup brown sugar
⅓ cup cake flour
½ teaspoon cinnamon
2 tablespoons butter or margarine

Cream ½ cup margarine, cream cheese, and sugar. Add eggs and vanilla. Sift together flour, baking powder, soda, and salt. Add dry ingredients, alternating with milk, to creamed mixture. Pour into 2 greased and floured 9-inch round pans or a 9x13-inch pan. Sprinkle with topping.

For topping, combine brown sugar, flour, cinnamon, and butter or margarine. Sprinkle over cake.

Bake at 350° for 30 to 35 minutes. Batter in pans can be frozen before you cook. Just defrost in the refrigerator the night before cooking.

Makes 16 servings.

Ginger Secrest—Shelby, North Carolina

A real roller coaster:

THELMA LOU (to Barney): Here's your cake.
ANDY: Hey, you gonna eat all that cake?
BARNEY: Well why not?
ANDY: Lot of calories in there.
BARNEY: Well, that's O.K.
ANDY: What do you weigh, anyway?
BARNEY: With or without my gun?

(Laughs all around the room.)

ANDY: Without.
BARNEY: Oh, it varies. 138, 138 1/2. I'm up and down.

Sheriff's Pay Day Cake

Check it out.

1 box yellow cake mix
2 sticks margarine, melted and divided
1 egg
2 cups miniature marshmallows
10 ounces peanut butter chips or
  butterscotch chips

2 cups white syrup
2 teaspoons vanilla extract
2 cups Rice Krispies cereal
2 cups salted peanuts

Mix cake mix, 1 stick margarine, and egg. Press into a 9x13-inch pan. Bake at 350° for 15 minutes. Pour marshmallows over hot cake. Mix remaining ingredients and pour over marshmallows.

Serves 15 to 18.

Carolyn and Sterling White—Florence, Alabama

Good reception for Aunt Bee's cooking by TV station owner:

CARL PHILLIPS: In our search we discovered that Miss Taylor has had innumerable recipes of her own published in local papers and has consistently won prizes at county fairs.

ANDY: Oh, yeah. She's been a winner, all right.

OPIE: I think she's the best cook in Mayberry.

Step-by-step directions for catching a cow thief:

BARNEY: I think that can use just a touch more plaster. Always like to make my moulages just a bit on the solid side.

ANDY: I like to use a little egg white in mine—makes 'em moister and fluffier.

Barney's Chocolate Moulage

"Oh, that kind of moulage."

4 whole eggs	1 cup butter
2 egg whites	2 teaspoons vanilla extract
2½ cups sugar	1¼ cups pecans, chopped
⅔ cup all-purpose flour	Chocolate syrup, optional
4 tablespoons cocoa	Ice cream

Beat eggs, egg whites, and sugar with a mixer for 10 minutes. Sift flour and cocoa together; then add, along with butter and vanilla, to mixture. Add nuts. Pour mixture into a greased 12x15x2-inch baking pan. Place pan in a pan of water while baking in a 300° oven for 55 to 60 minutes. (Bake 5 minutes longer if using a slightly smaller and deeper pan.) Drizzle with chocolate syrup before serving, if desired. Serve with your favorite ice cream (also drizzled), and don't worry about the calories because it all goes to muscle.

Makes 10-4 servings.

Don Knotts—Cast member

Fearless

Wise man of Mayberry

Candies

Taylor-Made Candy Strawberries

Andy candy.

1 large box strawberry gelatin
1 cup coconut
1 cup chopped nuts

¾ cup sweetened condensed milk
2 teaspoons vanilla extract
Red decorative sugar

Mix first 3 ingredients. Mix liquid ingredients. Pour liquid mixture into dry ingredients. Mix well. Chill for about 1 hour. Roll out and cut in strawberry shapes. Coat in red decorative sugar. Keep refrigerated.

Makes about 1½ pounds.

Lexa Holder—Gordo, Alabama

Raleigh Almond Butter Crunch

Capital idea.

1 cup butter
1⅓ cups sugar
1 tablespoon light corn syrup
3 tablespoons water

1 cup coarsely chopped blanched almonds,
   toasted
2½ pounds Hershey bars, melted
1 cup finely chopped blanched almonds,
   toasted

Melt butter in a large saucepan. Add sugar, corn syrup, and water. Cook, stirring slowly, to hard-crack stage (300° on a candy thermometer). Watch carefully after temperature reaches 290°. Quickly stir in coarsely chopped nuts and spread in an ungreased 13x9x2-inch pan. Cool thoroughly. Turn out onto waxed paper; spread top with half the melted chocolate, and sprinkle with half the finely chopped nuts. Cover with waxed paper; invert and spread again with chocolate. Sprinkle top with remaining nuts. If necessary, chill to firm chocolate. Break into pieces.

Makes about 4 pounds.

Melanie Corgill—Raleigh, North Carolina

89

Trey Bowden's Coconut Bon-Bons

Trey bon!

¾ cup white corn syrup
1 bag shredded coconut or 2½ cups
  dry macaroon coconut

12 ounces semisweet chocolate chips
4 tablespoons paraffin

Heat syrup until it's very hot. Pour over coconut on a cookie sheet. Let set for 2 to 3 hours or overnight. Roll into small balls. Dip in melted chocolate, to which paraffin has been added.

Makes about 1¾ pounds.

Vicki Venable Snow—Mount Airy, North Carolina

Who's minding the mints?

BARNEY: (on phone) Well, I'll discuss it with Andy. That's all I can promise. Yeah, All right. Good-bye. Andy?

ANDY: Another call from Gomer?

BARNEY: Yep. And he's just come from Pearson's Sweet Shop and he's riled up all over again. Now, Andy, there just might be something to his complaint.

ANDY: But all the years Pearson's run that store, he's been the soul of honesty.

BARNEY: Well, people do change. Now, this just could be something for the bunco squad to handle if there's swindling going on.

ANDY: Swindling's a mighty serious charge.

BARNEY: Well, look at the facts. Thursday, Gomer bought ten lucky peppermints—all white centers. Today, he bought twelve more—again, all white centers—every blessed one. Now, Gomer ain't saying that he expects to get the green one and win the flashlight right off. He's not being unreasonable. All he's saying is that out of twenty-two, he might expect to bite into one pink center for a free one.

ANDY: Well, I will admit that twenty-two whities in a row is mighty upsetting to a man. But I still can't believe that Jesse Pearson would ever run a fixed peppermint box.

BARNEY: Well, I don't know, Andy. Gomer's got some cash invested and I think there ought to be laws to protect him.

ANDY: All right. You call Gomer and tell him we do have laws against swindling.

BARNEY: Okay.

ANDY: While you're at it, tell him we've got a few laws against gambling, too.

BARNEY: Aw, come on, Andy. Now, that's not really gambling. I mean it's not like bingo or something like that.

Opie and Andy—Housekeepers extraordinaire

Good Ol' 14-A Nut Rolls

Hazel knows the key.

1 can sweetened condensed milk
1 pound large marshmallows
1 pound vanilla wafers, ground
1 pound black walnuts
  (can mix with pecans)

1 pound raisins (I use dark ones)
Melted margarine
2 cups ground walnuts or pecans

Pour sweetened condensed milk and marshmallows into a large double boiler. Stir occasionally until all is melted. In a large bowl, pour vanilla wafers, nuts, and raisins into marshmallow mixture, a few at a time until all are used (mixture will be very thick). Using a bowl of melted margarine, grease your fingers and pinch off prepared mixture (you determine size of pieces). Have a sheet of waxed paper with ground nuts spread on it to roll pieces in. (I usually make the rolls 4 or 5 inches long and about 1½ inches thick.) After you finish the rolls, you can immediately wrap them in foil (I use plastic bags and freeze). They will keep indefinitely.

Makes about 5 pounds.

Hazel Laxton—Lenoir, North Carolina

Taking aim

Colonel Harvey's Creamy Mocha Fudge

They're devils!

12 ounces semisweet chocolate chips
1 cup milk chocolate chips
2 tablespoons milk
1 14-ounce can sweetened condensed milk

1 tablespoon coffee-flavored Indian elixir
1 teaspoon vanilla extract
1 cup chopped nuts

Place chips, milk, sweetened condensed milk, coffee-flavored Indian elixir, and vanilla in a heavy saucepan. Place over low heat until melted. Remove from heat. Stir in nuts. Spread evenly in a foil-lined 9-inch square pan. Chill for 3 hours or until firm. Turn fudge onto a cutting board. Peal off foil and cut into squares. (Four teaspoons instant coffee dissolved in 1 tablespoon warm water can be substituted for coffee-flavored Indian elixir.)

Makes about 2 pounds.

Jan and Allan Newsome—Huntsville, Alabama

Briscoe's Brittle Brack Brittle

It's about the only thing that Briscoe can't get to come out of his jug.

2 cups sugar
⅔ cups white corn syrup
½ cup water

1 teaspoon salt
1 teaspoon baking soda
2 cups parched corn

Boil sugar, corn syrup, and water; do not stir. Boil until it threads; then add parched corn and stir until mixture turns golden. Remove from heat; stir in the salt and baking soda. Pour onto a buttered cookie sheet and cool before breaking it apart.

Makes about 1½ pounds.

Denver Pyle—Cast member

Call the Roll Pecan Roll

You'll always have perfect attendance at your table with this.

1 12-ounce box vanilla wafers, crushed
2½ cups chopped pecans
1 cup chopped dates

1 can sweetened condensed milk
Confectioners' sugar

Mix wafers, pecans, and dates; then add sweetened condensed milk. Combine until mixed. Put on waxed paper with confectioners' sugar. Slowly shape into logs or rolls. Refrigerate each log until ready to serve (best if refrigerated overnight).

Makes about 2½ pounds.

Melanie Corgill—Raleigh, North Carolina

Weaver's Peanut Butter Fudge

Goodness is in store for you here.

1½ cups brown sugar
1½ cups white sugar
1 cup milk

1 cup peanut butter
1 teaspoon vanilla extract
⅛ teaspoon salt

Combine sugars and milk. Cook to soft-ball stage. Remove from heat. Add peanut butter, vanilla, and salt; beat. When it starts getting dull looking and harder to beat, it is ready to be poured into a pan to harden.

Makes about 3 pounds.

Kim and Marvin Miller—Terre Haute, Indiana

93

Wednesday Night Chocolate Fudge

For when you've already used the cashew nuts on Tuesday.

2 cups sugar
¼ cup light corn syrup
½ cup milk
½ cup shortening

2 squares chocolate or 4 tablespoons cocoa
¼ teaspoon salt
1 teaspoon vanilla extract

Stir first 6 ingredients over low heat until chocolate and shortening melt. Bring to a full rolling boil, stirring constantly. Boil for 2 minutes at 220°. Remove from heat and beat until lukewarm. Stir in vanilla. Beat until a smooth, spreading consistency is reached. Pour into a lightly greased pan and allow to cool before serving.

Makes about 1½ pounds.

Susie Luguire—Tuscaloosa, Alabama

Dr. Pendyke's Peanut Brittle

It can cure anything.

½ cup white corn syrup
1 cup sugar
2 cups raw, shelled peanuts

1 tablespoon water
½ teaspoon salt
½ teaspoon baking soda

In a heavy saucepan, mix all ingredients, except soda. Cook on high or medium heat until peanuts pop open and syrup begins to brown (hard-crack stage, or 295 to 300° on a candy thermometer). Remove from stove and immediately add soda. Stir quickly until mixed. Pour on a buttered marble slab or hot platter (or the Sunday paper covered with tin foil, in a pinch). Spread thin. Cool and break into pieces.

(Option: Add a small handful of chopped black walnuts just before removing from heat.)

Makes about 1 pound.

Jennie Crevison—Smyrna, Tennessee

When a man's had cashew fudge every Tuesday for years:

ANDY: You go ahead. Besides, I wouldn't feel right having Thelma Lou spend the whole evening alone in a dark room with George Raft.

BARNEY: Well, she is probably expecting me, you know. I mean she's more than likely making up a whole pan of cashew fudge.

Pistol-Packin' Pecan Pralines

Give 'em a shot.

3 cups packed light brown sugar
1 cup milk
¼ teaspoon cream of tartar
⅛ teaspoon salt

2 tablespoons butter
1 teaspoon vanilla extract
2¼ cups pecan halves

In a heavy saucepan, cook and stir sugar, milk, cream of tartar, and salt over low heat until sugar is dissolved. Continue cooking without stirring to soft-ball stage (236° on a candy thermometer). Cool to warm (110°); beat in butter, vanilla, and pecans until creamy. Drop from a large spoon onto waxed paper and let stand until firm.

Makes about 2 pounds.

Linda and Jack Densmore—Denton, Maryland

Mayberry trio

Battle of Mayberry Bridge
Butterscotch Fudge Log

Maybe this is what they were fighting about.

6 ounces semisweet chocolate morsels
6 ounces butterscotch morsels
1 can sweetened condensed milk

1 cup coarsely chopped walnuts or pecans
1 teaspoon vanilla extract
1 cup walnut or pecan halves, divided

Melt chocolate and butterscotch morsels with condensed milk in a double boiler over hot water. Stir until morsels melt and mixture starts to thicken. Remove from heat and add chopped nuts and vanilla. Blend well and chill until thickened (about 1 hour). Spread a 12-inch piece of aluminum foil with ¾ cup nut halves in a strip about 2 inches wide. Spoon chilled mixture on top of nuts to form a flat log and decorate with remaining nut halves. Chill until firm and slice in half-inch slices.

Makes 30 to 36 slices.

Nancy Clark—Greensboro, North Carolina

"We're having a band concert—tonight!"

96

Lorraine's Fudge

From all the way over in Mt. Pilot.

1 large can evaporated milk
5 cups sugar
2 sticks margarine
1 pound marshmallows

12 ounces semisweet chocolate chips
4 squares unsweetened chocolate
2 cups chopped nuts, optional

In a large, heavy pan, mix milk, sugar, and margarine. Boil for 6 minutes. Time this from the first sign of boiling. Stir constantly. Remove from heat and add marshmallows, chips, and chocolate. Beat rapidly for 1 minute. Add nuts, if desired, and pour into a greased pan. Cut when cold.
    Makes about 5 pounds.

Lorraine Gilley—Pilot Mountain, North Carolina

Briscoe's Buckeyes

Eat 'em for luck.

1 pound confectioners' sugar
    (sifted 4 3/4 cups)
½ cup margarine, softened
1½ ounces creamy peanut butter

1 teaspoon vanilla extract
½ teaspoon salt
12 ounces semisweet chocolate pieces
½ block paraffin wax

Thoroughly blend confectioners' sugar, margarine, peanut butter, vanilla, and salt. Shape into ½-inch balls. Place chocolate pieces and paraffin in top of a double boiler. Heat over boiling water until melted. (The water in bottom of pan should not touch top pan.) Insert a toothpick in a candy ball. Dip ¾ of a ball into chocolate mixture. Place on waxed paper until set. Remove toothpick, smooth over toothpick hole, and place in bonbon cups.
    Makes 8 dozen.

Alma Venable—Mount Airy, North Carolina

Old Man MacKnight's Popcorn Balls

They're Grand!

¼ bar butter or margarine
Approximately 3 spoonfuls of molasses

Approximately 2 spoonfuls sugar
Popcorn

Mix butter, molasses, and sugar and boil in a skillet. While mixture is hot, pour over popcorn in a pan and mix well. Shape popcorn balls and eat.

Tommie and Nessie Mae Rogers—Woodbury, Tennessee

97

Full Moon Butterscotch Pecan Candy

They'll ride in from all directions for this.

½ cup sugar
1 cup light brown sugar, packed
2 tablespoons light corn syrup
⅓ cup water

½ teaspoon cider vinegar
6 ounces butterscotch morsels
1 cup pecan halves

Mix sugars, syrup, water, and vinegar and boil for 2 minutes. Remove from heat and mix in butterscotch morsels and pecan halves until morsels have melted. Drop by spoonful onto waxed paper with 2 pecan halves in each drop. Keep a few extra pecan halves for leftover syrup.

Makes about 1½ pounds.

Alice Schwenke—Houston, Texas

Irene Phlogg's Peanut Butter Fudge

Premiere attraction.

2 cups sugar
1 cup milk
½ cup butter

1 7-ounce jar marshmallow creme
12 ounces peanut butter
1 teaspoon vanilla extract

Combine sugar, milk, and butter. Bring to a full boil. Cook rapidly over medium heat for 12 to 15 minutes. Stir constantly. Remove from heat. Add marshmallow creme, peanut butter, and vanilla. Beat until blended. Pour into a greased 9-inch square pan. Let cool and cut into small squares.

Makes about 2 pounds.

Amy Wolfford—Elizabethtown, Kentucky

Claude's Crunchy Chocolate Fudge

They'll be beamin' after they try this!

12 ounces chocolate chips
1¼ cups crunchy peanuts

1 14-ounce can sweetened condensed milk

In a double boiler, melt chocolate chips and add crunchy peanuts. Remove from heat and stir in sweetened milk. Mix well. Pour mixture into an 8-inch pan lined with wax paper. Spread evenly; chill for 2 hours until firm. Turn fudge out, peel off waxed paper, and cut into squares.

Makes 2 pounds.

Harriet Patterson—Greensboro, North Carolina

PAIL BLUES—Gomer prepares to "take a think" under the bucket provided by Sgt. Carter.

Christmas Strawberry Divinity

Lots of fruits and nuts and candy.

3 cups sugar
¾ cup light corn syrup
¾ cup water
2 egg whites, stiffly beaten

1 3-ounce package strawberry gelatin
½ cup flaked coconut
1 cup chopped pecans

Combine sugar, corn syrup, and water. Bring to a boil, stirring constantly. Reduce heat and cook to hard-ball stage (252°), stirring constantly. Combine beaten egg whites and gelatin. Beat until mixture forms peaks. Pour hot syrup in thin stream into egg whites, beating until candy loses gloss and holds shape. Fold in coconut and nuts. Pour into a greased 9-inch square pan. Top with rows of chopped pecans and coconut.

Makes about 36 pieces.

Tim Simpson—Greensboro, North Carolina

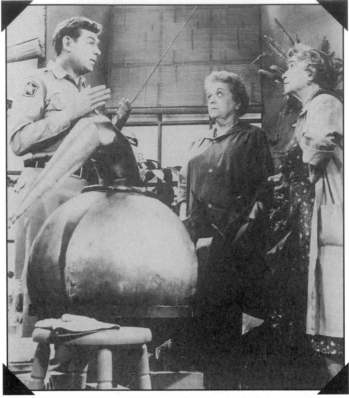

MAYBERRY STILL LIFE—Andy informs the Morrison Sisters that it's time to celebrate National Still-Smashing Day.

Morrison Sisters' Bourbon Balls

For special occasions only.

1 stick butter or margarine
1 can sweetened condensed milk
1 16-ounce can coconut
2 10-ounce boxes confectioners' sugar

12 ounces pecans
¼ to ⅓ cup mild bourbon
1 bar paraffin wax
12 ounces semisweet chocolate chips

Melt butter or margarine and let cool. Add milk. Mix with coconut, confectioners' sugar, pecans, and bourbon. Roll into little balls and refrigerate overnight. The next evening, melt paraffin and add semisweet chocolate chips. Use toothpicks to dip balls into paraffin. Candies will wax over in just a second, but you must keep paraffin and chocolate hot or it will set.
    Makes 3½ to 4 pounds.

Mable Helton—Readyville, Tennessee

Martha Washington Candy

By George, it's good.

1 stick margarine, softened
2 pounds confectioners' sugar
1 14-ounce can sweetened condensed milk
1 cup finely chopped pecans

1 cup flaked coconut
1 1-ounce block paraffin wax
4 ounces sweet chocolate squares

Beat margarine, sugar, and milk together well. Mix in pecans and coconut. Chill for 1 hour. Roll into little balls; place on a tray and refrigerate for 30 minutes. Melt paraffin and chocolate together over boiling water, or slowly in a microwave. Put a toothpick into each ball and dip in chocolate mixture to coat. Return to tray and cool thoroughly before serving or packaging as gifts.

Makes 4 pounds.

Janine Johnson—Orlando, Florida

Mrs. Wiley's Caramel Apple Slices Ankrum

It's very niece.

1 tart apple
1 carton caramel apple dip
    (can use nonfat)

Peanuts, almonds, pecans, walnuts, or
    any nut, crushed

Slice apple neatly. Dunk slices into caramel dip. Press caramelized slices into crushed nuts. Then munch and crunch. This is easier to eat than a whole candy apple and conserves on those little white sticks.

Makes 1 happy.

Jackie Joseph—Cast member

BARNEY'S CHEAP DATE QUIZ

1. How much does the Family Dinner for One cost when Barney takes Juanita to Mt. Pilot for Chinese?
   Answer: $2.75

2. Bread, Love, and Beans was the name of a movie playing in what town?
   Answer: Raleigh

3. What were the words on Barney's deputying anniversary cake?
   Answer: Congratulations Deputy Barney

Post Toasties Candy

They're gooood!

1 large box Post Toasties cereal
3 cups peanut butter
3 cups sugar

1½ cups white syrup
12 ounces semisweet chocolate chips
1 bar paraffin wax

Pulverize Post Toasties, then add peanut butter and mix thoroughly. Combine sugar and syrup and bring to a boil. Pour boiling mixture over peanut butter and Post Toasties and mix thoroughly. Put in a greased pan and flatten out. Use waxed paper and place over candy in pan and mash down over candy to get candy hard. Cool and cut into squares. Melt chocolate chips and paraffin; then use toothpicks to dip candies in paraffin and chocolate chips.

Makes about 5 pounds.

Mable Helton —Readyville, Tennessee

Ernest T. Bass Rock Candy

You can take it for granite that it's almost as sweet as Romeena.

3 cups sugar

1¼ cups water

First, you find a foil pan that's the size and shape of a window pane at Hogette Winslow's house (about 8x8 inches). Then at a point about half as deep as the pan is, you punch 7 or 8 pinholes, about as far apart from each other as your thumb is wide—all the way across a side of the pan, and then you do the same on the opposite side of the pan. Then you take some string and jab it through the holes from one side to the other like you were making a possum trap. Sometimes I like to put masking tape over the outside of the holes to cut down on stuff seeping out, but usually I just put the foil pan inside a larger pan to catch anything that drips out of the holes.

After you've got the pan ready, you dissolve the sugar in the water by cooking it in a pot on high (without stirring) until it's hot enough to make rocks (right at 250°). Next, you pour the syrup into the pan that has the strings. The strings should be covered with almost an inch of syrup. Cover the whole surface with foil. Now, you'll have time for dancing or for going off into the woods to kill a mockingbird because it might take a week for the rocks to form. (The bestest rocks take time.) Once the rock crystals have formed, cut the strings from the pan and pry the rocks loose. Wash off the rocks with cold water like a raccoon does and then put them in an oven that's just warm enough for the rocks to dry out and harden up just right. Now, the rocks are ready for throwin'—I mean, eatin'.

How to get a girl: Make flavored rocks by adding a few drops of your favorite extract. Try peppermint for Christmas or cherry for George Washington's birthday (see, I really was learning when I got my diploma from my "mother figure"!) And make different colors with food coloring. You'll have the purtiest rocks this side of Old Man Kelsey's ocean.

Makes about 1½ pounds, but who's counting?

Howard Morris—Cast member

"DIDN'T SAY NOTHING ABOUT NO BRICKS"—
Ernest T. promises not to throw any more rocks.

Mr. Potato Candy

Sets well.

1 small potato
¼ teaspoon vanilla extract

Confectioners' sugar
Peanut butter

Peel and boil potato. While it's still hot, mash and add vanilla. Add confectioners' sugar, a little at a time, until it reaches a doughlike consistency. Roll out and spread peanut butter on dough. Roll into a log and cut into pieces. Let set on waxed paper until firm. (For chocolate flavor, add 1 tablespoon cocoa when adding vanilla.)
    Makes about ½ pound.

Mary Lock—Stephens City, Virginia

Calvin Coolidge Cashew Fudge

You can enjoy this until you're at least 92.

The flavor of this fudge is affected by which brands of chocolate chips, marshmallows, and nuts you use—and by the balance of sugar and salt. After much experimentation, we decided we like this combination of brands best.

⅔ cup evaporated milk
1½ cups sugar
¼ teaspoon salt (½ teaspoon,
    if using unsalted nuts)
1 teaspoon vanilla extract

1½ cups small Kraft marshmallows
1½ cups milk chocolate chips
    (Guittard or Hershey perform best)
½ cup to ¾ cup Planters salted cashew
    pieces or cashew halves, chopped

In a large saucepan, combine evaporated milk, sugar, and salt. Heat to boiling over medium heat. Cook for 5 minutes, stirring constantly (4 minutes if making just half a batch, 6 minutes if making a double batch). Remove from heat and immediately stir in vanilla. (Vanilla should bubble when you add it. Don't let mixture cool before adding vanilla. If vanilla doesn't sizzle when you add it, the flavor will be different.) Add marshmallows and chocolate chips to the mixture. Stir for 1 to 2 minutes. Then stir in cashew pieces. (Option: Reserve a couple of tablespoons of nuts to sprinkle on the top).
    Pour into a buttered 9x9-inch pan. Cool and cut into squares. Watch that doctor show on TV.
    Makes about 1½ pounds.

Ellen, Martin, and Joel Simmons—Milton, Florida

104

Mayberry's top cops

BARNEY: Thelma Lou and I have always had a standing date on Tuesday nights. Every Tuesday night for as long as I can remember, we're setting on the couch, a pan of cashew fudge between us, watching that doctor show on TV.

Cool kid

Cookies

Opie's Trick or Treat Cookies

The best trick is to treat yourself to these.

½ cup butter or margarine, softened
1 cup sugar
1 cup firmly packed brown sugar,
  plus 2 tablespoons
3 eggs
2 cups peanut butter
¾ teaspoon light corn syrup

¼ teaspoon vanilla extract
4½ cups regular oats, uncooked
2 teaspoons baking soda
¼ teaspoon salt
1 cup M&M candies
6 ounces semisweet chocolate chips

Cream butter; gradually add sugar. Beat well with an electric mixer at medium speed. Add eggs, peanut butter, syrup, and vanilla. Beat well. Add oats, soda, and salt; stir well. Stir in remaining ingredients (dough will be stiff). Pack dough into a ¼ cup measure. Drop dough, 4 inches apart, onto lightly greased cookie sheets. Lightly press each cookie into a 3½-inch circle with fingertips. Bake at 350° for 12 to 15 minutes (centers of cookies will be slightly soft). Cool slightly on cookie sheets; remove to wire racks and cool completely.

    Makes 2½ dozen.

Maureen Arthur and Aaron Ruben—Writer, producer, and director

---

KIDS EAT THE DARNEDEST THINGS QUIZ

1. What food did Johnny Paul Jason once drop on the ground at school?
   Answer: His bacon, lettuce, and tomato sandwich

2. Goober once ate 57 of what in a contest?
   Answer: Pancakes

3. Who makes peanut butter and bologna, peanut butter and liverwurst, and peanut butter and peanut butter sandwiches for a hungry cowboy?
   Answer: Opie

Dobro Dunking Platters
They'll slide right into your mouth.

These are my all-time favorite cookies. Whenever my wife Jan and I travel in our motor home, I have a gallon of these scrumptious cookies right beside my seat. When I get the munchies, all I have to do is dip in. They also go with a hot cup of English tea with milk. Dunk them and enjoy!

2 cups margarine or butter, melted	2 cups corn flakes
2 cups brown sugar, packed	4 cups flour
2 cups sugar	2 teaspoons baking soda
4 eggs, beaten	2 teaspoons baking powder
2 teaspoons vanilla extract	1½ cups raisins
2 cups oatmeal	1 cup shredded coconut

Blend margarine and sugars. Stir in eggs and vanilla. Mix in oatmeal and corn flakes. Sift flour with soda and baking powder and combine thoroughly with oatmeal mixture. Stir in raisins and coconut. Drop by tablespoonful onto ungreased cookie sheet and bake at 350° for about 12 minutes. Keep cookies well separated because they will spread while baking.
Makes about 6 dozen large cookies.

LeRoy McNees—Cast member

Half Moon Trailer Park Pecan Crescents
They'll be rolling before you know it.

1 cup margarine	2 cups sifted flour
6 tablespoons confectioners' sugar,	½ teaspoon salt
plus extra for topping	1 cup chopped pecans
1 teaspoon vanilla extract	

Cream margarine; add sugar and vanilla. Mix well; then add flour and salt. Mix well; then add nuts. Taking a small amount of dough, roll in pen-

---

A KISS AND GOODBYE

Actor George Spence chuckles when recalling that he was accidentally too good in his one-episode appearance as boyfriend Frank in "Guest in the House" (Episode #151). His part called for him to kiss Andy's pretty "cousin" Gloria (Jan Shutan). But he laments that he did the scene so well that the director used the first take. No more kisses, by George.

---

cil shapes about 2 to 2½ inches long and form crescents. Bake on greased cookie sheets at 350° for 5 to 8 minutes. Cool and dust with confectioners' sugar.

Yields 2 to 3 dozen.

Carolyn and Sterling White—Florence, Alabama

Florrie's Fancy Nut Cookies
Frankly delicious.

2 sticks margarine
½ cup sugar
1 egg yolk

2 cups plain flour
Pecans, finely chopped
Red raspberry preserves

Cream margarine. Add sugar and cream again. Add egg yolk; then add flour, a little at a time. Shape into small balls and roll in chopped pecans. Make a dent in center of each cookie and bake at 250° for 1 hour. When finished, fill dent with red raspberry preserves (other flavors can be substituted).

Yields 2 to 3 dozen.

Mr. and Mrs. George Spence—Cast member

FRANK ENCOUNTER—*Frank the boyfriend makes his sole visit to Mayberry to reunite with his fiancée, Andy's "cousin" Gloria.*

Gifted Opie

Mayberry Holiday Sugar Cookies

They make even Scrooge smile.

4 cups flour
1 teaspoon baking powder
1 teaspoon baking soda
¾ teaspoon salt
¾ teaspoon nutmeg

1 cup soft butter or ½ butter,
  ½ shortening
1½ cups sugar, plus extra for topping
2 teaspoons vanilla extract
2 eggs
¾ cup sour cream

Grease a baking sheet lightly. Preheat the oven to 450°. Using a 3-quart mixing bowl, sift flour, measure; resift 4 times with next 4 ingredients. Cream butter until smooth. Add sugar gradually, creaming well. Stir in vanilla. Beat in eggs until fluffy. Add flour mixture alternately with sour cream in 2 or 3 portions, mixing until smooth after each addition. Cover bowl and chill in the refrigerator 1 hour or so to firm dough for easier rolling. Remove ⅓ at a time; roll out on a lightly floured pastry cloth. Cut out with cookie cutters. Place on a baking sheet and sprinkle with sugar. Bake for 9 to 10 minutes. Remove at once to cool. Store in a tightly covered cookie jar.
    Makes 40.

Don Scheib—Bradford, Ohio

Highway 6 Speedy Graham Cracker Goodie

If you give 'em one, they'll take two; if you give 'em two . . .

1 cup light brown sugar
2 sticks butter or margarine

1 cup chopped pecans
Graham crackers

Boil brown sugar, butter, and pecans for 2 minutes. Line a cookie sheet with aluminum foil and graham crackers. Pour mix over crackers. Bake at 350° to 400° for 5 minutes. Break apart immediately.

Makes about 2 dozen.

Jack and Jodie Ginn—Decatur, Georgia

Magical Mr. Dave Brownies

Tuscarora!

⅓ cup margarine
1 cup sugar
2 eggs
½ teaspoon vanilla extract
⅔ cup plain flour
3 tablespoons cocoa

⅓ cup chopped pecans
Frosting:
2 tablespoons cocoa
1 cup sugar
¼ cup milk
¼ cup margarine

Cream margarine and sugar. Add eggs and vanilla; beat until fluffy. Add flour and cocoa, which have been sifted together. Stir in chopped nuts. Spread into a greased 9-inch square pan and bake at 350° for 20 minutes or until done. Frost when cooled.

For frosting, combine cocoa, sugar, and milk in a saucepan. Boil for 3 minutes or until a ball forms in cold water. Remove from heat and add margarine; beat until cool. Spread on brownies.

Makes about 2 to 3 dozen.

Linda Snead—Tuscaloosa, Alabama

The Great Brownie Inquisition:

OPIE: How long does it take for brownies to cook?
AUNT BEE: Thirty minutes.
OPIE: After they come out of the oven, do they have to cool off before you can eat 'em? I like to eat 'em hot. You gonna put some conventionary sugar on 'em? Gee, I hope they come out nice and chewy. I think they're done. I'll get a plate ready.

Gomer's Gun-Drop Gum Drop Cookies

They'll always come back for these.

4 eggs
2¼ cups brown sugar
1 pound orange gum drop sections
  cut in small pieces
¼ cup flour for dredging gum drops
½ cup pecans

1¾ cups flour
1 teaspoon baking powder
Pinch of salt
1 teaspoon vanilla extract
Confectioners' sugar

Beat eggs; add brown sugar and gum drop pieces that have been dredged in ¼ cup flour. Add pecans. Mix in rest of flour sifted with baking powder and salt. Add vanilla. Line a 10x14-inch pan with waxed paper. (Size of pan can vary an inch or so.) Place spoonfuls of mixture all over pan as it does not spread until warm. Put in a 300° oven and cook for about 40 minutes. (Time will vary according to pan size). Turn out onto cloth or brown

Chance of a ghost?

paper. Remove waxed paper carefully. Cut into squares using 2 knives dusted with confectioners' sugar to help with cutting. Dust cookies well with confectioners' sugar.

Makes about 3 to 4 dozen.

Tonya Hamel—Greensboro, North Carolina

Cherry Berry Bin Bars
Something from the light classics.

½ cup butter
3 tablespoons confectioners' sugar
1¼ cups all-purpose flour, divided
2 eggs, beaten
½ cup flaked coconut

1 cup coarsely chopped, drained,
  maraschino cherries
½ teaspoon baking powder
¼ teaspoon salt
1 teaspoon vanilla extract

Preheat the oven to 350°. Using an ungreased 8x8-inch baking pan, combine butter, sugar, and 1 cup flour for crust. Pat into pan and bake for 20 minutes or until light brown. Mix eggs, coconut, cherries, baking powder, ¼ cup flour, salt, and vanilla. Spread over partially baked crust and bake for 30 minutes. Cool and cut into 2x1-inch bars.

Makes 2 to 3 dozen.

Annette Davis—Greensboro, North Carolina

Old Man Remshaw's Haunted House Pumpkin Bars
Yours for the axing.

1⅔ cups sugar
1 cup oil
4 eggs
2 cups canned pumpkin
2 teaspoons cinnamon
½ teaspoon salt
2 cups flour
2 teaspoons baking powder

1 teaspoon baking soda
Frosting:
3 ounces cream cheese
½ stick margarine, softened
1 tablespoon milk
2 cups confectioners' sugar
½ teaspoon vanilla extract

Combine first 9 ingredients and pour into an 11x17x1-inch ungreased pan. Bake at 350° for about 30 minutes.

For frosting, mix cream cheese, margarine, milk, confectioners' sugar, and vanilla. Spread evenly on bars.

Makes about 4 to 6 dozen.

Pat Rasmussen—Cokato, Minnesota

Sound Committee Potato Chip Cookies

Dig 'em; they're real cool.

1 cup shortening
1 cup brown sugar
1 cup white sugar
2 eggs, beaten
1 teaspoon vanilla extract

2 cups flour
1 teaspoon baking soda
½ to 1 cup chopped nuts
1 cup potato chips, crushed

Preheat the oven to 375°. Cream shortening and sugars. Blend in beaten eggs and vanilla. Sift flour and soda and add to mixture. Add nuts and chips. Drop by teaspoonful onto a lightly greased cookie sheet. Bake for 10 to 12 minutes. For variety, try different flavored potato chips!
    Makes about 3 dozen.

Karen Mol—Grand Rapids, Michigan

The Monster That Ate Minnesota Snowball Cookies

Even better than the ones in Anteaters from Outer Space.

¾ cup softened butter
1 teaspoon vanilla extract
1 tablespoon water
⅛ teaspoon salt
⅓ cup sugar

2 cups sifted flour
6 ounces chocolate chips
½ cup finely chopped nuts
Confectioners' sugar

Combine first 5 ingredients and blend well. Stir in flour, chips, and nuts. Form into 1-inch balls. Bake on an ungreased cookie sheet at 325° for 15 to 18 minutes. Roll cookies in confectioners' sugar while still warm.
    Makes 2 to 3 dozen.

Pat Rasmussen—Cokato, Minnesota

Opie's Better Batter Peanut Butter Cookies

A home run every time.

1 cup plain or crunchy peanut butter
1 cup white sugar
1 egg

1 teaspoon vanilla extract
Chocolate chips, optional

Mix all ingredients, except chocolate chips, well and form into small balls. Place on a greased cookie sheet. Flatten with a fork dipped in sugar.

Mayberry Giants

Bake at 325° for 8 to 10 minutes. (Option: Press a ball of cookie dough with your hand and place a chocolate chip in the middle of each cookie before baking.)

Makes 2 to 3 dozen.

Mary Ruth Lee—Wake Forest, North Carolina

Floss's Welsh Cakes

We bet you'll love 'em.

4 cups flour	1½ cups sugar, plus extra for topping
3 teaspoons baking powder	¼ teaspoon nutmeg
½ teaspoon salt	½ package currants
¼ pound margarine	2 eggs
¼ pound butter	Milk (if needed)

Mix ingredients in order; then roll out on a floured board to ¼ inch thick and cut with a cookie cutter or 2½-inch glass. Cook on a griddle at 350° until lightly brown. Sprinkle with sugar.

Makes 6 to 8 dozen.

Barbara Perry—Cast member

"Barney, why do you want to go to the duck pond?"

Tiger Fife's Low-Fat Brownies

It all goes to muscle.

2 ounces unsweetened chocolate	½ cup water
1 cup sugar	½ cup applesauce
1 egg	1 cup flour
1 teaspoon vanilla extract	1 cup chopped nuts, optional

Melt chocolate; add sugar and egg. Blend. Add vanilla, water, and apple-sauce. Mix well. Add flour and nuts. Stir until well blended. Spread in a greased square pan. Bake at 350° for 25 to 30 minutes.

Makes 2 to 3 dozen.

Kay and Dan Sisk—Albuquerque, New Mexico

George Barstow's Easy Butter Cookies

They deliver.

2 sticks butter	1 teaspoon almond extract
½ cup sugar	2⅓ cups all-purpose flour
1 egg	

116

Cream butter. Gradually add sugar and beat until light and fluffy. Beat in egg and extract. Gradually blend in flour. Fill a cookie press with ¼ cup of dough at a time; form desired shapes on an ungreased cookie sheet. Bake in a preheated 350° oven for 8 to 10 minutes. Remove immediately to a wire rack to cool.

Makes about 7 dozen cookies.

Pat Rasmussen—Cokato, Minnesota

Malcolm's Cheerio Cherry Squares
Cherries. Oh!

½ pound butter or margarine, softened
1 cup sugar
1 teaspoon vanilla extract
2 eggs

2 cups flour
1 cup chopped walnuts
1 can cherry pie filling
Confectioners' sugar

Cream butter and sugar. Add vanilla. Beat in eggs, 1 at a time. Stir in flour. Add nuts last. Spread ¾ of batter in a greased 13x9-inch pan. Cover with pie filling. Drop remaining batter by the spoonful on top and spread as best you can. Cherries should show through a bit. Bake at 325° for 45 minutes. Sprinkle with confectioners' sugar; cool slightly and cut into bars.

Makes 3 to 4 dozen.

Terry Quinsey—Fort Erie, Ontario

With Thelma Lou's brownie remedy, Opie forgets that he has another care in the world:

THELMA LOU: When I get home I'm gonna make some brownies. I sure could use a test pilot.

ANDY: You mean fudge brownies?

THELMA LOU: Uh-huh, to go with my homemade peach ice cream.

ANDY: Well how about that! Opie'd be glad to go with you, Thelma Lou, wouldn't you, Opie?

THELMA LOU: (to Andy) He's sure lovesick, isn't he?

ANDY: A batch of your fudge brownies just might be the antidote.

THELMA LOU: Which do you like?

OPIE: I like 'em with walnuts and pecans, and I just like 'em plain too.

Howard Sprague's Classy Cut-outs
They'll make history.

2 cups white sugar
1 cup lard
2 eggs
2 teaspoons vanilla extract
5 cups flour, divided

1 teaspoon baking soda
2 teaspoons baking powder
¼ teaspoon salt
1 cup buttermilk

Cream sugar and lard. Add eggs and vanilla and beat well. Sift 2 cups flour with soda, baking powder, and salt. Add to creamed mixture and stir. Alternate remaining cups of flour and buttermilk into batter and stir well. Refrigerate overnight. Roll out on a floured board, cut into desired shapes, and place on a cookie sheet. Bake for 10 minutes at 350°.
Makes 6 to 8 dozen.

Dorothy Menge—Jacksonville, Illinois

Carolina Moon Chocolates
They'll make you glow.

1 package dark chocolate cake mix
½ cup cooking oil
2 large eggs

1 cup chocolate chips
½ cup walnuts, chopped

Blend cake mix, oil, and eggs. Stir in chocolate chips and nuts. Drop from a spoon, leaving room to expand. Bake on an ungreased cookie sheet at 350° for 12 to 15 minutes.
Makes 3 to 4 dozen.

Terry Quinsey—Fort Erie, Ontario

Judy, Judy, Judy Cookies
You'll never take them for Granted.

2¼ cups flour
1 teaspoon baking soda
1 teaspoon salt
2 sticks butter, softened
¾ cup granulated sugar

¾ cup light brown sugar, packed
2 eggs
1 teaspoon vanilla extract
12 ounces chocolate chips
2 cups pecan halves

In a small bowl, combine flour, baking soda, and salt. Set aside. In a large bowl, blend butter and sugars until creamy. Add eggs and beat until very fluffy; add vanilla and gradually beat in flour mixture. Stir in chocolate chips and nuts. Drop by tablespoonful onto an ungreased baking sheet. Bake at 375° for 8 to 10 minutes. Do not overbake.

Makes 3 to 4 dozen.

Judy Vieira—Jacksonville, Illinois

Crosswaith Chocolate Chess Squares

You'll sit around and chit-chat about these for hours.

1 box chocolate cake mix	½ cup chopped nuts
3 eggs, divided	1 box confectioners' sugar
1 stick margarine, melted	8 ounces cream cheese, softened

Mix cake mix, 1 egg, margarine, and nuts and press into a 9x13-inch pan. Beat confectioners' sugar, 2 eggs, and cream cheese . Pour over crust. Bake at 350° for 30 to 40 minutes.

Makes 3 to 4 dozen.

Toni and Neal Brower—Lewisville, North Carolina

Smooth move

Ed Crumpacker's Snowball Cookies

Great offering.

¾ cup butter
½ cup sugar
1 egg
½ teaspoon salt
2 cups flour

2 cups chopped nuts
(walnuts or Brazil nuts)
2 teaspoons vanilla or almond flavoring
Confectioners' sugar

Cream butter and sugar and stir in egg. Beat well. Add remaining ingredients, except confectioners' sugar. Roll into balls. Bake at 350° for 15 to 20 minutes. Cool and roll in confectioners' sugar.
    Makes 2 dozen.

Teresa Thompson—Fergus Falls, Minnesota

Mayor Pike's Persimmon Cookies

Decisively delicious!

1 cup shortening
1 cup granulated sugar
1 cup brown sugar
2 eggs
2 teaspoons baking soda
2 cups persimmon pulp

4 cups flour
1 teaspoon nutmeg
1 teaspoon cinnamon
1 teaspoon baking powder
2 cups raisins, boiled and drained
1 cup black walnuts

There's always something to smile about in Mayberry.

120

Cream shortening and sugars. Add eggs and beat well. Dissolve soda in persimmon pulp; add to creamed mixture and stir. Sift flour with nutmeg, cinnamon, and baking powder. Add to batter and mix well. Fold in raisins and black walnuts. Drop by teaspoonful onto a greased cookie sheet. Bake at 350° for 12 minutes.

Makes 6 to 8 dozen.

Esther Morrison—Jacksonville, Illinois

Ernest Teasers

Riddled with flavor.

1 cup shortening	¼ teaspoon salt
1 cup brown sugar	1 cup flour
1 egg	1 cup chopped nuts
1 teaspoon vanilla extract	1 small package chocolate chips

Mix shortening, brown sugar, egg, and vanilla. Add salt and flour and fold in nuts. Pour into a 13½x9½x2-inch pan and bake at 350°. When half done, take out of the oven and add chocolate chips over top. Finish baking for 15 minutes. Cut into squares when cool.

Makes 3 to 4 dozen.

Diana Drummond—Jacksonville, Illinois

Genuine Ceramic Pelican Pecan Squares

A real prize.

1 box yellow cake mix, divided	½ cup brown sugar
1 egg	1½ cups dark corn syrup
1 stick margarine, melted	1½ cups ground pecans
3 eggs	

Reserve ⅔ cup dry cake mix and set aside. Mix remaining cake mix, 1 egg, and margarine. Press into a greased and floured 9x13-inch pan. Press dough up around sides of pan. Bake at 350° for 15 to 20 minutes, until golden brown. Cool.

Mix 3 eggs, brown sugar, corn syrup, and reserved cake mix. Spread over cooled crust and add pecans. Bake at 350° for 30 to 35 minutes.

Makes 3 to 4 dozen.

Joyce Blake Taylor—Princeton, West Virginia

Small Town Shortbread
Loved far and wide.

8 ounces butter
4 ounces confectioners' sugar

8 ounces plain flour
4 ounces cornflour (cornstarch)

Cream butter and sugar until white. Add flours and knead into a ball. Press into a Swiss roll tin (or something similar). Bake at 350° for 30 to 45 minutes.
    Serves 6 to 8.

Barbara Perry—Cast member

Guard the Cannon
Pumpkin Cookies
Goob food.

3½ cups sugar
7 cups flour
Pinch of salt
3½ teaspoons cinnamon
3½ teaspoons baking soda

1¾ cups vegetable oil
1 large can pumpkin
3½ teaspoons vanilla extract
2 cups pecans
2 cups chopped dates or raisins

Mix dry ingredients. Add vegetable oil and pumpkin. Mix well. Add vanilla, pecans, and dates. Spoon onto an ungreased cookie sheet. Bake at 375° for 8 to 10 minutes.
    Makes 7 to 8 dozen.

Judy Cannon—Mt. Juliet, Tennessee

Dud's Milk Dud Cookies
They taught him this one in the Army.

1 cup butter
21½ Milk Duds
½ cup brown sugar
6 egg whites

1 cup all-purpose flour
½ teaspoon baking soda
½ teaspoon salt
½ cup chopped walnuts

Heat butter on low and stir. Add 4 Milk Duds. Keep stirring. Add 2 Duds. Mix in brown sugar. Toss in 2 Duds and stir. Mix in egg whites and 3 Duds. Stir a bit and turn off heat. Throw in flour, 4 more Duds, baking soda, 2½ more Duds, salt, 4 more Duds, and chopped walnuts. Now stir until real thick and tacky. Grease and flour a cookie sheet; then tablespoon on big

WEDDING DUDS—Ernest T. Bass is in for a surprise after Barney pretends to be Charlene Darling marrying Dud Wash.

drops of mix. Bake at 350° for 15 minutes.

Serves from 9 to 12, depending on the size of the people.

Hoke Howell—Cast member

Gypsy Melody Ginger Snaps

Don't wait for a rainy spell to try these.

¾ cup shortening or margarine
1 cup white sugar
1 egg
⅓ cup molasses
2 cups plain flour (may need a little more)
½ teaspoon salt

1½ teaspoons baking soda
2 teaspoons ground ginger
1 teaspoon cinnamon
¼ teaspoon allspice
¼ teaspoon cloves
1½ tablespoons buttermilk, optional

Cream shortening and sugar. Add egg and molasses. Mix. Sift together flour, salt, soda, and spices. Add and mix well. Form into balls and place on a greased cookie sheet and bake at 325° to 350° until done. (To make chewy, add 1½ tablespoons buttermilk.) Do not overbake.

Makes about 3 dozen.

Mary Ruth Lee—Wake Forest, North Carolina

123

PAWS FOR APPLAUSE—Inspector Somerset approves of Mayberry's canine corps.

Goober's Gobs
Goobness!

1 cup corn oil	1½ teaspoons vanilla extract
2 cups brown sugar	**Filling:**
2 eggs, beaten	5 tablespoons flour
3½ cups flour	1 cup milk
¼ teaspoon salt	½ teaspoon salt
1 teaspoon baking soda	1 teaspoon vanilla extract
¼ cup cocoa	1 cup sugar
1 cup milk	1 cup shortening

Mix first 9 ingredients in order given and refrigerate for 30 minutes or overnight. Drop by teaspoonful onto a greased baking sheet. Bake at 375° for 8 minutes.

For filling, cook flour with milk until thick. Chill thoroughly. Beat, add remaining ingredients slowly, and continue beating until light and fluffy. Put a generous teaspoon of filling between 2 cookies.

Makes 6 to 8 dozen.

Debbie A. Fisher—Canton, Ohio

Hopscotch Butterscotch Cookies

Chalk this one up as a winner.

1 box yellow cake mix
½ cup oil
2 tablespoons water

2 eggs
6 ounces butterscotch morsels

Mix all ingredients. Spray a baking sheet lightly with nonstick cooking spray. Drop by tablespoonful onto baking sheet. Bake at 350° for 8 to 10 minutes.

Makes about 3 dozen.

Jeanne Swanner Robertson—Burlington, North Carolina

Inspector Somerset's Prune Cookies

Doggone good!

¾ cup butter, softened
⅓ cup honey
¼ cup brown sugar, packed
2 eggs
1 teaspoon vanilla extract
2 cups oats
¾ cup whole-wheat flour

⅓ cup bran
½ teaspoon baking soda
1 teaspoon ground cinnamon
1 teaspoon ground nutmeg
¼ teaspoon salt
1 cup chopped pitted prunes
1 cup chopped walnuts

Put butter, honey, sugar, eggs, and vanilla in a bowl and cream with all the elbow grease you can squeeze out of your electric mixer. In another bowl, throw oats, flour, bran, soda, cinnamon, nutmeg, and salt; stir 'em up and mix 'em into the creamed stuff. Rest a little if you feel the need and then stir in the prunes and walnuts. Drop by generous spoonfuls onto a couple of baking sheets. Flatten to about a half inch. Bake at 350° for 15 minutes. Remove the baking sheets from the oven and let the cookies cool on racks. You can store in airtight containers or freeze.

Makes about 12 large cookies.

Robert Cornthwaite—Cast member

I'LL BE DOGGED

It should have been no surprise that Inspector Somerset liked all of the dogs at the courthouse in "Dogs, Dogs, Dogs" (Episode #93). Among previous parts for actor Robert Cornthwaite was a co-starring role as John James Audubon in *The Adventures of Jim Bowie* during the 1950s. He is also a familiar face in the 1990s for his portrayal of the mayor on the critically acclaimed *Picket Fences* TV series.

HELLO, DOLL!—Fun girl Daphne has Andy cornered in the squad car.

Ford Galaxie Cream
Cheese Squares

The cruise favorite.

1 stick butter
1 box butter-flavored pudding cake mix
3 eggs, divided

8 ounces cream cheese, softened
1 box confectioners' sugar

Melt butter in a 9x13-inch pan in the oven. Lightly mix cake mix and 1 egg and press down over melted butter. In a separate bowl, mix cream cheese and 2 eggs until blended. Gradually add confectioners' sugar, reserving about 2 tablespoons. Mix well and pour over cake mix. Bake at 375° for 45 minutes or until golden brown. Cool and sift remaining sugar on top. Cut into squares.

Makes 3 to 4 dozen.

Robin and Tommy Ford—Tuscaloosa, Alabama

Sourwood Mountain Sour Cream Apple Squares

A Darling delight.

2 cups flour
2 cups brown sugar
½ cup margarine, softened
½ cup chopped nuts
1 to 2 teaspoons cinnamon
1 teaspoon baking soda
½ teaspoon salt

1 cup sour cream
1 teaspoon vanilla extract
1 egg
2 cups chopped apples
Whipped cream or confectioners' sugar, optional

Combine flour, brown sugar, and margarine; mix at low speed of an electric mixer until fine crumbs form. Stir in nuts. Press 2¾ cups mixture firmly into an ungreased 13x9-inch or a 15x10-inch pan. Combine all ingredients except apples, whipped cream, and confectioners' sugar in a large bowl; mix well. Stir apples into batter. Spoon batter evenly over crumb base. Bake at 350° for 30 to 40 minutes (for a 13x9-inch pan) and 25 to 35 minutes (for a 15x10-inch pan). Cool before cutting into squares or bars. Top with whipped cream or confectioners' sugar, if desired. Store loosely covered.

Makes 12 to 15 squares or 3 to 4 dozen bars.

Sandy and Dean Webb—Cast member

"Pain of heel, ache of toe, vanish now from my sweet beau."

Who's a Country Bumpkin Pumpkin Pie Dessert

This pie are square.

1 box yellow cake mix, divided
1 stick margarine, melted
3 eggs, divided
⅔ cup evaporated milk
½ teaspoon vanilla extract
½ teaspoon cinnamon
1 pound canned pumpkin
¾ cup sugar

⅛ teaspoon cloves
Pinch of salt
Topping:
1 cup reserved cake mix
¼ cup sugar
1 teaspoon cinnamon
½ stick margarine, softened

Grease bottom of a 9x13-inch pan. Set aside 1 cup cake mix for topping. Mix remaining cake mix, margarine, and 1 beaten egg. Press into pan. Beat 2 eggs; add milk, and then remaining ingredients. Pour over crust.

For topping, mix reserved cake mix, sugar, cinnamon, and softened margarine. Pour over filling. Bake at 325° for 45 to 50 minutes or until a knife inserted near the center comes out clean. Cut into bars.

Makes 3 to 4 dozen bars.

Judy B. Coleman—Asheboro, North Carolina

"LET'S PLAY JAIL!"—Daphne and Skippy are too much fun for Otis.

128

Aunt Bee's Canton Palace Morsels

Cookie fortunes.

1 small package butterscotch morsels
2 heaping tablespoons crunchy
   peanut butter

1 can Chinese noodles

Melt all ingredients over very low heat in a saucepan. Drop by spoonful onto waxed paper. Refrigerate to harden.
   Makes about 2 dozen.

Alice Schwenke—Houston, Texas

Chocolate Square Dances

Reel good.

4 cups quick oatmeal
1 cup margarine
½ cup sugar
1 cup brown sugar

1 teaspoon salt
1 tablespoon vanilla extract
12 ounces chocolate chips
¾ cup peanut butter

Mix first 6 ingredients and press on an 11x17-inch cookie sheet. Bake for 12 minutes at 350°. Melt chocolate chips and peanut butter. Spread over baked oatmeal crust. Cut into squares.
   Makes about 4 to 5 dozen.

Sue and Jack Fellenzer—Cedar Falls, Iowa

Daphne's Three-Layer Chocolate Squares

Don't skip these!

1½ cups graham cracker crumbs
¼ cup brown sugar
6 tablespoons butter or margarine, melted
Pinch of nutmeg
12 ounces semisweet chocolate chips

1 cup flaked coconut
1 cup pecans or walnuts
1 jar marshmallow cream
2 tablespoons milk
1 teaspoon vanilla extract

Combine crumbs, sugar, butter, and nutmeg. Press into a 9x13-inch pan. Bake at 350° for 10 minutes. Remove from the oven. Mix chocolate chips, coconut, and nuts. Spread over first layer. Thin marshmallow cream with milk and vanilla. Drizzle over top. Bake for an additional 15 minutes. Cool before cutting into squares.
   Makes about 30.

Jean Carson —Cast member

Crime-Free Caramel Safe Crackers

They're something to a door.

2 9-ounce boxes Ritz bits
1 cup dry-roast peanuts
½ cup butter
1 cup sugar

½ cup white corn syrup
1 teaspoon vanilla extract
1 teaspoon baking soda
M&M candies

Preheat the oven to 250°. Combine Ritz bits and dry-roast peanuts in a large, shallow, greased baking pan. In a saucepan, bring butter, sugar, and corn syrup to a boil. Cook for 5 minutes to caramelize. Remove pan from heat; stir in vanilla and baking soda. Pour caramel mixture over crackers and nuts; stir well. Bake for 1 hour, stirring every 15 minutes. Pour onto waxed paper to cool. Break apart after cooled. When serving, mix with M&M candies.
Makes about 3 dozen.

Sue and Jack Fellenzer—Cedar Falls, Iowa

Nip It in the Bud No-Bake Peanut Butter Balls

Taste bud, that is.

1 cup nonfat dry milk
½ cup peanut butter
½ cup honey

½ cup graham cracker crumbs
Chocolate sprinkles, chopped nuts, or
    confectioners' sugar

Mix first 4 ingredients. Shape into 1-inch balls and roll in chocolate sprinkles, nuts, or confectioners' sugar. Chill.
Makes about 3 dozen 1-inch balls.

Wanda C. Fields—Reidsville, North Carolina

Mayberry Jail Cells

There's a good life behind these bars.

1 cup dark syrup
1 cup sugar
1 cup chunky peanut butter

6 cups Special K cereal
1 cup butterscotch chips
1 cup chocolate chips

Bring syrup and sugar to a boil. Remove from heat and stir in peanut butter. Mix in Special K. Spread in a buttered 9x13-inch pan. Melt butterscotch chips and chocolate chips. Stir and spread on top. Cut into bars.
Makes 3 to 4 dozen.

Nancy and Richard Stout—Anamosa, Iowa

*SAVING FACE—Farmer Flint begins to see
Andy and Ellie's point about his daughter.*

Robert Golden's Chocolate Chip Cookies

This is a recipe you'll make over and over.

¾ cup margarine or butter
1 cup brown sugar
1 cup sugar
1 teaspoon vanilla extract
2 eggs
1 cup flour
¼ teaspoon baking soda

Pinch of salt
1½ cups oats
½ cup nuts (walnut, pecan, or
   macadamia)
½ cup coconut
½ cup raisins
A whole lot of chocolate chips

Cream margarine and sugars. Add vanilla and eggs and mix. Sift flour with baking soda and salt. Add to the creamed mixture. Combine with remaining ingredients. Preheat the oven to 350°. Drop by teaspoonful about 2 inches apart onto a greased cookie sheet. Bake for about 10 minutes.

Makes about 36 two-inch cookies.

Mary and R.G. Armstrong—Cast member

QUITE A CHARACTER

Renowned character actor R.G. Armstrong was memorable in his one Mayberry appearance as farmer Flint in "Ellie Saves a Female" (Episode #27). A friend of Andy Griffith's since their days together in North Carolina's famed "Lost Colony" outdoor drama, he is well-known for his countless roles in movie and TV westerns, and recently as Pruneface in the *Dick Tracy* movie.

PROUD MOMENT—*Everybody's happy when Otis arrives to receive a plaque honoring his ancestor and Revolutionary War hero Nathan Tibbs.*

Otis Campbell Oatmeal Chocolate Chip Cookies

You'll lock yourself in jail to get these.

1 cup brown sugar
½ cup granulated sugar
2 sticks butter or margarine, softened
¼ cup molasses
2 eggs
1 tablespoon milk
1 tablespoon vanilla extract
1 cup unbleached flour

¾ cup whole-wheat flour
1 teaspoon cinnamon
1 teaspoon baking soda
½ teaspoon salt
2 cups quick-cooking oats
12 ounces semisweet chocolate chips
1½ cups coarsely chopped pecans

Preheat the oven to 375°. Combine sugars and mix well. Add butter and beat to creamy consistency. Add molasses, eggs, milk, and vanilla to sugar mixture. Mix well. In a medium bowl, mix flours, cinnamon, baking soda, salt, and oats. Stir to combine. Add flour-oat mixture to sugar mixture slowly, while stirring. Add chocolate chips and pecans; mix well. Drop by tablespoonful onto an ungreased cookie sheet. Bake for 8 to 10 minutes. Cool on a wire rack. Transfer to a covered tin to keep moist.

Makes 4 to 5 dozen 2-inch cookies.

Bill and LuAnne Dugan—Wynne, Arkansas

Goober Blossoms
Will bring Goober out of his shell.

½ cup sugar, plus additional	1 teaspoon vanilla extract
½ cup brown sugar	1¾ cups flour
½ cup shortening	1 teaspoon baking soda
½ cup peanut butter	½ teaspoon salt
1 egg	Chocolate candy kisses

Cream sugars, shortening, and peanut butter. Add egg and vanilla. Add sifted dry ingredients. Roll teaspoons of dough into balls. Roll balls in additional sugar. Bake at 350° for about 10 minutes. Take out of the oven and press a chocolate candy kiss in the center of each cookie and return to the oven for 2 to 5 minutes.

Makes about 3 dozen.

Nancy and Richard Stout—Anamosa, Iowa

Regis's Gold Shipment Bars
Setting the standard.

1½ cups flour	2 tablespoons flour
½ cup brown sugar	½ teaspoon baking powder
1 stick margarine	¼ teaspoon salt
2 eggs	½ teaspoon vanilla
1 cup brown sugar	1 tablespoon margarine
1¼ cups coconut	2 tablespoons lemon juice
½ cup chopped pecans	1 cup confectioners' sugar

Mix first 3 ingredients and press into a 9x13-inch pan. Bake at 275° for 10 minutes.

Mix next 8 ingredients and pour over baked pastry. Bake for an additional 20 minutes at 350°. Remove from oven. Glaze with mixture of last 3 ingredients. Cool and cut.

Makes 3 to 4 dozen.

Sally and Jim Lord—Seattle, Washington

Ebum, Shoobum, Shoobum, Shoobum Peanut Butter Bars

Watch 'em disappear.

½ cup butter or margarine
½ cup sugar
½ cup brown sugar
1 egg
⅓ cup peanut butter
½ teaspoon baking soda

½ teaspoon salt
½ teaspoon vanilla extract
1 cup flour
1 cup quick rolled oats
6 ounces chocolate chips

Cream butter and sugars. Blend in egg, peanut butter, baking soda, salt, and vanilla. Stir in flour and oats. Spread in a greased 9x13-inch pan. Bake at 350° for 20 to 25 minutes. Sprinkle with chocolate chips. Let stand for 5 minutes. Spread evenly and cool before cutting.
    Makes 3 to 4 dozen.

Sally and Jim Lord—Seattle, Washington

Sam Browne Belt Brownies

Every deputy needs one.

2 sticks margarine
4 eggs
2 cups sugar
6 tablespoons cocoa
1½ cups flour

2 teaspoons vanilla extract
Pinch of salt
Nuts, optional
Chocolate or vanilla frosting, optional

Melt margarine and combine with other ingredients, except nuts and frosting. Mix until smooth. Pour into a greased 9x13-inch pan and bake at 350° for 20 to 25 minutes. Cool and frost, if desired.
    Makes 3 to 4 dozen.

Bill and Evonne Williams—Omaha, Nebraska

"In the case of the delicious brownies, how do you plead?" "Guilty!":

AUNT BEE: Now, I have a surprise for us. I made us some brownies.
JURY FOREMAN: Brownies?
AUNT BEE: I thought they'd be nice to nibble on while we discuss the case. We might even send some in to Judge Cranston while he's waiting.

Beasto Maristo Low-Fat, High-Fiber Brownies

Not pretty, but good.

Brownies, mix or scratch   6 tablespoons water
8 ounces pitted prunes

Start with your favorite brownie mix or from-scratch recipe, but do not add oil, butter, or margarine. Instead, prepare a prune paste by putting prunes and water in a food processor. Pulse on and off several times to create paste. Add prune paste to other ingredients and prepare brownies as usual.

Makes about 3 dozen.

Robert Pulciani—Rockford, Illinois

*"Andrew Paul Lawson" and Floyd prepare to fool Floyd's lonely
hearts club pen pal.*

Count Istvan Teleky Brownies

Every wish comes true with these.

2 cups flour
2 cups sugar
2 sticks margarine
1 cup cold water
4 tablespoons cocoa
2 eggs
½ cup buttermilk
1 teaspoon baking soda

1 teaspoon vanilla extract
Icing:
2 sticks margarine
4 tablespoons cocoa
6 tablespoons milk
1 box confectioners' sugar
1 cup broken nuts
1 teaspoon vanilla extract

Mix flour and sugar and set aside. Melt margarine. Mix water and cocoa. Add to melted margarine. Add this to flour and sugar mixture. Beat eggs and add. Add buttermilk, baking soda, and vanilla. Bake in a 15½x10¼x1-inch pan at 400° for 20 minutes.

For icing, melt margarine; add cocoa and milk. Sift and add confectioners' sugar. Add nuts and vanilla. Mix well and pour over warm brownies.

Makes 4 to 5 dozen.

Peggy Mode Metzger—Clarksville, Indiana

Drive-thru service

136

Reverend Tucker's Toffee Bars

Our Sunday best.

2 sticks butter
1 cup light brown sugar
1 egg yolk
1 cup flour

¼ teaspoon salt
1 teaspoon vanilla extract
6 Hershey bars
Chopped pecans

Cream butter and sugar. Add egg yolk, flour, salt, and vanilla and cream well. Spread into a 9x15x2-inch pan lined with aluminum foil that has been sprayed with nonstick cooking spray. Bake at 350° for 20 minutes. Remove from the oven and immediately spread Hershey bars over top. Spread chocolate evenly; then sprinkle pecans over and press into chocolate. Cool in refrigerator or freezer until hardened. Cut into desired pieces. Freezes well.
Makes 4 to 5 dozen.

Marcia and Tom Hotchkiss—Birmingham, Alabama

Mayberry Deputy Almond Cookies

They'll grow on you.

½ cup margarine
½ cup confectioners' sugar
½ cup flour

1 teaspoon vanilla extract
¼ teaspoon salt
Almonds

Cream margarine and sugar until smooth. Add flour, vanilla, and salt. Work until smooth; scoop up a tablespoon at a time. Roll into a ball. Flatten out and place an almond on top. Bake at 325° until cookie turns slightly brown around edges.
Makes about 2 dozen.

Mikel Snow—Mount Airy, North Carolina

Mrs. Mendelbright's Bulb-Snatchers

Watt a treat!

1 cup white sugar
1 cup white corn syrup

1 cup chunky or plain peanut butter
5 cups cornflakes

Bring first 2 ingredients to a boil in a large pan. Stir in peanut butter. Remove from heat. Stir in cornflakes. Drop by tablespoonful onto waxed paper. (Hint: Spray waxed paper with nonstick cooking spray, or you may eat the added treat of waxed paper.)
Makes about 4 dozen.

Sue and Jack Fellenzer—Cedar Falls, Iowa

Emmett's Harvest Ball Pumpkin Bars

Clark bars.

2 cups flour
1 teaspoon baking soda
2 teaspoons cinnamon
1 cup vegetable oil
1 large can pumpkin (with spices)
2 teaspoons baking powder
½ teaspoon salt
2 cups sugar

4 eggs
Icing:
3 ounces cream cheese
¾ stick butter
½ teaspoon vanilla extract
2 cups confectioners' sugar
1 tablespoon milk

Mix all ingredients until well blended. Pour into 2 greased and floured 9x13-inch pans or a jelly roll pan. Bake at 350° for 25 minutes. Cool well; then ice.

For icing, mix cream cheese and butter thoroughly. Add vanilla, confectioners' sugar, and milk. Beat well and spread on cake. Cut into bars. Refrigerate.

Makes 3 to 4 dozen.

Peggy Seil—Scottsdale, Arizona

Edgar Coleman's Gluey, Chewy Oatmeal Cookies

They've got you covered.

1 cup sifted all-purpose flour
¾ teaspoon baking soda
½ teaspoon salt
1 teaspoon cinnamon
¼ teaspoon nutmeg
¾ cup shortening

1⅓ cups packed brown sugar
2 eggs
1 teaspoon vanilla extract
2 cups old-fashioned oats, uncooked
1 cup raisins (can omit and use 1/2 cup
    more oats)

Sift together flour, soda, salt, cinnamon, and nutmeg in a bowl. Add shortening, sugar, eggs, and vanilla; beat with an electric mixer until smooth, about 2 minutes (don't overmix). Stir in oats and raisins (don't crush). Drop by teaspoonful onto greased cookie sheets. Bake in a preheated 350° oven for 12 to 15 minutes.

Makes 3 to 4 dozen.

Berry Stout—Greensboro, North Carolina

Couple of special couples

Charlotte's Concrete Jungle Blocks

They live up to the build-up.

⅔ cup melted butter
1 box light brown sugar
3 eggs
1 teaspoon vanilla extract
2¾ cups cake flour, sifted 3 times

2½ teaspoons baking powder
¼ teaspoon salt
1 package semisweet chocolate bits
1 cup nut meats

Pour butter into a mixing bowl. Add brown sugar and mix well. Let cool. Add eggs, 1 at a time, beating well after each addition. Add vanilla. Sift together dry ingredients and add to mixture. Add chocolate bits and nuts. Spread into a well-greased pan. Bake at 350° for 30 minutes. Let cool in pan and cut into squares. Do not overbake.

Makes 3 to 4 dozen.

Charlotte Womack—Greensboro, North Carolina

Salt-and-pepper sugar

Weary Willie's Brown Sugar Cookies
You'll be truly grateful for these.

1 cup butter
¾ cup brown sugar
2 cups flour
¼ teaspoon allspice
⅛ teaspoon nutmeg

2 tablespoons orange juice
Topping:
⅓ cup sugar
⅓ teaspoon cinnamon
4 dashes of cloves, optional

Cream butter and brown sugar. Sift in flour, allspice, and nutmeg. Add orange juice and blend well. Chill dough for 1 hour. Roll out thin onto a floured board and cut out.

For topping, combine sugar, cinnamon, and cloves and sprinkle over cookies. Bake on ungreased cookie sheets at 350° for 10 minutes.

Makes about 4 dozen.

Tim Simpson—Greensboro, North Carolina

Saturday Night Date Chews

Something to look forward to all week.

1 stick butter
1 cup sugar
1 tablespoon water
8 ounces dates

2 cups Rice Krispies cereal
2 cups nuts
1 teaspoon vanilla extract
Confectioners' sugar

Melt butter and add sugar, water, and dates. Cook for 4 to 5 minutes over medium heat, stirring constantly. Take off stove; add Rice Krispies, nuts, and vanilla. Pour onto a buttered plate; let cool. Make into balls and roll in confectioners' sugar.

Makes about 3 dozen.

Beverly Stump—Lebanon, Indiana

Jelene Naomi Conners Scotch Shortbread

Enjoyed with conviction.

1 pound butter
1 pound light brown sugar

4 to 5 cups flour

With an electric mixer, combine butter, sugar, and as much flour as possible. Finish mixing with hands. Roll out to ¼-inch thickness. Use a thimble to make impressions of 3 intertwined rings and cut. Bake at 350° for about 10 minutes, until barely brown on edges. Do not overbake. Store in a tight tin box.

Makes 6 to 8 dozen.

Jean Carson—Cast member

Walker's Drugstore Candy Bar Cookies

A sweet remedy.

1 cup margarine, softened
¾ cup sugar
¾ cup brown sugar
2 eggs

1 teaspoon vanilla extract
2½ cups self-rising flour
3 candy bars, any kind

Mix margarine, sugars, eggs, and vanilla. Add flour and mix. Cut or chop candy bars into pieces and mix into dough. Drop by teaspoonful onto a cookie sheet. Bake at 350° for 10 to 12 minutes.

Makes about 3 dozen.

Becky Owsley—Elizabethtown, Kentucky

Barney's Thins
They're the mark of the Fifes.

1 stick margarine
1 stick butter
1 cup sugar
1 egg, separated

2 cups flour
1 teaspoon vanilla extract
1 cup pecans, finely chopped

Cream margarine, butter, and sugar. Add egg yolk, flour, and vanilla. Mix well (mixture will be somewhat dry). Spread very thin in a greased jelly roll pan. Brush with egg white and sprinkle with finely chopped pecans. Bake at 300° for 30 to 40 minutes or until golden brown. Do not overbake. Cool and slice into 2-inch pieces.
    Makes about 3 dozen.

Camille Townsend—Greensboro, North Carolina

Mayberry Cherry Cookies
Yea!

2 sticks margarine
1½ cups sugar
2 eggs
3 cups flour
1 teaspoon baking powder

1 teaspoon baking soda
1 teaspoon salt
1 cup raisins
2 cups chopped maraschino cherries
    (red or green)

Cream margarine and sugar; beat in eggs. Add dry ingredients; mix well. Fold in fruit. Drop onto lightly greased cookie sheets by rounded tablespoonful. Bake at 325° for 12 to 15 minutes.
    Makes 6 dozen.

Janine L. Johnson—Orlando, Florida

Clarence Earp's Cowboy Cookies
They're right.

2 sticks margarine
1 cup sugar
1 cup light brown sugar
2 eggs
1 teaspoon vanilla extract
2 cups flour

½ teaspoon salt
½ teaspoon baking soda
½ teaspoon baking powder
2 cups quick-cook oats
6 ounces chocolate chips

Cream margarine and sugars; beat in eggs and vanilla. Combine flour, salt, baking soda, and baking powder and add to mixture. Fold in oats and chocolate chips. Drop by rounded tablespoonful about 3 inches apart onto lightly greased cookie sheets. Bake for 15 minutes at 350°.

Makes 3 dozen.

Janine Johnson—Orlando, Florida

Old Country Lemon Squares

"From somewhere's else."

1 cup flour
¼ cup confectioners' sugar, plus extra
    for topping
¼ pound butter
2 eggs, slightly beaten

1 cup granulated sugar
1 tablespoon flour
½ teaspoon baking powder
3 tablespoons lemon juice

Mix flour with ¼ cup confectioners' sugar. Melt butter and mix with flour and sugar. Put into a greased and floured 8x8-inch square pan. Bake at 350° for 18 to 20 minutes. Mix eggs, granulated sugar, flour, baking powder, and lemon juice. Pour over baked crust. Bake at 350° for 20 to 25 minutes. Cool and sprinkle with confectioners' sugar before cutting into squares.

Makes 2 to 3 dozen.

Jane Ellis—Albuquerque, New Mexico

Above all, Mayberry is a nice place to be.

143

Courthouse Christmas Tree Cookies

Seasoned greetings!

1 stick butter
1 cup sugar
½ teaspoon vanilla extract
1 egg
2 cups flour

1 teaspoon baking powder
¼ teaspoon salt
Colored sugars, chocolate sprinkles, and
    silver dragées for decorating

Cream butter and sugar; beat in vanilla and egg. Stir dry ingredients together and mix well into dough. Chill for a couple hours, until fairly

PIPE DOWN!—With an "amazing resemblance to Frank Sinatra," Barney is long one of Mayberry's most eligible bachelors. (Barbara Perry is pictured at far right.)

144

firm. Roll out on a lightly floured countertop or smooth tabletop to ⅛-inch thickness. Cut. Bake a scant 8 minutes at 325°. Cool completely and decorate. For super easy decorating, top with colored sugars, chocolate sprinkles, silver dragées, etc., before popping into the oven.

Makes 4 to 5 dozen.

Janine Johnson—Orlando, Florida

Floss's Australian Munchies
Indigenous deliciousness, by dogged!

1 cup quick-cook or regular oatmeal	½ cup part butter, part margarine
½ cup coconut, shredded or grated	1 tablespoon honey
½ cup sugar	¾ tablespoon boiling water
⅓ cup flour	¼ teaspoon baking soda

Mix oatmeal, coconut, sugar, and flour. Melt honey and butter together and add to oatmeal mixture. Pour boiling water on soda and stir; then add to mixture. Flatten ⅔ teaspoon dough on a greased cookie sheet, widely spaced. Bake 3 to 5 minutes at 370° until light brown. Remove from sheet when firm but warm.

Makes about 1 dozen.

Barbara Perry—Cast member

Briscoe's Hill Country Cookies
Mouthwatering mountain mounds.

1 cup real butter	1 cup raisins
1½ cups brown sugar	1 cup nuts
3 eggs	Icing:
1 teaspoon allspice	1 tablespoon butter
2 cups plus 2 tablespoons flour, sifted	2 tablespoons milk
Pinch of salt	1 cup confectioners' sugar
1 teaspoon baking soda in ½ cup hot water	

Cream butter, sugar, and eggs. Combine dry ingredients and baking soda water; mix. Stir in raisins and nuts. Drop by teaspoonful onto buttered cookie sheets. Bake at 350° until light brown. Cool.

For icing, melt butter and stir in milk and confectioners' sugar until smooth. Spread on cookies.

Makes about 3 dozen.

Jane Ellis—Albuquerque, New Mexico

Andy's Apricot Queen Squares
Outstanding!

1 cup water	¼ teaspoon salt
½ pound dry apricots	½ cup brown sugar
¾ cup honey or ½ cup sugar	1 cup quick-cook oatmeal
1 cup sifted flour	½ cup shortening
½ teaspoon baking soda	Whipped cream

Add water to apricots and cook until tender. Add honey or sugar and chill. Sift together flour, soda, and salt. Add brown sugar and oatmeal. Cut in shortening until mixture is crumbly. Put ⅔ of mixture in bottom of a 7x11-inch pan. Pat down and spread apricot mixture on top. Cover with remaining crumbs. Bake at 350° for 30 minutes. Cut into squares and serve with whipped cream.
    Makes about 2 dozen.

Dee Boquist—Minneapolis, Minnesota

Barney's Bloodhound Chocolate Chip Cookies
Blue's favorite.

½ cup and 2 tablespoons butter or margarine, softened	1½ teaspoons vanilla extract
½ cup sugar	2¾ cups flour
¾ cup brown sugar	1½ teaspoons baking soda
2 eggs	½ teaspoon salt
	12 ounces chocolate chips

Blend butter and sugars. Add eggs and vanilla and blend until smooth. Sift flour, baking soda, and salt 5 times; this is necessary to create soft, thick cookies. Gradually add flour mixture to butter, sugar, and egg mixture until completely blended. Mix in chocolate chips. Form cookie mixture into fairly large balls, place on ungreased cookie sheet, and bake in 325° oven for 12 to 15 minutes.
    Makes about 3 dozen.

Paula Phillips Blue—Angola, Indiana

TAKING A GOOD LOOK—
Barney and Blue get ready to hit the trail.

Mayberry's favorite aunt

But true beauty's in the taste buds of the beholder:
AUNT BEE: I've always felt that food that looks good, tastes good.

Frostings, Toppings, and Preserves

Aunt Bee's Homemade Watermelon Rind Pickles

You knew Aunt Bee couldn't do a cookbook without at least one pickle recipe!

1 large watermelon
1 tablespoon slaked lime
  (calcium hydroxide)
3 gallons water, divided
1 tablespoon alum
½ pound ginger root

16 cups sugar
8 cups vinegar
5 cups water
1 tablespoon whole allspice
1 tablespoon whole cloves
2 sticks cinnamon

Select watermelon with as thick a rind as possible. Peel and cut off all red and cut green outside into 1½ to 2 by 1-inch pieces, or of desired size and shape. Soak prepared pieces overnight in slaked lime dissolved in 1 gallon water.

The next day, remove from lime water and soak for 5 minutes in alum dissolved in 1 gallon water.

Remove from alum and simmer for 30 minutes in ginger root (be sure you get the whole root) and 1 gallon water. Remove from ginger root water and plunge into cold water 7 times.

Meanwhile, make the syrup by combining sugar, vinegar, 5 cups water, and spices. Simmer rinds in syrup for 3 hours.

Some pickle makers tie spices in a small cheesecloth bag or let them float with the pickles. Put pickles in hot, sterilized jars, cover with syrup, and seal. If your watermelon is extra large, you may need to increase the amount of syrup by ¼. Good enough to eat as a dessert.

Makes 10 to 12 pints, if well packed.

Eudora Garrison—Charlotte, North Carolina

149

Floyd's Mocha Frosting

Perfect topping for your crew.

½ cup shortening	1 teaspoon vanilla extract
⅓ cup cocoa	2 teaspoons instant coffee
¼ teaspoon salt	4 cups confectioners' sugar
1 egg	6 tablespoons milk

Blend shortening, cocoa, salt, and egg. Add vanilla, coffee, sugar, and milk. Blend. (If coffee has large grains, warm 2 tablespoons of the milk and dissolve coffee before adding.)

Jan and Allan Newsome—Huntsville, Alabama

Bank Job Baked-On Frosting

A safe choice.

5 tablespoons brown sugar	2 tablespoons cream (sweet or sour)
3 tablespoons butter	½ cup coconut, grated

Melt brown sugar, butter, and cream. Add coconut. When cake is done, spread over top of cake. Broil until bubbly and slightly brown.

Dee Boquist—Minneapolis, Minnesota

"Yep, that's a pickle."

150

Barney braves Andy's gibes during rehearsal for the Centennial Pageant:
ANDY: (as James Merriweather) Greetings to you, great chief.
BARNEY: (as Noogatuck) How.
(They walk off stage for a break.)
ANDY: Hey, Barn. I know how you can learn your part real good.
BARNEY: How?
ANDY: See.

White Horse Icing for Angel Food Cake
Its rider is dressed in black.

¾ cup sugar
⅜ cup white corn syrup
3 tablespoons water
3 egg whites

⅛ teaspoon cream of tartar
1 teaspoon vanilla extract
2 squares unsweetened chocolate
½ teaspoon butter

Blend sugar, corn syrup, and water in a saucepan. Boil hard until it spins an 8-inch thread. Beat egg whites and cream of tartar until stiff and peaks hold. Pour hot mixture into stiff egg whites in a fine stream, while beating, until it holds its shape. Add vanilla. Ice angel food cake. Melt chocolate with butter. Drop with tip of spoon around edges of cake and let it run down.

Noogatuck's Honey Nougatine Frosting
Piece piping.

2 egg whites
1½ cups sugar
4 tablespoons water
2 tablespoons light corn syrup

2 tablespoons honey
¼ teaspoon cream of tartar
⅛ teaspoon salt
1 teaspoon vanilla extract

Put all ingredients, except vanilla, in top of a double boiler. Mix thoroughly. Place over rapidly boiling water and beat with an electric mixer or rotary beater until mixture holds a peak (about 7 minutes). Remove from heat. Add vanilla and beat until thick enough to spread. Good on any cake, but wonderful on chocolate or spice cake.

Tonya Hamel—Greensboro, North Carolina

Eleanora's Praline Ice Cream Sauce

So good, it'll make you Blush.

1 cup firmly packed light brown sugar
¼ cup light corn syrup
½ cup half-and-half
2 tablespoons butter

1 teaspoon vanilla extract
⅛ teaspoon salt
1 cup pecan halves
Vanilla ice cream

Combine all ingredients in a saucepan. Cook over medium heat, stirring constantly, for 10 minutes or until sauce is thick and smooth. Cool slightly. Serve over vanilla ice cream. May be refrigerated in a covered container for several days. Before serving, add a small amount of cream, then heat, stirring until smooth.
Makes 1½ cups.

Lydia's Vanilla Sauce

Plain good.

¾ cup water
½ cup sugar
1 tablespoon cornstarch

1 teaspoon butter
1 teaspoon vanilla extract

Boil water. Add sugar and cornstarch. Stir until thickened; then add butter and vanilla. This sauce is especially good with bread pudding.

Jane Roberts—Jacksonville, Illinois

Fruit Dip Warren Ferguson

Know what we mean when we say it's good, huh, huh? Yeah.

8 ounces cream cheese, softened
1½ cups confectioners' sugar

8 ounces nondairy whipped topping
⅛ teaspoon cinnamon

Beat cream cheese until smooth, add confectioners' sugar, and then gradually fold in whipped topping and cinnamon. Refrigerate. Tastes great with fresh strawberries, apples, grapes, or pineapple chunks!

Shirley Phillips Friel—Angola, Indiana

Peter Piper Pepper Jelly

It's a pick.

1 pound red bell peppers
  (clean out stems and seeds)
3 chili (or other hot) peppers
  (clean out stems and seeds)
1 tablespoon salt

½ cup lemon juice
½ cup vinegar
1½ pounds sugar
1½ to 2 packs Sure-Gel
  (or equivalent pectin)

Mince peppers fine to medium in a blender; add salt, lemon juice, and vinegar. Boil for 10 minutes. Stir in sugar and boil for 5 minutes (skim off foam, if necessary). Turn down heat, add pectin, boil for 1 minute, and take off the stove. Put into clean jars and seal with clear foil.

This is a wonderful condiment for meat and poultry, as well as a topping for cream cheese with crackers. Because it can be kept (like jam or marmalade) for quite a long period of time, consider making a large batch. It makes a wonderful gift for gourmet cooks and other connoisseurs.

Makes about 1 to 3 one-pound jars.

Irmela Vontilius—Alexandria, Virginia

Salt-and-peppered pickled pepper picker

153

Cousin Eudora's Strawberry Preserves
Leon's first choice.

2 quarts strawberries, capped and washed
8 cups sugar

3 to 4 tablespoons vinegar (or part lemon
    juice and part vinegar)
Paraffin wax

Put prepared berries over very low heat and warm until juice is drawn; add sugar and vinegar or lemon juice and bring to boil. Reduce heat, but continue boiling for 15 to 20 minutes, skimming when necessary. Remove from heat, skim, pour in shallow containers (nonmetal), and allow to stand for 24 hours, stirring occasionally. Put cold preserves into jars and seal with paraffin.

Makes about 4 pints.

Eudora Garrison—Charlotte, North Carolina

Last Strawberry Preserves
They won't last long!

4 cups fresh strawberries
5 cups sugar

¼ teaspoon cream of tartar
Paraffin wax

Place alternate layers of berries and sugar in large kettle, with sugar as the first layer. Bring slowly to a boil. When contents are boiling, cook for 9 minutes. Remove from heat and add cream of tartar. Let stand overnight.

On the second day, boil for 9 minutes. Cool. Place in glasses. Seal with paraffin.

Makes 4 half-pints.

Patsy Caldwell—Charlotte, Tennessee

Rodney Darling's Persimmon Pucker Up
The Darlings' favorite courtin' dish.

Find a green persimmon tree (usually on the north side of the holler). Run off possum. Pick 1 pound green persimmons. Chunk and burn for 10 minutes in lard and molasses

Serve on cold biscuits and "pucker up." (One hour afterpucker guaranteed.)

Serves notice.

Beverly and Rodney Darling Dillard—Cast member
(Chefs of the Month at the Chat 'n' Gobble Cafe in Booger Hollow)

154

Leon's Blackberry Jelly

His secret is out!

Blackberries   **1½ cups sugar**

Rinse berries and place in a container to cook. Do not add water, only the amount that clings to the fruit. Boil until tender. Strain in a cheese-cloth. For jelly, bring 1 cup juice to a boil. Add sugar. Bring to a rolling boil for 1 minute. Pour into sterilized jars and seal. You may use this method for any tart juice that you have cooked.

Patsy Curtis—Charlotte, Tennessee

BOY FULL OF JELLY—Sandwiches, that is

Gomer pie

Pies, Cobblers, and Pastries

Gomer's Hana Key Lime Pie

Shazam, it's good!

4 eggs, separated
1 cup sugar, divided
½ cup fresh lime juice
½ teaspoon salt
1 or 2 drops green food coloring

1 tablespoon unflavored gelatin
¼ cup cold water
1 cup heavy whipping cream
1 pie shell, baked

Combine egg yolks, ¾ cup sugar, lime juice, and salt in top of a double boiler. Cook until thick, stirring constantly. Add food coloring slowly. Soften gelatin in cold water and add slowly to lime-egg mixture. Cool until partially set. Beat egg whites until foamy. Add remaining ¼ cup sugar and beat until stiff. Whip cream into soft peaks and add to egg-white mixture, mixing well. Fold into cooled lime-egg mixture. Pour into baked pie shell and refrigerate until set.

Serves 6 to 8.

Jim Nabors—Cast member

Barney's waiting for a call, so keep that line open:

AUNT BEE: (on phone) Marie, may I call you back? I've got some cherry popovers in the oven. Sure, they turn out nice and fluffy. The secret is in the batter, Marie. Sure I'll give it to you. You take a pound of cherries—

(Barney clears his throat impatiently)

AUNT BEE: (continuing) I'll give you the recipe when I call you back, Marie. Bye.

157

Checkerboard Chess Pie

Aunt Bee's crowning glory.

1 stick butter or margarine
1½ cups sugar
3 eggs, beaten

1 tablespoon dark vinegar
1 teaspoon vanilla extract
1 pie shell, unbaked

Cream butter and sugar. Add eggs, vinegar, and vanilla. Mix and pour into an unbaked pie shell and bake at 350° for 45 minutes.
Serves 6 to 8.

Martha Jean Bundy—Bristol, Tennessee

Peekaboo Pecan Pie

Worth writing home about.

3 tablespoons margarine
¾ cup sugar
3 eggs
1 cup white corn syrup

1 teaspoon vanilla extract
1 cup chopped pecans
1 pie shell, unbaked

Cream margarine and sugar. Beat in eggs, 1 at a time, adding separately. Add white corn syrup, vanilla, and pecans. Pour into pie shell and bake for 10 minutes at 350°. Finish baking at 325° for about 35 more minutes.
Serves 6 to 8.

Linda Snead—Tuscaloosa, Alabama

Miss Crump's Peanut Butter Pie

Has class and great taste.

1 cup peanut butter
8 ounces cream cheese
1 cup granulated sugar
2 tablespoons softened butter
8 ounces whipped topping

1 tablespoon vanilla extract
1 9-ounce chocolate or graham cracker
  crust
Reese's Peanut Butter Cups, optional

Blend first 6 ingredients until smooth. Pour into pie crust. Refrigerate overnight or until pie is cold throughout. Garnish with peanut butter cups, if desired. (Option: For more filling, add an extra 3 ounces cream cheese and more whipped topping.)
Serves 6 to 8.

Tracy Smitherman—Gordo, Alabama

Drum and Fife Corps Cherry Crunch
Cymbal of great flavor!

½ cup brown sugar
½ cup sugar
¼ cup melted butter
¼ cup melted shortening
1 cup quick-cook oatmeal
1 cup flour

2 teaspoons baking powder
½ teaspoon cinnamon
¼ teaspoon salt
1 can cherry pie filling
Ice cream

In a bowl, cream sugars, butter, and shortening. Add oatmeal and stir well. Sift together flour, baking powder, cinnamon, and salt. Add to other mixture and stir. Press half of this mixture into a 11½x7½x2-inch pan. Pour pie filling on top. Cover with rest of mixture. Bake at 350° for 30 minutes. Serve topped with ice cream.

Serves about 10.

Diana Drummond—Jacksonville, Illinois

TUBA TWOSOME—Andy and Barney get the town band ready to perform.

159

Clara's Cherry Cobbler

Honest goodness.

1 cup flour
3 teaspoons baking powder
1 teaspoon salt
1 cup sugar

1 cup milk
¼ pound butter
1 16-ounce can cherry pie filling
Vanilla ice cream or whipped cream

Sift together dry ingredients, except sugar; add sugar and milk. Melt butter; pour half of butter into a 9x4-inch pan. Add remaining butter to batter. Pour batter into pan; spoon cherry filling into batter gently. Bake at 350° for 35 to 40 minutes. Serve warm with vanilla ice cream or whipped cream.

Serves 4 to 6.

Christine and Brad Born, The Mayberry Cafe—Danville, Indiana

BEE FRIEND—Clara

160

Ernest T.'s E-Z Coconut Pie

There goes a happy nut.

1 stick margarine
4 eggs
2 cups sugar
½ cup self-rising flour

2 cups milk
1 can flaked coconut
½ teaspoon vanilla extract
½ teaspoon coconut flavoring

Soften margarine and beat in eggs. Add sugar, flour, and milk. Mix in coconut and flavorings. Pour into a deep-dish pie pan. Bake for 40 to 45 minutes at 350°. Better if refrigerated overnight.

Serves 6 to 8.

Linda Snead—Tuscaloosa, Alabama

Wilbur Finch's Peach Cobbler

It'll make you a star.

3 tablespoons butter
1 cup flour
1 cup sugar

⅔ cup milk
1 pint peaches, or 1 can any flavor
    pie filling

Melt butter in a casserole dish. Mix flour, sugar, and milk. Pour over melted butter. Pour fruit over flour mixture. Bake at 350° for 30 minutes or until done.

Serves 4 to 6.

Jan and Allan Newsome—Huntsville, Alabama

Welcome to Mayberry Pineapple Dessert

Southern hospitality you can taste!

20 ounces unsweetened crushed
    pineapple, drained
¾ cup sugar
3 tablespoons flour

¼ cup margarine, melted
1 cup Cheddar cheese, grated
2 cups Ritz crackers, crushed

Combine all ingredients, except crackers. Pour into a buttered 8x8-inch dish. Top with crushed Ritz crackers. Bake at 350° for 30 minutes.

Makes 4 servings.

Tracy Smitherman—Gordo, Alabama

161

Charlotte Chocolate Pie

Businessman's special.

2 egg yolks	Pinch of salt
2 cups milk	½ teaspoon vanilla extract
1 cup sugar	1 teaspoon butter
⅓ cup cocoa	1 9-inch pie shell, baked
⅓ cup plain flour	Whipped cream for topping

Beat egg yolks; add milk. Sift together dry ingredients. Stir ⅓ egg-milk mixture into dry ingredients to form a paste. Add remaining liquid. Cook in a double boiler, stirring frequently. When thickened, add vanilla and butter. Pour into baked pie shell. Top with whipped cream. Refrigerate for about 2 hours before serving.

Serves 6 to 8.

Susie Luguire—Tuscaloosa, Alabama

Bachelor Barney's Blackberry Cobbler

Even Mrs. Mendelbright doesn't mind when you cook this.

1 stick butter	½ cup milk
1 cup sugar	1 teaspoon vanilla extract
1 cup flour	3 to 4 cups blackberries
1 egg	

Melt butter in a 9x12-inch casserole dish. Mix remaining ingredients, except blackberries, in a separate bowl and gently pour into casserole dish. Place blackberries along the middle of casserole dish. Bake at 350° for approximately 30 minutes. Don't burn.

Serves 10 to 12.

Gary Cannon—Old Hickory, Tennessee

Barney has a burning desire to cook in his room:

ANDY: Reckon Mrs. Mendelbright smelled it?
(Knock-knock-knock at the door.)
BARNEY: She smelled it!
MRS. MENDELBRIGHT (entering room): Mr. Fife! How could you?
BARNEY: So I cooked a little! Is that so terrible?

Gunfighters don't get paid by the bullet.

Barney's Deluxe Special Fudge Pie

Just like Mom used to make.

1 stick margarine or butter	2 eggs
1 square unsweetened chocolate	1 teaspoon vanilla extract
1 cup sugar	Pinch of salt
½ cup flour	

Preheat the oven to 325°. Put stick of margarine or butter in pie pan with square of chocolate on top. When melted, remove from the oven and add sugar and flour. These 2 ingredients will form a mound in pan. In the middle of the mound add eggs, vanilla, and salt. Stir ingredients until blended. Bake for 30 minutes. (Option: Add raisins, drained cherries, nuts, etc.)
    Serves 6 to 8.

Patty and David Browning—Bristol, Virginia

Man in a Hurry Cobbler Topping

Ready to go.

1 stick margarine
1 cup sugar

1 cup all-purpose flour
Canned fruit of your choice

Melt margarine. Mix in sugar and flour (it will be lumpy). Drain most of juice from big can of fruit. Pour fruit into a casserole dish. Sprinkle topping mixture across top. Bake at 300° until topping is light brown. Keep cans of fruit on hand and whip up a "homemade" cobbler in no time flat. Serves 4 to 6.

Jeanne Swanner Robertson—Burlington, North Carolina

Man in a hurry slows down.

Oh, he'll be staying, all right. Don't you worry:

AUNT BEE: Andy, would you give me a hand?

ANDY: Mr. Tucker's car is ready, Aunt Bee. He's leaving.

AUNT BEE: Oh, oh, what a shame. We were going to have ice cream.

MR. TUCKER: Sounds wonderful, but I really do have to be going.

BEE'S NICE QUIZ

1. What food that Aunt Bee makes does Briscoe Darling say is "larrapin"?
   Answer: Blueberry muffins
2. Where did Aunt Bee buy her 150 pounds of "bargain" beef?
   Answer: Diamond Jim's
3. What two main dishes is Aunt Bee most likely to make for Sunday dinner?
   Answer: Roast beef and fried chicken

Butter and Egg Man Buttermilk Pie
Hard to beat.

2 eggs
1 stick butter
¼ cup buttermilk
1½ cups sugar

1 tablespoon flour
1 teaspoon vanilla extract
1 9-inch pie shell, unbaked

Mix first 6 ingredients; pour into pie shell. Bake for 40 minutes at 350°. Serves 6 to 8.

Rhonda Brewington—Lebanon, Tennessee

Lawman Barney's Fruit Pizza
It stands for something.

½ cup sugar
1 tablespoon cornstarch
Dash of salt
½ cup orange juice
2 tablespoons lemon juice
¼ cup water

1 box sugar cookie mix, 1 roll refrigerated
   sugar cookies, or your own recipe
8 ounces cream cheese
8 ounces nondairy whipped topping
3 tablespoons confectioners' sugar
Fresh fruit slices

For glaze, bring sugar, cornstarch, salt, orange juice, lemon juice, and water to a boil; remove from heat. Beat and let begin to cool. Spread cookie dough onto a pizza pan. Bake for 10 to 12 minutes and let cool.

For filling, use an electric mixer to beat cream cheese, whipped topping, and sugar. Pour over cookie. Top with fruit slices, such as strawberries, kiwi, and bananas. Drizzle glaze over fruit.

Serves 10 to 12.

Joyce Blake Taylor—Princeton, West Virginia

Clyde Plaunt's Coconut Caramel Pie

Aces.

1 7-ounce package coconut
½ cup chopped pecans
¼ cup margarine, melted
8 ounces cream cheese, softened

1 can sweetened condensed milk
16 ounces nondairy whipped topping
2 deep-dish pie crusts
12 ounces caramel ice cream topping

Sauté coconut and pecans in margarine in a large skillet until light brown. Set aside. Beat cream cheese and milk until smooth. Fold in whipped topping. Make ¼-inch layers of cream cheese mixture in each pie shell. Drizzle caramel on each. Sprinkle coconut mixture on top and cover with remaining cream cheese. Cover and freeze. Leave out for 5 minutes before serving. Thaws quickly.
   Serves 12 to 16.

Judy Cannon—Mt. Juliet, Tennessee

Rafe Hollister's Sweet Tater Pie

It really shines!

1½ cups mashed sweet potatoes, cooked
1 cup sugar
1 cup milk
2 beaten eggs
½ teaspoon cinnamon

2 tablespoons melted margarine
½ teaspoon salt
½ teaspoon allspice or nutmeg
1 pie shell, unbaked

Mix well all ingredients, except pie shell. Pour into pie shell. Bake at 400° for 40 minutes.
   Serves 6 to 8.

Teri Cannon—Old Hickory, Tennessee

Bribery will land Rafe Hollister in jail—if he's smart:

ANDY: If you'll do that, I'll make you just as comfortable as I can while you're here.
RAFE: Huh?
ANDY: Yes, and Aunt Bee, she'll bring some chicken and dumplings and sweet tater pie for supper.
RAFE: She will?
ANDY: She will.
RAFE: I'll do it! Chicken and dumplings?
ANDY: And sweet tater pie.
RAFE: I should have give myself up years ago.

OTIS CAMPBELL—One of Mayberry's best

Oatmeal Pie Otis

O'tis delicious!

3 eggs, well beaten
1 stick butter
1 cup brown sugar
1 cup light corn syrup

1 cup instant oatmeal, uncooked
1 teaspoon vanilla extract
1 pie shell, unbaked
¼ cup crushed pecans

Mix all ingredients, except pie shell and pecans, thoroughly and pour into an uncooked pie shell. Bake at 350° for 45 minutes and place the pecans on top.
    Serves 6 to 8.

Vickie and Larry Russell
(current owners of Frances Bavier's last residence)
Siler City, North Carolina

Frozen Lemon Pie

1 cup finely crushed Post
    Grape-Nuts Flakes
¼ cup butter, melted
2 egg yolks
¼ cup sugar
    Dash of salt
½ teaspoon grated lemon rind
¼ cup lemon juice
¾ cup heavy cream
2 egg whites
¼ cup sugar

Mix cereal and butter. Press ¾ cup firmly on bottom and sides of an 8-inch pie pan. Blend egg yolks and ¼ cup sugar in top of double boiler. Mix in salt, lemon rind, and lemon juice. Cook and stir over boiling water, until slightly thickened — about 5 minutes. Cool. Whip cream just until soft peaks will form and fold in lemon mixture. Beat egg whites until foamy throughout. Add ¼ cup sugar gradually and continue beating until stiff peaks will form. Fold in cream mixture and pour into crust. Sprinkle with remaining cereal mixture. Freeze until firm—about 4 hours. Makes 6 to 8 servings.

This is one of my favorite desserts — it's frozen and cool, the lemon flavor is tart and refreshing, and oh boy, the filling sure is smooth. It's that li'l ole crunchy crust that sets it off. *ANDY GRIFFITH STAR OF ANDY GRIFFITH SHOW CBS-TV MONDAY NIGHTS*

POST AND GRAPE-NUTS ARE TRADEMARKS OF GENERAL FOODS CORP.

Aunt Bee's pie recipe sure is good!

COURTESY OF DENNIS HASTY COLLECTION

Charlie Foley's Frozen Lemon Pie

Always keep some in your freezer.

4 egg yolks
Juice and grated rind of 1 large lemon
½ cup sugar
3 tablespoons lemon gelatin
1 cup hot water

1 cup whipping cream
¼ cup sugar
2 egg whites
Crushed vanilla wafers or cinnamon
    wafers

Combine egg yolks, lemon juice, rind, and ½ cup sugar in a double boiler and cook until thickened. While cooking, dissolve gelatin in hot water and add to first mixture. Cool. Whip cream; add ¼ cup sugar and 2 egg whites beaten stiff. Fold all together and put in a loaf pan. Cover with crumbs and freeze.

Serves 6 to 8.

Blair Bowers—Bethesda, Maryland

Manhunt Chocolate Almond Pie

Magnetic.

½ square unsweetened chocolate
8 ounces Hershey bars with almonds
1 graham cracker crust

1 12-ounce container nondairy
whipped topping

Melt chocolate and Hershey bars over low heat. Mix in ¾ of the whipped topping. Pour into graham cracker crust. Cool. Cover with remaining whipped topping. Refrigerate.
Serves 6 to 8.

Melanie Corgill—Raleigh, North Carolina

Henry "Shopping Bag" Leonetti's Apple Pie

Most wanted.

Approximately 5 to 6 apples for filling
½ cup sugar
2 tablespoons flour
½ teaspoon nutmeg, optional
½ teaspoon cinnamon

1 pie shell, unbaked
Topping:
½ cup sugar
½ cup flour
½ cup margarine

Toss apples with sugar, flour, nutmeg, and cinnamon. Place in pie shell.
For streusel topping, mix sugar, flour, and margarine. Sprinkle over apples in pie shell. Put into an oven roasting bag; fold down end and paper clip. Bake at 425° for 45 minutes to 1 hour.
Serves 6 to 8.

Beverly Stump—Lebanon, Indiana

Opie outfoxes a fox:

AUNT BEE: Andy, did you take an apple pie from home this morning? I've lost my apple pie.

ANDY: I didn't take it.

AUNT BEE: This is strange. Heavens, what do you think it is?

ANDY: I don't know.

BARNEY: You know what I think it is?

ANDY: What?

BARNEY: A fox.

ANDY: A fox?

BARNEY: Yeah, a fox come down out of the hills. You know we've had this dry spell. Well, it came down out of the hills for food and water. That's what it is—a hungry fox foraging around.

Fattening up Barney:
AUNT BEE: Just a little bit more? Then, I'll get the dessert—banana
cream chocolate pie.
BARNEY: Mmm, no.
AUNT BEE: No dessert? Oh, it'd be so helpful. It's nothing but sugar
and starch.

Sweet Juanita's Sweet Potato/Banana Pie
Take a tip: It's delicious.

2 eggs
½ cup brown sugar
¾ cup granulated sugar
1 cup cooked, mashed sweet potatoes
2 large mashed bananas
Dash of salt

1 teaspoon cinnamon
1 teaspoon vanilla extract
1 cup milk
¼ cup melted butter or margarine
½ cup chopped pecans, if desired
Pie shell(s), unbaked

Beat eggs with sugars. Add and mix well sweet potatoes, bananas, salt, cinnamon, and vanilla. Blend in milk and butter or margarine. Sprinkle pecans on top, if desired. Bake in uncooked pie shell(s) at 400° for 10 minutes; then reduce heat to 350° and bake for 35 to 40 minutes.
    Serves 6 to 8.

Linda Stewart—Dallas, Texas

Briscoe's Declarin' Mocha Eclairs
Put on your square wheels and slow down for these!

½ cup margarine
1 cup boiling water
1 cup sifted flour
½ teaspoon salt

4 eggs
2 small boxes or 1 large box instant
    vanilla pudding
Floyd's Mocha Frosting (p. 150)

Combine margarine and boiling water and heat until margarine melts. Add flour and salt all at once, stirring vigorously. Cook while stirring until mixture leaves sides of pan. Remove from heat and cool for 1 minute. Add eggs, 1 at a time, beating until smooth. Drop by rounded tablespoonful onto greased cookie sheet. Bake in a preheated 450° oven for 10 minutes. Turn oven to 400° for 25 minutes. Cut off tops and fill with pudding. Ice with Floyd's Mocha Frosting.
    Makes about 3 dozen.

Diane and Steve McCarty—New Freedom, Pennsylvania

Skippy's Cherry Torte

Oh, Bernie, it's a scream.

1 cup cake flour
5 tablespoons confectioners' sugar
½ cup soft butter
2 eggs
1½ cups sugar
¼ teaspoon salt

¼ cup flour
¾ teaspoon baking powder
1 teaspoon vanilla extract
1 can sour cherries, drained
½ cup chopped nuts
Whipped cream or ice cream

Mix well cake flour, confectioners' sugar, and butter. Line an 8x11-inch pan with mixture. Bake for 20 minutes in a 350° oven. Mix eggs, sugar, salt, flour, baking powder, and vanilla. Fold in sour cherries and chopped nuts. Pour over baked layer and return to oven and bake for 30 to 40 minutes at 350°. Serve with whipped cream or ice cream.

Serves 10 to 12.

Dee Boquist—Minneapolis, Minnesota

Barney: "Our only crime is that we're attractive to women."

171

BABY STEPS—When Opie finds a baby on the courthouse steps, he can only hope pal Arnold will have a good plan when he comes along.

Arnold's Easy Apple Dumplings
It's good, friends.

1 pie crust, unbaked
6 cooking apples, peeled, cored, and cut
3 cups sugar, divided
2¼ teaspoons ground cinnamon, divided

1½ teaspoons ground nutmeg, divided
1 pat, plus ¼ cup melted butter
2 cups hot water
Ice cream

Cut pie crust into 5-inch squares. Place 4 to 5 pieces of apple in each square. Mix 1 cup sugar, 2 teaspoons cinnamon, and 1 teaspoon nutmeg. Sprinkle mixture over apple squares. Top each square with pat of butter. Pinch 4 corners together with a little cold water. Put aside.

To make syrup, stir remaining sugar, cinnamon, nutmeg, and butter with hot water. Pour into a baking dish. Place dumplings on top of syrup. Bake at 375° for 40 minutes. Serve individually with ice cream.

Makes 12 servings.

Sheldon Golomb—Cast member

Slimy River Bottom Pie

It'll make you dance till your stockings are hot and raveling.

1½ cups gingersnap crumbs
6 tablespoons melted margarine
1 tablespoon unflavored gelatin and
　½ cup cold water
1½ cups milk and 2 tablespoons margarine
4 eggs, separated
1½ tablespoons cornstarch and
　¼ cup cold milk

1 cup sugar, plus 1/2 cup
½ teaspoon salt
4 tablespoons cocoa and 1½
　tablespoons margarine
1 teaspoon vanilla extract
2 tablespoons rum or 1 tablespoon
　rum flavoring
1 cup whipping cream

Mix well gingersnap crumbs and melted margarine. Line a 10-inch pan, patting along sides and bottom to make crust. Soak gelatin in water for 2 to 5 minutes. Scald milk and margarine in top of a double boiler, water softly boiling, until margarine melts. Beat yolks slightly. Make a paste of cornstarch and milk. Add 1 cup sugar to hot milk. Stir slightly to dissolve. Add salt. Combine egg yolks and cornstarch paste. Add a small amount of milk to this slowly; then return it to milk in double boiler over hot water. Stir constantly until mixture coats spoon, about 2 minutes. Remove from heat; add gelatin, stirring until dissolved. Divide filling in half. Add cocoa mix to half. Stir in vanilla. Pour into pie crust and chill. Beat egg whites until stiff, gradually adding ½ cup sugar while beating. Fold into remaining custard with rum. Pile on top of cooled chocolate layer. Chill overnight, covered with a top that does not touch it. When ready to serve, cover with whipped cream.
　Serves 10 to 12.

Mrs. A. C. Rhodes—Greensboro, North Carolina

Cock-a-doodle-doo Nests

One of Barn's favorites.

2⅔ cups flaked coconut
⅔ cup sweetened condensed milk

1 teaspoon vanilla extract
Ice cream

Mix well all ingredients, except ice cream. Drop by heaping tablespoonful onto a baking sheet covered with brown paper. Shape into 2-inch rings, making a hollow in each center. Bake at 350° for 17 minutes or until golden brown. Remove from paper at once. Cool and fill with ice cream.
　Makes 6 to 8.

Carolyn Thrower—Opelika, Alabama

173

Bluegrass Blueberry Cobbler
Finger lickin' pickin'.

1 stick margarine
1 pint fresh or frozen blueberries
1 teaspoon lemon juice
Approximately ¼ cup water
2 cups sugar, divided

1 cup sifted flour (if all-purpose, add
  1 teaspoon baking powder and ½
  teaspoon salt)
½ cup milk
½ teaspoon vanilla extract

Preheat the oven to 375°. Put margarine in a large deep-dish pan; set in oven to melt. Meanwhile, put blueberries, lemon juice, water, and 1 cup sugar in a saucepan. Heat to boiling.

For batter, mix remaining ingredients until well blended and smooth. When margarine is melted, pour batter over melted margarine; then pour blueberry mixture on top of batter. Bake until top is golden brown and crusty, about 25 to 30 minutes.

Serves 8 to 10.

Autice Culbreath—Union Grove, Alabama

Sam's Chocolate Pineapple Pie
Eat up with the Joneses.

3 tablespoons butter
4 tablespoons flour
2 cups milk
4 tablespoons sugar (rounded),
  plus 6 tablespoons
3 eggs, separated

2 squares baking chocolate, melted
1 teaspoon vanilla extract
1 pie crust, baked
1 medium can pineapple tidbits, drained
¼ teaspoon cream of tartar

Melt butter in top of a double boiler. Add flour and mix until smooth; add milk and stir well until smooth. Add 4 tablespoons sugar. Beat egg yolks until light. Take a little of the custard and add to egg yolks and melted chocolate squares; pour back into custard and cook until thick and smooth. Add vanilla. Cool filling and put into baked pie crust. Add drained pineapple tidbits by poking individually into cooled filling.

Beat egg whites and cream of tartar with an electric mixer until foamy. Gradually add 6 tablespoons sugar. Beat at medium speed for 1½ to 2 minutes until stiff peaks form. Place on pie, sealing meringue to edge of pie crust. Bake in a preheated 350° oven for 15 minutes or until meringue is golden brown. Cool at room temperature.

Serves 6 to 8.

Bernice Berry (mother of Ken Berry)—Cast member

174

Favorite farmer Sam Jones

County Clerk Chocolate Coconut Pecan Pie

Sure to receive the stamp of approval.

1 box light brown sugar
3 tablespoonfuls plain flour
5 tablespoons cocoa
1 stick margarine, melted
4 eggs

1 large can evaporated milk
1 teaspoon vanilla extract
1 cup chopped nuts
1 can flaked coconut
3 regular or 2 deep-dish pie shells, unbaked

Mix sugar, flour, and cocoa. Add margarine, eggs, milk, and vanilla. Add nuts and coconut. Pour into crusts. Bake at 350° for 30 to 35 minutes.
Serves 12 to 16.

Sara Brower—Asheboro, North Carolina

Malcolm's Jam Roly Poly

Jelly good.

½ recipe for Short-Cut Short Crust   3 tablespoons jam
   Pastry (p. 177)

Roll out pastry into an oblong pan, about 9 inches long. Spread with jam to about ½ inch from edge. Don't go too close or it will squeeze out. Roll up carefully and press edges together. Bake at 400° for 30 to 40 minutes. You can make a hearty variation on this by using suet paste instead of short crust and boiling the roly poly in a cloth for 3 hours. (For suet paste, substitute 8 ounces suet and 2 tablespoonfuls baking powder for lard and butter.)

   Serves 6 to 8.

Bernard Fox—Cast member

HALE ON WHEELS—Robust pedaler Malcolm Merriweather

Malcolm's Short-Cut Short Crust Pastry

Just follow this map.

4 cups flour
1 teaspoon salt
½ cup butter

½ cup lard
Cold water

Sift flour and salt; mix in butter and lard. When well blended, add water to make a dry dough. You can put other delightful fillings into a roly poly. Try currants, raisins, mashed dates, or mincemeat. I always thought it was called roly poly because that's the shape you're in if you eat too much of it.

Makes pastry for 2 pies or 2 Roly Poly recipes.

Bernard Fox—Cast member

Earlie Gilley's Pecan Pie

Worth the drive to Mt. Pilot any day.

4 eggs
½ cup brown sugar
1 cup dark corn syrup
½ teaspoon salt

1 teaspoon vanilla extract
1 pie shell, unbaked
1 cup pecans
Butter

Beat eggs; add sugar, corn syrup, salt, and vanilla. Pour into an unbaked pie shell and dot pie with pecans and butter. Bake at 350° for 40 to 50 minutes.

Serves 6 to 8.

Lorraine Gilley—Pilot Mountain, North Carolina

Pilot Pines Pineapple Chess Pie

Heavenly.

1 box light brown sugar
3 tablespoons flour
1 stick margarine, melted
3 eggs, beaten

1 teaspoon vanilla extract
1 large can crushed pineapple, slightly
    drained (can use applesauce)
2 pie shells, unbaked

Preheat the oven to 450°. Mix ingredients in order, except pie shells. Pour into 2 unbaked pie crusts. Reduce oven temperature to 325° and bake for 30 minutes.

Makes 2 pies.

Judy B. Coleman—Asheboro, North Carolina

Blue-vue Blueberry Delight

Something special.

3 cups blueberries, fresh or frozen,
thawed and drained
1 small can crushed pineapple
¾ cup sugar, divided

1 box yellow cake mix
1 cup chopped pecans
1 stick butter, melted

Preheat the oven to 350°. Grease a 13x9x2-inch baking dish. Mix blueberries, pineapple, and ½ cup sugar in dish and spread evenly along bottom. Pour dry cake mix over fruit and smooth out to edges of dish. Sprinkle pecans evenly over cake mix and then follow with ¼ cup sugar, being careful not to sprinkle too much sugar in one spot. Drizzle melted butter over mix and bake for 45 minutes or until golden brown on top.
Serves 12.

Anne Hood—Duluth, Georgia

Backwoods Blackberry Dumplings

They always come back for more.

4 cups blackberries
1¼ cups sugar, divided
½ cup water

1¼ cups biscuit mix
1 egg
¼ cup milk

Put blackberries with 1 cup sugar and water in a large saucepan and bring to a boil. In a separate pan or bowl, mix biscuit mix with egg, ¼ cup sugar, and milk to make dumplings. Drop dumpling mixture by teaspoonful into boiling berries. Cover and simmer for 5 minutes. Serve warm.
Makes 5 or 6 servings.

Alice Schwenke—Houston, Texas

We probably don't have to wonder who's going to be served the bigger piece:
FLORA: We have fresh blueberry pie, and the peach is simply fantastic, and the apple is real, real yummy.
ANDY: OK, apple.
(To Helen):Want a piece of pie?
HELEN: Fine.
ANDY: What kind?
HELEN: Whichever one's the yummy one.

Crabman Comic Cranberry Apple Pie

Goober's favorite.

1 9- or 10-inch pie pastry, unbaked
1½ cups sugar, divided
¾ cup flour, divided
1 teaspoon cinnamon

12 ounces fresh cranberries
2 cups sliced peeled apples
⅓ cup unsalted butter

Preheat the oven to 425°. Line a pie pan with pastry; prick with a fork. Freeze until filling is ready. In large bowl, combine 1¼ cups sugar, ¼ cup flour, and cinnamon. Rinse and remove any bad cranberries; drain well. Add to sugar mixture. Add chopped apples and stir to mix well. Pour into unbaked pie shell. In a small bowl, combine ½ cup flour, ¼ cup sugar, and ⅓ cup unsalted butter that has been diced in a food processor. Pulse in processor or blend with a fork until crumbly. Sprinkle over filling. Bake for 15 minutes. Reduce heat to 350° and continue baking for 45 minutes or until crust is lightly browned. Cool before serving. A holiday favorite!

Serves 6 to 8.

Thayer Wine—Nashville, Tennessee

Comic relief

Ask a silly question:

AUNT BEE: (to Andy and Opie) Well, how would you boys like a nice apple pie for dessert tonight?

LIFE OF HARD KNOCKS—
Door-to-door salesman visits Mayberry.

Martin Phillips' French Strawberry Pie
Oui like it.

1 9-inch pie shell, baked	1 cup sugar
3 ounces cream cheese	3 tablespoons cornstarch
Milk	Whipped cream
1 quart strawberries	

Spread baked pie shell with cream cheese moistened with milk to make it easier to spread. Clean berries, leaving half of them whole, and place in cream cheese. Mash remaining strawberries in a saucepan; add sugar and cornstarch. Cook for 10 minutes, stirring constantly until thick (like jam) and clear. Pour over berries in pie shell. Refrigerate for several hours and serve with whipped cream.

Serves 6 to 8.

Alvy Moore—Cast member

MOORE TO THE STORY

Actor Alvy Moore's role as the lucky kitchenwares salesman in "A Baby in the House" (Episode #184) bailed Aunt Bee out of her babysitting worries. But Alvy, who is best-known for his decisive portrayal of county agent Hank Kimball in *Green Acres*, also was considered for the role of Mayberry deputy after Don Knotts departed the show (and Barney Fife moved to Raleigh). Had Alvy not already been headed to Hooterville, he might have been wearing a badge in Mayberry.

Pie for later:
AUNT BEE: They'll be some rhubarb pie for you when you get home.

Rube Sloan's Rhubarb Crumble
Folks won't be still till they have some.

1 cup brown sugar	4 cups rhubarb, cut into pieces
½ cup oatmeal	1 cup sugar
1 cup flour	2 tablespoons cornstarch
½ cup margarine	1 cup water
1 teaspoon cinnamon	1 teaspoon vanilla extract

Mix first 5 ingredients. Reserve ¼ of mixture. Add rhubarb to ¾ of mixture. Put in a buttered 8x8-inch glass baking dish.

Cook sugar, cornstarch, water, and vanilla until thick. Pour thickened mixture over rhubarb mixture. Sprinkle remaining ¼ of dry mixture over top. Bake at 350° for 30 to 45 minutes or until lightly browned and crisp on top.

Serves 8 to 10.

Donna M. Fisher—East Canton, Ohio

Above Your Raisin-Pecan Pie
Tops.

2 eggs, separated	½ cup raisins
1 cup sugar	1 tablespoon melted butter
1 teaspoon cinnamon	1 tablespoon vanilla extract
1 teaspoon cloves	1 8-inch pastry shell, unbaked
½ cup pecan halves	Whipped cream, optional

Beat egg yolks until light and thick. Gradually add sugar, which has been sifted with cinnamon and cloves. Then add pecan halves, raisins, and butter. Beat egg whites until stiff but not dry and fold them gently into sugar mixture. Do not beat. As you fold them in, add vanilla. Pour into pastry shell. Bake at 450° for 10 minutes; then reduce heat to 350° and bake for 25 minutes more. Serve with whipped cream, slightly sweetened, if desired.

Serves 6 to 8.

Alice Schwenke—Houston, Texas

All God's Children Got a Chocolate Pie

After you've a-tried it, you'll say you've a-loved it.

2 cups sugar
2 cups milk
4 eggs
2 tablespoons cocoa

4 heaping tablespoons flour
1 teaspoon vanilla extract
1 tablespoon butter
1 9-inch pie shell, baked

Mix first 5 ingredients and cook in a double boiler until thick. Add vanilla and butter. Pour into a baked pie shell. Top as desired.
Serves 6 to 8.

Autice Culbreath—Union Grove, Alabama

Anniversary Waltz Apple Crisp

A popular request.

¾ cup sugar
¾ cup flour
Pinch of salt
½ cup butter or margarine

4 cups sliced apples
2 tablespoons water
½ teaspoon cinnamon

Butter an 8x8-inch baking dish. Mix sugar, flour, and salt. Add butter and mix until fine crumbs are formed. Put apples in a baking dish. Pour water on apples and sprinkle cinnamon over apples. Spread flour mixture over apples and bake at 375° until apples are tender, approximately 1 hour.
Makes 9 servings.

Bill and Evonne Williams—Omaha, Nebraska

The timer's ticking on Aunt Bee during her TV quiz show appearance:

HOST: All right, Miss Taylor. You have just ten more seconds. Think, Miss Taylor. Think. Just four more seconds.

AUNT BEE: Cinnamon with custard filling.

HOST: That's right! Cinnamon with custard filling!

GOOBER (watching the show on TV): My ma always made that pie with lemon filling. 'Course, it never was any good. I'm gonna have to tell her to make it out of custard.

HOST: That's a tricky one, Miss Taylor. Most people think that's made with a lemon filling.

GOOBER: See, I told you my ma always made that with lemon filling.

ANDY: Goober!

Ellie's Apple Crisp
A welcome addition.

6 large apples, peeled and sliced
½ cup orange juice
½ cup sugar
½ teaspoon cinnamon

¾ cup sifted flour
½ cup light brown sugar, packed
¼ teaspoon salt
6 tablespoons butter or margarine

Arrange apples in a greased baking dish. Pour orange juice over apples. Combine granulated sugar and cinnamon and sprinkle over apples. Combine flour, brown sugar, salt, and butter to make a crumbly mixture. Spread over apples. Bake at 350° until apples are tender and crust is lightly browned, about 45 minutes. (Option: For a nutty flavor, add ¼ cup rolled oats and an additional tablespoon butter to flour mixture.)

Makes 6 servings.

Elinor Donahue—Cast member

Firearms inspection

183

Chocolate Mikado

Yum-yum!

1 tablespoon sugar	16 ounces nondairy whipped topping
1 package graham crackers	1 3-ounce box vanilla pudding
½ stick butter, softened	1 3-ounce box chocolate pudding
8 ounces cream cheese	3 cups milk

For crust, combine sugar, graham crackers, and butter.

For filling, mix cream cheese softened with whipped topping. Beat until smooth. Mix vanilla pudding and chocolate pudding with milk. Pour ½ whipped topping mixture on crust. Add pudding mixture. Top with whipped topping mixture.

Serves 10 to 12.

Kay Disher—Kernersville, North Carolina

BRANCHING OUT—*Barney has figured out how Revolutionary War hero Nathan Tibbs fits into his family tree.*

184

Fearless Fife Fruit Cocktail Dessert

Deadly delicious.

1 cup sugar
1 cup flour
1 teaspoon baking soda
Dash of salt
1 egg, beaten
1 1-pound, 13-ounce can fruit cocktail,
   drained

½ cup brown sugar
½ cup chopped pecans
Whipped cream or ice cream, optional
½ cup sugar, optional
½ cup butter, optional
½ cup heavy cream, optional

Mix sugar, flour, soda, salt, and beaten egg. Add fruit cocktail. Mix well and pour into an 8x8-inch pan. Sprinkle brown sugar and chopped pecans over top. Bake at 350° for about 50 minutes. May serve cold with whipped cream or ice cream.

    When served hot, I like to heat, but not boil, ½ cup sugar, ½ cup butter, and ½ cup heavy cream (can be reheated over boiling water). Grand over cranberry pudding also!

    Serves 8 to 18.

Dee Boquist—Minneapolis, Minnesota

Mayberry Says Thanks Pumpkin Pie

We appreciate it.

2½ cups fresh pumpkin
1½ cups brown sugar
¾ cup sugar
2 tablespoons butter

5 eggs
1 cup evaporated milk
1 tablespoon cinnamon
1 pie shell, unbaked

Mix all ingredients, except pie shell. Pour into pie shell. Bake at 375° for 1 hour.

    Serves 6 to 8.

Kay Disher—Kernersville, North Carolina

Andy sings praises for the meal. Speaking of which:

ANDY: About all we need now to have a perfect meal is pumpkin pie à la mode.

AUNT BEE (entering room): And now for dessert—pumpkin pie à la mode. Here we are.

OPIE: Is this what we call bribery, Pa?

ANDY: You mean is she working on me for the choir robes? I'd say yes.

Thomas A. Moody's Easy Key Lime Pie

For your guests of honor.

3 egg yolks
1 14-ounce can sweetened condensed milk
¾ cup lime juice

1 graham cracker crust
Whipped cream

Whip egg yolks with sweetened condensed milk. Gradually beat in lime juice. Pour into graham cracker crust. Chill for 6 hours. Serve with whipped cream.
    Serves 6 to 8.

Marcia and Tom Hotchkiss—Birmingham, Alabama

Mayberry Union High Apple Pie

Alma mater pie.

1 pie crust, sprinkled with flour
2 cups tart apples, thinly sliced
¾ cup sugar
¼ cup brown sugar

¼ cup flour
1 teaspoon cinnamon
½ stick butter

Add apples to pie crust. In a bowl, mix sugars, flour, cinnamon, and butter. Sprinkle on top of apples. Bake at 350° for about 45 minutes or until done.
    Serves 6 to 8.

Alma Venable
Mayberry Motor Inn—Mount Airy, North Carolina

Eatin' doesn't always speak loud enough:

AUNT BEE: There's another piece left, if you'd like it. 'Course, it didn't turn out quite right this time, did it? Hmm? A little too much cinnamon? Hmm?

ANDY: Well, I'd say there maybe was just the least little bit of too much cinnamon, yeah.

AUNT BEE: Hmm, do you think so?

ANDY: Well, maybe your apples was too ripe.

AUNT BEE: Andy Taylor, that was one of the best apple pies I ever made!

ANDY: Well, I tell you. Since it was so bad, maybe we better eat it up and get it out of the way, so we'll make room for another pie. Aunt Bee you're a bird in this world. You have to have a little bragging, don't you?

"Will you help us?"

Mayberry Minutemen Concord Grape Pie

You won't find anything this good in your history book.

1½ pounds (4 cups) Concord grapes	1½ tablespoons melted unsalted butter
1 cup sugar	1 9-inch pastry shell, unbaked
¼ cup flour	½ cup flour
¼ teaspoon salt	¼ cup sugar
1 tablespoon lemon juice	⅓ cup unsalted butter

Preheat the oven to 400°. Slip skins from grapes; set skins aside. Place pulp in a saucepan and bring to boiling point, reduce heat, and simmer for 5 minutes. Press pulp through a sieve to remove seeds. Add skins to pulp. Combine sugar, flour, and salt. Add lemon juice, butter, and grape pulp and skins. Pour into pastry-lined pie plate.

For crumb topping, whisk ½ cup flour with ¼ cup sugar. Cut in ⅓ cup unsalted butter until crumbly. Sprinkle over pie filling. Bake in a preheated oven for 40 minutes. Have a napkin handy as the mouthwatering aroma fills your kitchen.

Serves 6 to 8.

Patty Hridel—Chagrin Falls, Ohio

187

Laura Hollander, the best cook in neighboring Walnut Hills

Laura Hollander's Camp Winokee Pie
A wealth of flavor.

20 saltines
1¼ teaspoons baking powder
4 egg whites
1⅓ cups sugar

1 teaspoon vanilla extract
1 cup chopped pecans
1 cup heavy cream, whipped
Strawberries

Crush crackers into fine crumbs, using a rolling pin, or pulverize in a blender. Add baking powder; mix well, and set aside. Beat egg whites until stiff but not dry. Beat in sugar slowly, until stiff. Gently fold in vanilla, pecans, and crumbs, mixing well. Pour into a well-greased 9-inch pie plate. Bake at 350° for 30 minutes or until golden brown and firm. Let cool. Garnish with whipped cream and strawberries. Yum Yum Yummy.

Serves 6 to 8.

Joyce Van Patten—Cast member

Apple Pizza à la Morelli

Pound for pound, it's the best.

2 tablespoons flour
1 cup brown sugar
1 teaspoon cinnamon
1 can biscuits

1 cup grated mild cheese
2 apples, peeled
Butter or margarine

Mix flour, brown sugar, and cinnamon in a bowl. Press biscuits into flat circles and put on a slightly greased cookie sheet. Sprinkle grated cheese on biscuits. Slice apples and put a slice on each biscuit. Put brown sugar mixture on top. Dot with butter and bake at 350° for 20 to 30 minutes. Cool. Serves 10.

Freda and Mike Creech—Plainfield, Indiana

Aunt Bee's Summer Dessert

A favorite of front porch fans.

1 cup flour
1 stick margarine, softened
1 cup chopped nuts
8 ounces cream cheese, softened
1 cup confectioners' sugar

2 packages instant chocolate pudding mix
3 cups milk
12 ounces nondairy whipped topping
Semisweet chocolate, grated

Mix flour, margarine, and nuts and pat into bottom of a flat rectangular dish (a 2-quart dish works well). Bake at 350° until slightly browned. Cool. Blend cream cheese and confectioners' sugar until smooth. (A food processor works well for this.) Spread cheese-sugar mixture on cooled crust. It helps if you can let this set up a bit before adding the next layer. Combine instant pudding mix with milk and blend into this 1¼ to 1½ cups whipped topping. Spread on top of cream cheese-sugar layer. Spread remaining whipped topping on top of pudding layer and garnish with grated semisweet chocolate. Chill. This simple but delicious summer dessert is better made a day ahead. (Other pudding flavors can be used.) Serves 10 to 12.

Berry Stout—Greensboro, North Carolina

ACTING CLASS

As Laura Hollander in "Opie Steps Up in Class" (Episode #225), Joyce Van Patten gave Opie and the Taylors a taste of richly deserved friendship outside of Mayberry.

And Now a Word from Our Sponsor Pie

Brought to you by Grape-Nuts.

½ cup Grape-Nuts cereal
½ cup warm water
1 cup packed brown sugar
1 cup dark corn syrup
⅛ teaspoon salt

¼ cup butter
3 eggs
1 teaspoon vanilla extract
1 9-inch pastry shell, unbaked
Whipped cream, optional

Soak Grape-Nuts in water until water is absorbed. Combine sugar, syrup, salt, and butter in a saucepan and bring to a boil, stirring until sugar dissolves. Remove from heat. Beat eggs until foamy. Add small amount of hot mixture to eggs, beating well. Add remaining hot mixture to eggs, mixing well. Stir in softened Grape-Nuts and vanilla. Pour into pastry shell. Bake at 375° for 45 to 50 minutes. Serve with whipped cream, if desired.

Serves 6 to 8.

Nancy Clark—Greensboro, North Carolina

Your Harvards and Your Yales Chocolate Pie

It's rich.

Meringue Crust:
3 egg whites
1 cup sugar
½ cup chopped nuts
10 saltine crackers, loosely crumbled
¼ teaspoon salt
Filling:
¾ cup milk
1 cup semisweet chocolate chips

3 egg yolks
Pinch of salt
1 tablespoon Kahlua liqueur or 1
    tablespoon vanilla extract
Topping:
2 cups heavy cream
3 tablespoons sugar
3 1.5-gram milk chocolate bars

Preheat the oven to 300°. For crust, beat egg whites until stiff. Gradually add remaining crust ingredients. Bake crust in a 9-inch pie plate for 35 minutes. Let cool.

For filling, heat milk to boiling and place in a blender with remaining filling ingredients. Blend on low speed for 1 minute. Pour into cooled pie shell. Refrigerate for 2 to 3 hours.

For topping, whip cream and add sugar. Pile on top of chilled filling and top with chocolate shavings or curls. (Try cheese slicers or vegetable peelers to make shavings.)

Serves 6 to 8.

Ann McIver—Greensboro, North Carolina

Andy's Apple Pie Order

Straight from the diner.

2 cups grated apples
1 tablespoon lemon juice
1 cup sugar

1 egg, beaten well
½ stick margarine or butter, melted
1 9-inch pie shell, unbaked

Mix first 5 ingredients well. Pour into pie shell. Bake in a 325° oven for 40 minutes or until nice and brown.

Serves 6 to 8.

Anna Dale—Morganton, North Carolina

Filling in for Aunt Bee. Pie filling, that is:

CLARA: Oh, it'll be so nice to have someone to cook for.
ANDY: Well, we're looking forward to it. Huh, Ope?
OPIE: Yeah boy.
ANDY: Boy, I can't wait for some of that fine apple pie you make.
CLARA: Why, we'll have some every night if you like.
OPIE: Pie every night? Wow!

*The face of a man who is about to enjoy
a nice big slice of apple pie.*

A Regular Sin City Cinnamon Apple Puffs

Clean your plate and all is forgiven.

1 cup sugar
1 cup water
½ teaspoon red food coloring
1½ pounds tart apples (4 to 5 apples), peeled and thinly sliced
1½ cups sifted flour
½ teaspoon salt

2 teaspoons baking powder
¼ cup shortening
¾ cup milk
2 tablespoons melted butter
2 tablespoons sugar
½ teaspoon cinnamon
Cream, optional

Boil sugar, water, and food coloring until syrupy (about 5 minutes). Place apples in a greased, shallow 8x12-inch baking dish. Pour syrup over apples. Sift together flour, salt, and baking powder; cut in shortening with pastry blender, and then add milk to make a soft dough. Drop 12 spoonfuls of dough on top of apples and make a dent in top of each. Place in the dents a mixture of 2 tablespoons melted butter, 2 tablespoons sugar, and ½ teaspoon cinnamon. Bake for 25 to 30 minutes at 450°. Serve warm, with cream, if desired.

Serves 8 to 10.

Dee Boquist—Minneapolis, Minnesota

Crime stoppers

Charlene's Rhubarb Fluffs

There is a time for this—always!

2½ pounds pink rhubarb, cut into
    1-inch pieces (about 7½ cups)
⅔ cup water
1 to 1½ cups sugar

Dumpling dough (2 cups Bisquick,
    ¾ cup milk)
Fresh cream

Bring to boil rhubarb, water, and sugar in a deep 4-quart saucepan. Make dumpling dough. Drop spoonfuls of dumpling dough onto hot rhubarb. Cook, uncovered, over medium heat for 10 minutes and 10 minutes covered. Serve with fresh cream.

    Makes 6 to 8 servings.

Maggie Peterson—Cast member

Floss's Australian Pavlova

From way over yonder somewhere.

4 large fresh egg whites
6 ounces castor sugar
12 ounces soft fruits

½ pint whipped cream
A little icing

Preheat the oven to 300°. Lightly oil a baking sheet and line it with greaseproof paper, also lightly oiled. Whisk eggs and add sugar, 1 ounce at a time. Make the desired number of individual nests on baking sheet. Place in oven and turn down to 275°. Cook for 1 hour; then turn off and leave in oven until cold. Fill with fruit and top with whipped cream. Dinah Shore used to put canned passion fruit over the top, so I stole that tip from her recipe and put it with this one.

    Serves 6 to 8.

Barbara Perry—Cast member

LIFE OF THE PARTY

Barbara Perry plays four different but equally enthusiastic characters in four episodes of *The Andy Griffith Show*. She's reunion organizer Mary Lee in "Class Reunion" (Episode #82), one of Barney's prospects as a mate for Andy in "A Wife for Andy" (Episode #92), Doris Williams (who played the part of Mary Merriweather) in "The Pageant" (Episode #138), and class reunion organizer Flossie in "The Return of Barney Fife" (Episode #176).

Ellie's Pretty as a Peach Cobbler

Keen.

¼ cup melted margarine
½ cup flour
1 teaspoon baking powder

½ cup sugar
½ cup milk
1 pint canned or fresh fruit with juice

Pour melted margarine into a 9-inch square baking dish. Combine flour, baking powder, sugar, and milk in a separate bowl. Pour batter over melted margarine. Pour fruit and juice on top. Bake in a preheated 400° oven for about 25 to 35 minutes or until batter comes to top.
Serves 8.

Jane Ellis—Albuquerque, New Mexico

Southern Pecan Pie

Simply delicious.

1 cup pecan halves
1 9-inch pie shell, unbaked
3 eggs
1 cup light (or dark) corn syrup

1 tablespoon melted butter
½ teaspoon vanilla extract
1 cup sugar
1 tablespoon flour

Arrange nuts in pie shell. Beat eggs and blend syrup, butter, and vanilla. Combine sugar and flour. Blend with egg mixture and pour over nuts in pie shell. Let stand until nuts rise. Bake at 350° for 45 minutes. (Oven temperature and time may vary.) Bake until filling is no longer soupy.
Serves 6 to 8.

Bettina and Richard O. Linke—Associate Producer

Chase the Crooks Lemon Chess Pie

Captures great flavor.

2 cups sugar
1 tablespoon cornmeal
4 eggs, unbeaten
¼ cup melted butter

¼ cup milk
4 tablespoons grated lemon rind
¼ cup lemon juice or more to taste
1 9-inch pie shell, unbaked

Toss sugar and cornmeal in a large bowl. Add eggs, butter, milk, lemon rind, and lemon juice. Beat until smooth and pour into pie shell. Bake at 375° for 35 to 45 minutes or until golden brown.
Serves 6 to 8.

Nancy Clark—Greensboro, North Carolina

*SURE SHOT—It would take Eagle-Eye Annie
for Andy to win against Thelma Lou's Cousin
Karen in a sporting competition.*

Karen's Perfect Lemon Pie

Right on target.

3 egg yolks
1 14-ounce can sweetened condensed milk
½ cup real lemon juice concentrate

1 8-inch graham cracker crust
8 ounces nondairy whipped topping

Preheat the oven to 325°. Beat egg yolks with milk and lemon juice. Pour into crust and bake for 30 minutes. Cool. Spread with whipped topping. Refrigerate.

Serves 6 to 8.

Gail Davis—Cast member

STRAIGHT SHOOTER

Gail Davis, who portrayed Thelma Lou's Cousin Karen from Arkansas in "The Perfect Female" (Episode #57), made skeet shooting against Andy look easy. During the 1950s, she starred in her own TV series, *Annie Oakley*.

At ease in Mayberry

Aunt Florence's Rum Parfait Pie

A special treat.

1 egg white	4 to 6 Heath Bars (crushed, then
⅔ cup sugar	chopped fine and chilled)
1 teaspoon lemon juice	2 9-inch pie crusts or chocolate graham
1 tablespoon rum flavoring	cracker crusts, baked
½ pint whipping cream	Chopped almonds or pecans for topping

Beat egg white, sugar, lemon juice, and rum flavoring with an electric mixer until soft peaks form. Whip cream until thick. Combine egg-white mixture and whipped cream. Fold in Heath Bars, reserving some to sprinkle on top of pie, and pour into pie shells. Sprinkle pie with chopped almonds or pecans. (Cool Whip can be substituted for whipped cream for lighter pies.) Freeze for several hours before serving.

Makes 2 small pies.

George Spence—Cast member

Sewin' Love Apricot Dessert

Perfect for hem or her.

1 6-ounce can frozen lemonade
½ gallon vanilla ice cream
1 12-ounce jar apricot preserves

3 pie crusts or graham cracker crusts, baked

Thaw lemonade and soften ice cream. Mix lemonade and preserves and fold into ice cream. Spread into 3 pie crusts and freeze.
Makes 3 pies.

—Gramma's Sewing Club

Leonard Blush's Lemon Cheese Pie

It sings.

8 ounces cream cheese
1 can sweetened condensed milk
Juice and rind of 2 lemons

1 graham cracker crust
Nondairy whipped topping, optional
Fruit, optional

Mix first 3 ingredients and pour into crust. Chill and serve. Top with whipped topping or fruit, if desired.
Serves 6 to 8.

Edna Weatherly—Charlotte, North Carolina

Happy Valley Chocolate Pie

Settles well in Mayberry.

6 ounces chocolate morsels
1 package Heath Bar bits

9 ounces nondairy whipped topping
1 graham cracker crust

Melt chocolate morsels and Heath Bar bits (bits won't melt completely) in a double-boiler over hot water. Mixture will be stiff. Fold with whipped topping (chop mixture to blend.) Pour into crust and chill. Very rich, but so good.
Serves 6 to 8.

Alcie Sturgill—Newland, North Carolina

Crump crumb:

ANDY (on phone): Wait a minute, Helen, don't tell me. Let me guess. A lemon pie? What? Apple crumb. Wow, better and better. This is going to be a picnic.

Claudette Beamon's Chocolate Pie

A favorite overbite.

4 eggs	Dash of salt
1 large can evaporated milk	1 stick butter, melted
5 tablespoons (or more) cocoa	2 cups coconut
3 cups sugar	1 cup chopped pecans
1 teaspoon vanilla extract	2 pie shells, unbaked

Combine eggs and milk; add cocoa and sugar. Stir in vanilla and salt. Add butter, coconut, and nuts. Pour into shells. Bake at 350° for about 40 minutes.

Serves 12 to 16.

Alcie Sturgill—Newland, North Carolina

Clara's Vinegar Pie

When she's not making pickles, she has to use the vinegar for something.

3 eggs	1 teaspoon vanilla extract
1½ cups sugar	1 stick butter, melted
1 tablespoon vinegar	1 8-inch pie shell, unbaked

Beat eggs with sugar. Add remaining ingredients. Pour into pie shell and cook for 10 minutes at 300° and then for 20 minutes at 350°. If pie is not solid when shaken, cook longer.

Makes 1 small pie.

Annie Mae Murray—Greensboro, North Carolina

Scene of the Crème de Menthe Pie

Worth investigating.

1½ cups crushed Oreos	Crème de menthe to taste
1 to 2 tablespoons margarine	Chocolate sauce
2½ cups softened vanilla ice cream	Whipped cream

Mix Oreos and margarine and press into pie pan to form crust. Mix softened vanilla ice cream with crème de menthe (as much as desired). Spoon filling into crust. Cover and refreeze. Serve with chocolate sauce and whipped cream on top.

Serves 6 to 8.

Jane Ellis—Albuquerque, New Mexico

All Souls Church Cherry Burst Pie

A good recipe to a choir.

1 14-ounce can sweetened condensed milk	1 cup crushed pineapple, drained
¼ cup lemon juice	½ cup maraschino cherries, chopped
½ teaspoon vanilla extract	1 graham cracker crust
4 ounces nondairy whipped topping	

Combine milk, lemon juice, and vanilla. Mix until well blended. Fold in remaining ingredients, except crust, 1 at a time, mixing well after each addition. Add to crust. Freeze for 23 hours. Let stand for 20 minutes before serving.

Serves 6 to 8.

Kim and Tim White—Blountville, Tennessee

Famous pie maker Emma Brand

Blue Ribbon Chocolate-Almond Torte

Winner at the county fair.

8 ounces Ghiradelli semisweet chocolate
1 ounce strong coffee
1 ounce Chambord (or Amaretto,
Kahlua, Grand Marnier)
Cream of tartar

8 ounces butter
8 ounces granulated sugar
8 large eggs, separated
8 ounces ground almonds
Blue Ribbon Ganache (p. 201)

Melt chocolate with coffee and Chambord over a double boiler. Cream butter and sugar; add yolks 1 at a time. Blend in almonds; blend in chocolate. Whip egg whites with a pinch of cream of tartar until stiff but not dry; then fold into chocolate mixture. Preheat the oven to 375°. Pour mix into a buttered and floured 9-inch springform pan. Level with a rubber spatula, making sides slightly higher than center. Bake for approximately 40 to 50 minutes. Cool; then chill. Top with Blue Ribbon Ganache (p. 201).
Serves 8.

Elinor Donahue—Cast member

"Well, looky here, Ellie."

Blue Ribbon Ganache

Tops.

1 pound Ghiradelli semisweet chocolate
1 ounce dark coffee

3 ounces heavy cream
Toasted almonds, ground, for garnish

Heat chocolate, coffee, and cream slowly over a double boiler. Pour over top of torte and brush sides with ganache. Garnish sides with ground toasted almonds.

Serves 6 to 8.

Elinor Donahue—Cast member

Class of '45 Fast Lemon Pie

Will create happy memories.

1 can sweetened condensed milk
1 small can frozen pink lemonade
   concentrate

1 small container nondairy whipped
   topping
1 graham cracker crust

Mix milk, lemonade, and whipped topping, and pour into graham cracker crust. Refrigerate for 1 hour.

Serves 6 to 8.

Barbara Perry—Cast member

Tom's Mother's Chocolate Pie

Ol' Tom Montgomery was one of the best fried catfish cooks and cattle callers
west of the Mississippi. But the family favorite was his chocolate pie,
and he always attributed the recipe to his mother. Y'all enjoy it!

1 "heaping" tablespoon flour
Dash of salt
2 cups sugar, plus 2 tablespoons
2 tablespoons cocoa

2 cups milk
1 tablespoon vanilla extract
5 eggs, separated
1 pie crust, baked

Mix flour, salt, 2 cups sugar, cocoa, milk, and vanilla. Add egg yolks, beaten. Stir over medium heat until cocoa cooks and thickens. (Ol' Tom used to say that it should "drop off of a spoon like jelly.") Let filling cool. Pour into a cooked, cooled pie crust.

Beat egg whites until stiff, adding 2 tablespoons sugar as you beat. Pile on top of filling, touching crust on all sides. Bake at 300° for 15 to 20 minutes.

Serves 6 to 8.

Dana H. Snyder—Fort Worth, Texas

O-Pie
Oh, so easy.

20 marshmallows
1 large Hershey almond bar
½ cup milk

½ pint cream
Graham cracker crust
Almonds for topping

Put first 3 ingredients in a double boiler to melt. Allow to cool. Whip cream. Fold in marshmallow-chocolate mixture. Pour over graham cracker crust and top with almonds. Also good on a baked meringue crust.
Serves 6 to 8.

Mrs. Roy Boquist—Minneapolis, Minnesota

Goober's Beanie Brownie Pie
From our nation's capital.

1 stick butter or margarine, melted
1 cup sugar
3 tablespoons cocoa
¼ cup flour

2 unbeaten eggs
1 teaspoon vanilla extract
1 cup chopped pecans
Whipped cream or ice cream

Blend butter and sugar. Add cocoa, flour, eggs, vanilla, and pecans. Pour into a greased, 8-inch pie plate and bake at 350° for 20 minutes. Serve with whipped cream or ice cream.
Serves 6 to 8.

Mary Umbarger—Washington, DC

Ethel Montgomery St. John's Nesselrode Pie
Sainted.

8 ounces cream cheese
½ cup sugar
2 cups whipped topping
½ cup coconut

½ cup candied fruit, chopped
¼ cup chopped pecans
1 graham cracker crust

Beat softened cream cheese and sugar until smooth and creamy and sugar crystals have begun to dissolve. Carefully fold in whipped topping, then coconut, fruit, and pecans. Mound into a graham cracker crust (it will be poofed up nicely). Decorate with additional candied fruit, if desired.
Serves 6 to 8.

Janine Johnson—Orlando, Florida

202

Thelma Lou's Chocolate Meringue Birthday Pie

Sweet as can be.

¾ cup sugar
3 tablespoons cornstarch
½ teaspoon salt
2½ cups milk
2 squares semisweet melted chocolate

3 egg yolks
1 tablespoon vanilla extract
1 9-inch pie shell, baked
3 egg whites
¼ cup sugar

Combine sugar, cornstarch, and salt with milk. Add melted chocolate. Cook in a double boiler over hot water or low heat until slightly thickened (about 20 minutes).

Beat egg yolks. Add small amount of first mixture. Add egg yolk mixture to first mixture, stirring constantly. When thick, remove from heat (about 5 minutes). Add vanilla and pour into pie shell. Let cool. Beat egg whites with ¼ cup sugar until stiff enough to hold peaks. Place meringue on cooled pie and brown in a 325° oven for about 15 minutes.

When I was a very little girl, my grandmother made this for me on my birthday, because I liked it better than cake.

Serves 6 to 8.

Betty Lynn—Cast member

Darling Baby Chess Pies

Hard to match.

3 ounces cream cheese, softened
1 stick butter, softened
1 cup flour
1 egg

¾ cup light brown sugar
Dash of salt
1 teaspoon vanilla extract
⅔ cup broken pecan pieces

For shells, let cream cheese and butter soften; then mix. Stir in flour and let chill for 1 hour. Shape into 1-inch balls. Place balls in mini muffin pans or tins, spreading them out to form small, pie-like shells.

Beat remaining ingredients, except pecan pieces. Put a teaspoonful of filling into each pie shell. Sprinkle pecans over each pie shell. Bake for 25 minutes at 325°

Makes 24 baby pies.

Betsy Mebane—Chapel Hill, North Carolina

NICE CASTING

As Andy's high-school sweetheart, Sharon DeSpain in "Class Reunion" (Episode #82), Peggy McCay made quite a splash in her one appearance in the little pond of Mayberry. Beyond Mayberry, Peggy has performed in countless episodes for TV and was awarded an OBIE for her performance as Sonya in Chekhov's *Uncle Vanya*. She is the only actress to receive nominations for both a daytime Emmy (for her role as Caroline Brady on *Days of Our Lives*) and a prime-time Emmy (which she won for a guest appearance on *The Trials of Rosie O'Neil*) in the same season (1991).

CLASS COUPLE—Andy visits with high-school sweetheart Sharon DeSpain.

Sharon's Easy Cherry Cobbler Dessert

Hometown favorite.

¼ cup margarine, shortening, or
    vegetable oil
¾ cup all-purpose flour (if self-rising,
    omit baking powder and salt)
½ cup sugar
1 teaspoon baking powder

¼ teaspoon salt
¼ teaspoon almond extract
½ cup milk
2 cups (20-ounce can) prepared cherry
    pie filling

Melt margarine in an 8-inch or 9-inch round pie pan. In a mixing bowl, combine remaining ingredients, except pie filling. Mix until smooth. Pour over margarine, but do not mix. Spoon pie filling over top. Bake at 350° for 35 to 40 minutes, or until cake springs back when touched lightly in center. Serve warm or cool.

Makes 6 servings.

Peggy McCay—Cast member

Doug Darling's Makes-Its-Own-Crust Coconut Pie

Great dessert after a meal of his white beans!

4 eggs
1¾ cups sugar
½ cup flour
¼ cup melted margarine

2 cups milk
1½ cups coconut
1 teaspoon vanilla extract

Combine ingredients in order and mix well. Pour mixture into a greased 10-inch pie pan or 2 small pans. Bake in a 350° oven for 45 minutes or until golden brown. The middle will appear rather soft. The pie should have a delicate crust on top, sides, and bottom. Cool before serving.

Makes 8 servings.

Doug Dillard—Cast member

GOING THE LONG WAY AROUND—
Shy Miss Rosemary delivers a pie to Andy and Barney.

Best for Last Strawberry Pie

Our berry best to you.

1 cup sugar
6 teaspoons cornstarch
Dash of salt
1 cup water

4 tablespoons strawberry gelatin
1 quart fresh, ripe strawberries
1 pie shell, baked
Whipped cream

Combine sugar, cornstarch, and salt. Add water and cook until clear. Add gelatin; stir well until dissolved and cool. Add strawberries. Pour into cooled, baked pie shell. Refrigerate until serving. Top with whipped cream.

Serves 6 to 8.

Mary Jane and David Allan—Birmingham, Alabama

Food for thought:

ANDY: Did you hear that Aunt Bee? What do you think of a boy who get. all A's?

AUNT BEE: I know. Isn't it wonderful?

OPIE: I fooled you didn't I? You thought there were going to be some black marks there, but I fooled you didn't I?

ANDY: You sure did, you little buzzard. Am I ever proud of you. Aunt Bee, what are we gonna do to reward a boy like this?

AUNT BEE: I baked him a special pie.

ANDY: You did?

AUNT BEE: Uh-huh, his favorite—butterscotch pecan.

ANDY: Mmm, mmm.

OPIE: A whole pie just for me?

ANDY: Why not?

AUNT BEE: Well, your head's so full, we might as well fill your tummy to balance you.

ANDY: That's right. Fill up your tummy. Anybody who gets all A's ought to have a little tum-tum full of pie-pie-pie.

Happy eater!

Puddings

Goober's Banana Pudding
Have a Pyle!

¾ cup sugar
2 tablespoons cornstarch
Pinch salt
2 cups milk
4 egg yolks, beaten

1 teaspoon vanilla extract
1 cup fresh whipped cream
Vanilla wafers
5 ripe bananas, sliced

Mix first 3 ingredients in a double boiler. Slowly add milk and cook, covered, over boiling water without stirring for 9 minutes. Uncover and cook for 9 more minutes. Add egg yolks and stir while cooking for 2 more minutes. Cool; then add vanilla. Fold in whipped cream. Line a casserole dish with vanilla wafers. Fill with alternating layers of pudding and bananas. Begin and end with pudding.
    Serves 6 to 8.

George Lindsey—Cast member

Floyd and Al's Banana Pudding
Onvictscay erehay.

2 small boxes instant vanilla pudding
2 cups cold milk
1 cup sour cream

8 ounces nondairy whipped topping
Vanilla wafers
2 to 5 bananas

Mix pudding in milk. Add sour cream. Add whipped topping. Mix with a spoon. Line bottom and sides of a 9x13-inch glass dish with vanilla wafers. Pour half of pudding mix over wafers. Slice bananas and place over pudding mixture. Put remaining pudding mixture on top of bananas. (For those who wish to remain "light" on their feet, low-fat ingredients may be used.)
    Serves 12.

Audrey and Phil Lee—Wake Forest, North Carolina

Mary Grace's Bread Pudding

She's Thelma Lou's cousin—need we say more?

2 cups milk
⅔ cup sugar
4 tablespoons butter
½ cup chopped dates
½ cup chopped dry apricots
　(any dried fruit can be substituted)
2 eggs, beaten
½ teaspoon salt

1 teaspoon vanilla extract
4 cups dry bread, cubed (French bread
　is best)
1 teaspoon cinnamon
1 teaspoon nutmeg
⅛ teaspoon allspice
Whipped cream, optional

Scald milk and add sugar, butter, and fruits. Cool slightly; then add beaten eggs, salt, and vanilla. Butter an 8x10-inch glass baking dish and line with bread cubes (about 1 inch square). Put spices on top of bread. Pour warm liquid mixture over bread. Stir to moisten. Bake at 350° for about an hour. Cover while baking. Serve warm while pudding is still puffy. Can add whipped cream.

　　Serves 6 to 8.

Mary Grace Canfield—Cast member

SHE'S NICE—Mary Grace

Oliver Gossage's Date Nut Pudding

A favorite at Mrs. Wiley's.

2 cups brown sugar, divided	1 cup chopped dates
2½ cups water	1 cup chopped nuts
2 tablespoons butter	1 teaspoon vanilla extract
½ cup milk	Whipped cream
1¼ cup biscuit mix, such as Bisquick	

Mix 1 cup brown sugar, water, and butter in a saucepan. Boil for 5 minutes and pour into an 8x8x2-inch pan.

Mix 1 cup brown sugar, milk, biscuit mix, dates, nuts, and vanilla in a bowl. Spoon batter on top of first mixture. Bake for 45 minutes in a 350° oven. Serve warm with whipped cream.

This recipe was given to me by my good friend Mae Chesney in Knoxville.

Serves 8 to 10.

Martha Jean Bundy—Bristol, Tennessee

Persimmon Pudding Pyle

Perfect.

2 cups persimmon pulp	½ teaspoon baking soda
2 eggs	½ teaspoon salt
3 cups milk	¼ teaspoon cinnamon
1½ cups sugar	¼ teaspoon nutmeg
2 cups flour	3 tablespoons melted oleo

Mix pulp, eggs, and milk. In another bowl, stir sugar, flour, baking soda, salt, cinnamon, and nutmeg. Add pulp mixture to flour mixture. Then add melted oleo. Bake in a greased 13x9x2-inch pan at 300° for 1 hour.

Serves 12.

Kim and Marvin Miller—Terre Haute, Indiana

GRACE IS HER MIDDLE NAME

As Thelma Lou's nice cousin Mary Grace Gossage, actress Mary Grace Canfield caught the eye of Gomer in "A Date for Gomer" (Episode #105). Mary Grace (the actress, that is) went on to play the hilarious role of Ralph, one of the Monroe Brothers on *Green Acres*.

Plane to Mexico Flan de Queso (Spanish Custard Dessert)

Everyone agrees it's great.

¾ cup sugar (to make caramel)
½ cup and 1 teaspoon sugar
8 ounces cream cheese
1 13-ounce can condensed milk
1 cup fresh milk

4 large eggs
¼ teaspoon salt
1 teaspoon vanilla extract
1 teaspoon lemon extract

To make the caramel, melt ¾ cup sugar over low heat, mixing constantly. Pour caramel into bottom of a round baking dish quickly before caramel hardens.

Mix ½ cup and 1 teaspoon sugar with cream cheese until well blended. Add rest of ingredients and blend well. Pour mix into caramel dish. Bake in a warm water bath for 1½ hours at 350°. Chill in refrigerator for 1 hour after removing from oven.

Serves 8 to 10.

Maria and Don Teague—Lexington, North Carolina

Opie's Banana Split Dessert

Fantastic!

¼ cup sugar
⅓ cup melted butter
1¼ cups graham cracker crumbs
6 bananas
16 ounces cream cheese
2 cups confectioners' sugar
1 teaspoon vanilla extract

1 20-ounce can crushed pineapple with
    heavy syrup
⅓ cup milk
16 ounces nondairy whipped topping
Chocolate syrup
½ cup chopped nuts
Maraschino cherries

To make crust, mix sugar, butter, and crumbs and press firmly in bottom of 9x13-inch dish. Do not bake. Set aside while making filling.

For filling, drain pineapple (save juice); cut bananas in half lengthwise. Soak bananas in pineapple juice. In a medium bowl, mix cream cheese, confectioners' sugar, milk, and vanilla until smooth. Pour over graham cracker crust. Put pineapple over mixture; place bananas cut side down over pineapple.

For topping, spread whipped topping over top. Drizzle with chocolate syrup, nuts, and cherries.

Serves 12.

Judy Vierra—Jacksonville, Illinois

Smooth operator

Sarah's Steamed Cranberry Pudding
Receives lots of calls.

1½ cups flour
1 teaspoon baking powder
¼ teaspoon salt
½ cup molasses
⅓ cup warm water (can use hot water
   and melt shortening in it)
2 tablespoons shortening, melted
2 teaspoons baking soda

⅔ cup canned cranberry sauce, drained
   (may use 2 cups cranberries cut in half)
Sauce:
1 cup sugar
½ cup cream
¼ cup butter
1 teaspoon vanilla extract

Stir together first 3 ingredients; mix molasses, water, shortening, and soda. Combine and fold in cranberry sauce. Pour into a greased, lidded mold and steam for 1 hour and 15 minutes. (Put waxed paper between dough and lid of mold. The container holding water should also be covered. Water should surround pudding mold about ¾ of the way up sides of mold.) Unmold pudding and serve with sauce.

For sauce, heat sugar and cream (don't boil); remove from heat and add butter in small chunks so that they melt. Add vanilla.

Serves 6 to 8.

Dee Boquist—Minneapolis, Minnesota

THE WRITE WAY—Harvey Bullock and Andy Griffith review a script.

Very Last Minute Chocolate Mousse

A wink, a blink, and a nod—and it's done!

½ cup hazelnuts
12 ounces semisweet chocolate chips
1 ounce unsweetened chocolate
4 tablespoons milk

1 cup light cream
4 egg yolks
Dash of salt

Grind hazelnuts to powder in a blender. Add semisweet chocolate chips, unsweetened chocolate, and milk. Heat light cream until a skin forms on top. Pour into blender and blend until racket stops. Add egg yolks and salt. Blend again; then chill for an hour.

Serves 6.

Betty and Harvey Bullock—Writer

214

Mayberry Hotel Pistachio Pudding
Masterful.

9 ounces nondairy whipped topping
1 package pistachio pudding
1 cup miniature marshmallows
1 cup chopped pecans
1 large can pineapple chunks

Mix all ingredients. Use part of the pineapple juice to make it moist. Pour in a mold and refrigerate.

Serves 4 to 6.

Teri Cannon—Old Hickory, Tennessee

John Danby's Rice Custard Pudding
Much more interesting than U.S. Steel.

2 cups cooked rice (about 1 cup uncooked)
½ cup sugar
¼ teaspoon salt
1½ cups milk
2 well-beaten eggs
⅓ cup raisins
1 teaspoon vanilla extract
Cinnamon
Nutmeg

Combine all ingredients, except spices, and pour into a buttered casserole dish. Sprinkle top with cinnamon. Add a dash of nutmeg. Bake in a 350° oven for about 50 minutes or until a knife inserted in center comes out clean.

Serves 4 to 6.

Mabel R. Austin and the family of
Brad (Joe Bolleter) Olson—Cast member

WRITE ON!

Legendary writer Harvey Bullock penned some of the all-time classic episodes of *The Andy Griffith Show*. Beginning with "Opie's Hobo Friend" (Episode #40) and "The Pickle Story" (Episode #43), he went on to write such favorites as "Jailbreak" (Episode #50) and "Wedding Bells for Aunt Bee" (Episode #58). He developed an especially good touch with episodes centering around Opie, such as "Mr. McBeevee" (Episode #66, written with Ray Saffian Allen), and one of the most often cited episodes of the entire series, "Opie the Birdman" (Episode #101). Ironically, one of Harvey's recent hobbies has been building birdhouses, some of which he donated as a fundraiser for victims of Hurricane Andrew.

Among Harvey's many other best-loved episodes are "The Haunted House" (Episode #98), "Barney and the Cave Rescue" (Episode #109), and all episodes featuring popular visitor Malcolm Merriweather (Bernard Fox). Harvey also teamed with Everett Greenbaum, another Mayberry writing legend, on the script for *Return to Mayberry* in 1986.

Otis's Bananas Foster Rum Pudding

Yummy rummy tummy.

3½ tablespoons all-purpose flour
1⅓ cups sugar
Dash of salt
3 egg yolks
3 cups milk
1 teaspoon vanilla extract
½ cup butter or margarine
½ cup firmly packed brown sugar
1 teaspoon ground cinnamon

6 bananas, split and quartered
2 tablespoons Crème de Banane (banana liqueur) or 2 tablespoons banana extract
½ cup light rum
1 12-ounce package vanilla wafers
1 cup whipping cream
⅓ cup sifted confectioners' sugar
2 tablespoons rum

Combine flour, sugar, and salt in a heavy saucepan. Beat egg yolks; combine egg yolks and milk, mixing well. Stir in dry ingredients; cook over medium heat, stirring constantly until smooth and thickened. Remove from heat. Stir in vanilla.

Melt butter in a large skillet; add brown sugar and cinnamon. Cook over medium heat until mixture is bubbly. Add bananas; heat for 2 to 3 minutes, basting constantly with syrup. Stir in banana extract or liqueur. Put rum in a small saucepan and heat. Remove from heat, ignite with a long match, and pour over bananas. Baste bananas with sauce until flames die down.

Beat whipping cream until foamy; gradually add confectioners' sugar until soft peaks form. Beat in rum.

Layer ⅓ of wafers in a 3-quart baking dish. Cover wafers with ⅓ of banana mixture. Pour ⅓ of custard over bananas. Repeat layers twice. Cover with whipped cream.

Serves 8.

Maureen Arthur and Aaron Ruben—Writer, producer, and director

Dr. Harrison Everett Breen
of New York City Rice Pudding

New York City?!

2 large eggs
2½ cups milk
2 cups rice, cooked
1 cup sugar

2 tablespoons margarine, melted
1 teaspoon vanilla extract
½ cup raisins

Mix all ingredients. Bake in a buttered pan for 40 minutes at 350°.
Serves 6 to 8.

Toni and Neal Brower—Lewisville, North Carolina

WINNER'S CIRCLE—*While working undercover to investigate illegal off-track betting in Mayberry, Barney pauses behind the scenes with producer Aaron Ruben.*

IN GOOD HANDS

In addition to being producer for the first five seasons of *The Andy Griffith Show*, Aaron Ruben also wrote several episodes and directed "Gomer Pyle, U.S.M.C." (Episode #107), which was the pilot for the series by the same name. Aaron was executive producer (with Sheldon Leonard) and line producer of the *Gomer Pyle* series, and he later served as producer for hit shows such as *Sanford and Son* and *Too Close for Comfort*.

Men Are Orbiting the Earth Brownie Pudding

Out of this world!

1 cup sifted flour
¾ cup sugar
2 tablespoons cocoa
2 teaspoons baking powder
½ teaspoon salt
½ cup milk
2 tablespoons salad oil or melted
   shortening

1 teaspoon vanilla extract
¾ to 1 cup chopped walnuts or pecans
¾ cup brown sugar
¼ cup cocoa
1¾ cups hot water
Ice cream or nondairy whipped topping

Stir together first 5 ingredients. Add milk, salad oil, and vanilla. Mix until smooth. Stir in nuts. Pour into a greased 8x8x2-inch pan. Mix brown sugar and cocoa. Sprinkle over batter. Pour hot water over all. Bake at 350° for about 45 minutes. Serve warm or chilled with ice cream or whipped topping.

Mary Ellis—Albuquerque, New Mexico

NOT OUT TO LAUNCH—Men may be orbiting the
earth, but Andy is happy to stay in Mayberry.

218

Mrs. Pendleton's Persimmon Pudding

Approved by the school board.

2 cups persimmon pulp
1½ cups sugar
3 eggs
1½ cups flour
1 teaspoon baking soda
1 teaspoon baking powder
½ teaspoon salt

1 teaspoon cinnamon
¼ teaspoon cloves
¼ teaspoon allspice
2 cups milk
½ cup butter, melted
2 teaspoons vanilla extract

Mix persimmon, sugar, eggs, and flour with baking soda, baking powder, salt, and spices. Use an electric mixer to stir in milk and melted butter. Add vanilla. Put mixture in a greased baking dish and bake at 325° for a little more than an hour, depending on depth of pan.
Serves 8 to 10.

Esquire Club Lemon-Pineapple Chiffon Pudding

Well, they don't have Baked Alaska every night.

1 box lemon pie and pudding mix
   (not instant)
1 8-ounce can crushed pineapple

2 egg whites
Maraschino cherries or seasonal berries

Prepare pie and pudding mix according to package directions. Place in a bowl and cool. Add crushed pineapple. Beat egg whites until stiff (add sugar if desired) and fold into pudding. Put into parfait glasses and top with maraschino cherries or seasonal berries.
Serves 4.

Renée Austin Bolleter and the family of
Brad (Joe Bolleter) Olson—Cast member

GOOBER'S INCREDIBLE INEDIBLES QUIZ

1. Mrs. Foster on Elm Street makes what dish that tastes like wallpaper paste?
Answer: Chicken à la king

2. Who makes hoot owl pie?
Answer: The Darling boys (but they aren't talking)

3. Who in Mayberry makes meatballs that are described as being ninety-nine percent bread crumbs?
Answer: Lillian (last name withheld)

LISTEN TO THIS STORY ABOUT A MAN NAMED PAUL

Paul Henning is best known among most fans of TV as the creator of such classic sitcoms as *The Beverly Hillbillies*, *Green Acres*, and *Petticoat Junction*. But Mayberry also benefitted from his genius in one episode. He wrote "Crime-free Mayberry" (Episode #41), which includes examples of his knack for writing hilarious lyrics (supposedly written by Barney): "The Ballad of Andy and Barney (or the Gangster's Mistake)" and "Oh, My Darin' Barney Fife."

Tom Strongbow's Baked Indian Pudding
How good!

½ cup yellow cornmeal
4 cups hot milk
½ cup maple syrup
¼ cup light molasses
2 eggs, slightly beaten
2 tablespoons butter or margarine, melted

⅓ cup brown sugar, packed
1 teaspoon salt
¼ teaspoon cinnamon
¾ teaspoon ginger
½ cup cold milk
Vanilla ice cream or light cream

In top of a double boiler, slowly stir cornmeal into hot milk. Cook over boiling water, stirring occasionally for 20 minutes. Preheat the oven to 300°. Lightly grease a 2-quart round baking dish. (I use a soufflé dish.) In a small bowl, combine remaining ingredients, except cold milk. Stir into cornmeal mixture; mix well. Turn into prepared casserole. Pour cold milk on top without stirring. Bake, uncovered, for 2 hours or until just set, but quivery on top. Do not overbake. Let stand for 30 minutes before serving. Serve warm with vanilla ice cream or light cream.
    Serves 6 to 8.

Ruth (Mrs. Paul) Henning—Writer

Summit Meeting Advokaat (Brandy Custard)
A true leader.

12 egg yolks
12 level teaspoons sugar

½ cup brandy

Break egg yolks in top of a large double boiler. Add sugar. Beat with egg beater until light lemon colored and thoroughly blended. Add brandy. Beat thoroughly again. Place boiling water in lower part of a double boiler. Cook egg yolk mixture in double boiler for about 5 minutes or until it begins to thicken. While cooking, be sure to beat constantly. Do not allow to boil. Remove from stove immediately at first sign of bubbling. Cool. Place in refrigerator. Serve hot or cold in sherbet or parfait glasses.

Makes 12 servings.

Marie Faulkner—Greensboro, North Carolina

Dean Darling's Favorite Bread Pudding
He'd rather eat this than talk.

5 cups soft bread crumbs
3 cups scalded milk
½ cup margarine, melted
1 cup sugar
3 eggs, beaten
½ cup raisins (plumped by soaking in
   1 cup of boiling water)

¼ teaspoon salt
1½ teaspoons cinnamon
½ teaspoon nutmeg
½ teaspoon cloves
½ teaspoon vanilla extract
½ cup chopped nuts

Preheat the oven to 325°. Combine crumbs and milk in a large bowl. Mix until crumbs are thoroughly soaked. Add remaining ingredients. Mix well. Spoon into a greased 2-quart baking dish. Bake for 1½ hours or until a knife inserted in center comes out clean. Bread pudding will be firm. Refrigerate leftovers.

Serves 6.

Sandy and Dean Webb—Cast member

Banker's Baked Custard
Makes a good statement.

3 eggs
4 tablespoons sugar
¼ teaspoon salt

½ teaspoon vanilla extract
1⅔ cups milk
Nutmeg

Beat eggs lightly in 1½-quart casserole dish. Mix in sugar, salt, and vanilla, stirring well. Measure milk into a 1-quart measure. Microwave for 3 to 4 minutes on high power, or until about to boil. Stir gradually into egg mixture. Sprinkle with nutmeg. Place in an 8x8-inch baking dish. Pour 1 cup very hot water into baking dish. Microwave for 9 minutes (on #6 power), or until custard is almost set. Custard will become firm as it cools. Serve chilled.

Serves 6.

Margie and Norris Mode—Clarksville, Indiana

Spot the Goober

Andy's Petunia Pot de Crème
Giant hit!

3 large egg yolks
⅓ cup sugar
Pinch of salt
1¼ cups milk

6 ounces semisweet chocolate, chopped
1 teaspoon vanilla extract or 1
    tablespoon Kahlua

Whisk yolks, sugar, and salt in a medium bowl and blend. Heat milk in a heavy, medium saucepan over medium heat until bubbles form around sides. Whisk milk with egg mixture slowly. Return to saucepan and stir over medium-low heat until thickened (about 3 minutes). Do not boil. Remove from heat and add chopped chocolate and vanilla. Whisk until melted and smooth. Pour into 4 custard or demitasse cups. Cover tightly.
    Makes 4 servings.

Nancy Clark—Greensboro, North Carolina

222

Otis is just horsing around, but Barney has a cow!

Thelma Lou

TRIVIA SNACK: The three names Cousin Bradford considered using to market Aunt Bee's strawberry ice cream are: Bee's Homemade Ice Creams, Mayberry Pride Ice Creams, and Bradford International Ice Creams.

Refrigerator Treats

Aunt Bee's Homemade
Strawberry Ice Cream
Loved around the world.

6 cups sliced strawberries, fresh or frozen   ½ teaspoon vanilla extract
2 cups sugar, divided   ½ teaspoon almond extract
3 cups light cream   ⅛ teaspoon salt
3 cups heavy cream

Sprinkle strawberries with half the sugar. Mix creams and remaining sugar, extracts, and salt. Freeze until partially frozen. Stir in sugared fruit and continue to freeze.

Thelma Lou could use this recipe with peaches instead of strawberries, and it would turn out just peachy.

Makes 1 gallon.

Patsy Caldwell—Charlotte, Tennessee

Aunt Bee's cousin may be a handful, but he still can't get his fill of her homemade ice cream:

COUSIN BRADFORD: Strawberry, my favorite. Mmm, mmm. Bee, this is delicious.

AUNT BEE: Thank you. I made it myself.

COUSIN BRADFORD: Homemade, oh. I haven't had that in years.

GOOBER: Aunt Bee makes the best.

ANDY: First prize at the county fair.

COUSIN BRADFORD: Really? Well, I can believe that. You know something, I've been all over the world and this is by far the best I've ever tasted.

AUNT BEE: Well, it's just an old family recipe.

Ed's Refrigeration Fruit Ice Cream

You'll have no beef from anybody about this one.

Juice of 3 oranges
Juice of 3 lemons
3 bananas, chopped
2 pints strawberries, fresh or frozen
2 cups sugar

2 cups milk
4 eggs, beaten
½ pint whipping cream
1 pint half-and-half

Combine all ingredients, slightly crushing the strawberries. Mix well and freeze in a gallon ice cream freezer.
   Makes about 1 gallon.

Patsy Caldwell—Charlotte, Tennessee

Mr. Schwamp's Chocolate Ice Cream

Gets nods of approval.

8 ounces chocolate syrup
1 can sweetened condensed milk
1 pint whipping cream

½ gallon chocolate milk
Whole milk

Combine first 4 ingredients and pour into a freezer can. Add whole milk to fill line. Use hand crank or electric freezer to make this cool, tasty treat.
   Makes about 1 gallon.

Donny Whitehead—Greenwood, Mississippi

Deputy Fice Ice Cream Sandwich Dessert

Delicious—any way you spell it.

12 or more ice cream sandwiches
2 teaspoons almond extract (or to taste)
9 to 12 ounces nondairy whipped topping

1 package slivered almonds, sliced
1 small can coconut, flaked or shredded

Layer a 13x9-inch pan with ice cream sandwiches. Add almond extract to whipped topping. Spread a layer of whipped topping over sandwiches. Repeat with another layer of sandwiches. Spread remaining whipped topping over sandwiches. On a cookie sheet, spread almonds and coconut in 2 stacks. Preheat the oven to 325°. When coconut and almonds begin to brown, stir. Remove when completely brown. Spread coconut first, then almonds. Freeze.
   Makes about 2 dozen squares.

Jodie and Jack Ginn—Decatur, Georgia

It's a Fun Day Fresh Peach Ice Cream

Thelma Lou knows this goes great with brownies.

3 eggs, separated
1½ cups sugar
1 can sweetened condensed milk
1 large can evaporated milk

1½ teaspoons vanilla extract
4 cups fresh peaches, diced
Whole milk

Mix egg yolks and sugar and beat well. Add sweetened condensed milk and evaporated milk. Beat egg whites until stiff and then fold into milk mixture.

Add vanilla extract and peaches. Pour into freezer and fill ¾ full with whole milk. Freeze and eat until you pop.

Makes about 1 gallon.

Linda Stewart—Dallas, Texas

Not being one "to get some ice cream for later,"
Goober enjoys some ice cream for now!

After the Sunday offering, Barney needs to borrow from Andy:

BARNEY: Can you lend me fifty cents? I promised Thelma Lou I'd pick up a Sunday paper and then get her a couple of frozen Sunny Jim Bars.

SUNDAE AFTERNOON—Arnold enjoys one of Opie's special ice cream creations.

Dr. Bailey's Homemade Orange Sherbet

Aunt Bee reminds you to brush after all meals and snacks.

1 large can crushed pineapple   2 liters orange soda
1 can sweetened condensed milk

Mix pineapple with milk. Pour into an ice cream container. Fill with orange soda. Prepare according to ice cream maker manufacturer's instructions.

Makes about ¾ gallon.

Sheldon Golomb—Cast member

Well, what do you expect for just 35 cents?

ARNOLD: More syrup.
    OPIE: That's all we give.
ARNOLD: But I'm your friend.
    OPIE: Look, Arnold. I can't give every friend who comes in here more than he's supposed to get. Now we want your business, Arnold, but this stuff costs money. How is it?
ARNOLD: Not bad. You make a pretty good banana split for a kid.
    OPIE: Thanks.

They're going to spoil the boy:

AUNT BEE: Well, I think I'll get the ice cream freezer.

ANDY: Oh, yeah. We wanna make some ice cream.

AUNT BEE: Come on, Barney. Give me a hand.

RON BAILEY: You can buy it at the store. What do you want to make it for?

ANDY: Haven't you ever eaten any homemade ice cream?

RON BAILEY: No.

BARNEY: Well, you're in for a treat.

Inspector Upchurch's Ice Cream Churn
The Big Freeze.

Vanilla:
5 eggs
3 cups sugar

1 can evaporated milk
2 to 3 tablespoons vanilla flavoring
Whole milk

Beat eggs until light and fluffy. Add sugar and beat well. Add evaporated milk and vanilla flavoring. Add regular milk to fill line on freezer. Ready to freeze.

Chocolate:
1 cup cocoa
3 cups sugar, divided

1 cup milk
5 eggs
Whole milk

Combine cocoa, 1 cup sugar, and milk. Bring to boil and cook for about 3 minutes to make syrup. Beat eggs with 2 cups sugar. Add syrup. Add milk to fill line, as in Vanilla recipe. Freeze.

Strawberry or Other Fruit:
3 cups sugar, divided
Mashed fruit (as much as you want)

5 eggs
Whole milk

Add 1 cup sugar to mashed fruit. Set aside while you beat eggs with 2 cups sugar. Add fruit and milk, as in Vanilla recipe. Freeze.

Makes about 1 gallon.

Marie Fields—Summerfield, North Carolina

EXTRACTION FROM MAYBERRY

Who would have thought that Sheldon Golomb, who played Opie's pal Arnold Bailey (son of a Mayberry doctor), would grow up to be a doctor? But he did. He's a dentist. So he means business when he says brush and floss after eating all these delicious desserts!

Peggy's Chocolate Nut Crunch
Nice and rich.

2 cups vanilla wafer crumbs
1 cup chopped nuts
1 cup butter
2 cups sugar

6 eggs, separated
3 squares unsweetened chocolate, melted
1 teaspoon vanilla extract
Whipped cream

Combine vanilla wafer crumbs with chopped nuts. Line bottom of a 9x13-inch pan with half the crumbs. Thoroughly cream butter and sugar. Add well-beaten egg yolks. Add chocolate and vanilla. Mix well. Fold in stiffly beaten egg whites. Pour over cookie crumbs. Top with remaining crumbs. Chill overnight. Top with whipped cream.

Makes about 2 dozen squares.

Peggy Seil—Scottsdale, Arizona

Bannertown Banana Brittle Dessert
Quite a find.

2 bananas
¾ cup crushed peanut brittle

1 teaspoon vanilla extract
1 cup whipped cream

Slice bananas thin. Fold bananas, peanut brittle, and vanilla into whipped cream. Spoon into 4 sherbet dishes. Chill for 1 hour. Top with more crushed peanut brittle and serve.

Makes 4 servings.

Helen Robinson—Jacksonville, Illinois

Coconut Macaroon Dessert
You'll be hank-hankering for more.

1 package Nabisco macaroons, rolled
1 cup English walnuts, finely chopped

3 envelopes Dream Whip (prepare
    according to package directions)
3 pints frozen sherbet (assorted flavors)

Fold cookies and nuts into Dream Whip. Put half of mixture in a 9x15-inch pan. Drop frozen sherbets (lime, orange, and raspberry or any sherbet of your choice) by the teaspoonful. Mix colors. Top with remaining Dream Whip mixture. Freeze.

Makes about 3 dozen squares.

Alvy Moore—Cast member

Favorite teacher

Old Lady Crump's Butterscotch Ice Cream Crunch Squares

Great discovery!

1 cup sifted flour
¼ cup quick-cook oatmeal
¼ cup brown sugar
½ cup butter

½ cup chopped nuts
1 12-ounce jar butterscotch or
    caramel sauce
1 quart chocolate or coffee ice cream

Combine flour, oatmeal, and sugar. Cut in butter until crumbly. Stir in nuts. Put mixture in a 9x13x2-inch baking pan. Bake at 400° for 15 minutes. Watch carefully. Stir while still warm to crumble. Cool. Spread half the crumbs in a 9x9x2-inch pan. Drizzle about half the ice cream topping over crumbs in pan. Stir ice cream to soften. Spoon carefully into pan. Drizzle with remaining topping. Sprinkle with remaining crumbs. Freeze.
   Makes 8 servings.

Ann Clark—Charlotte, North Carolina

Mayor's Chocolate Ribbon Delight

Ribbon-cutting treat.

1 cup flour
1 stick margarine, softened
1 cup pecans, finely chopped
8 ounces cream cheese, softened
1 cup confectioners' sugar

1 cup nondairy whipped topping, plus
   additional for layering
1 box instant chocolate pudding mix
2 cups milk
Grated chocolate or chopped nuts
   for topping

For first layer, mix flour, margarine, and pecans and spread over bottom of a baking dish. Bake for 20 minutes at 350°. Cool. (May use graham crackers instead of flour.)

For second layer, cream cream cheese, confectioners' sugar, and whipped topping. Spread over first layer.

For third layer, beat pudding mix and milk thoroughly and spread over second layer.

Finally, spread whipped topping over third layer. Sprinkle grated chocolate or finely chopped nuts on top and refrigerate.

Makes about 2 dozen squares.

Marie Fields—Summerfield, North Carolina

Mayor Stoner

Cousin Bradford just can't say enough about Aunt Bee's ice cream:

COUSIN BRADFORD: Well, it's your ice cream, Bee. It has a magic quality, a quality that could cause a major readjustment in the ice cream industry.

AUNT BEE: Oh, I knew you liked it.

COUSIN BRADFORD: Liked it. Liked it. My dear, why it's ambrosia!

Barney's Deadly Game Dessert
Quick and cool.

2 small boxes French vanilla instant pudding
3 cups evaporated milk

9 ounces nondairy whipped topping
Graham Crackers
1 can chocolate fudge frosting

Mix pudding with milk. Fold in whipped topping. Line a 9x13-inch pan with whole graham crackers. Spoon half of pudding mixture on top. Add another layer of graham crackers, then rest of pudding, and top with graham crackers. Frost with chocolate fudge frosting and refrigerate overnight.

Makes about 2 dozen squares.

Zoe Bass—Greensboro, North Carolina

Opie's First Date Dessert
You'll develop a crush.

12 Hydrox cookies, crushed
1 8-ounce package (1 cup) dates, cut into pieces
¾ cup water
¼ teaspoon salt

2 cups miniature marshmallows or 16 regular size
½ cup chopped walnuts
1 cup whipping cream
½ teaspoon vanilla extract

Reserve ¼ cup cookie crumbs. Spread the rest in a 10x6x1½-inch baking dish. Combine dates, water, and salt in a saucepan and bring to a boil. Reduce heat and simmer for 3 minutes. Remove from heat and add marshmallows and stir until they are melted. Cool to room temperature. Stir in chopped nuts. Spread date mixture over crumbs. Whip cream and add vanilla. Swirl over dates. Sprinkle with rest of crumbs. Chill overnight. Cut into squares.

Serves 8.

Dee Boquist—Minneapolis, Minnesota

Mavis Neff's Ambrosia
Snuggly-wuggly good!

1 small jar maraschino cherries
1 can pineapple
1 can mandarin orange segments

1 small container light sour cream
1 cup small marshmallows
1 cup shredded coconut

Cut cherries and pineapple in small pieces and mix with remaining ingredients. Chill in refrigerator until cold. This is a delightful dessert that can be served with breakfast, lunch, or dinner.
Serves 6 to 8.

Elaine Joyce—Cast member

Bookie Barber's Chocolate Icebox Dessert
They'll race for this one.

1 stick butter, softened
¾ cup sugar
4 egg yolks
1 1-ounce square bitter chocolate, melted
1 teaspoon vanilla extract
¾ cup pecans, coarsely chopped

16 2½-inch-in-diameter almond
    macaroons, crumbled
18 double ladyfingers
4 egg whites, beaten
1 pint whipping cream
3 tablespoons sugar

Cream butter and sugar; add egg yolks 1 at a time, beating well after each addition. Stir in melted chocolate, vanilla, pecans, half of macaroon crumbs, and 2 crumbled ladyfingers. Fold in beaten egg whites. Pour mixture into a shallow bowl lined with 16 ladyfingers; sprinkle with remaining macaroon crumbs. Whip cream with sugar; spread over all, leaving tips of ladyfingers exposed. Cover with waxed paper and refrigerate overnight.
Serves 8.

Mrs. James Parrish—Paris, Kentucky

Trivial Trivialities Amaretto Trifle
No time to discuss it—it's terrific.

1 devil's food cake mix
½ cup Amaretto (or less to taste)
6 Heath or Skor bars, crumbled

1 small can Hershey syrup
16 ounces nondairy whipped topping
1 small jar maraschino cherries, optional

Bake cake according to package directions in a 9x13-inch pan. When cool, punch holes in cake with a toothpick or fork. Pour Amaretto evenly over top of cake. Cover with foil and refrigerate overnight. Cut cake into 1-inch squares. Make 3 layers in a trifle bowl: ⅓ of cake pieces, 2 crushed candy bars, ⅓ can of syrup, ⅓ of whipped topping. Continue to layer ingredients. Top may be garnished to taste, possibly with cake crumbs or candy bar crumbs, along with any remaining syrup. A cherry or creative cherry design adds a colorful touch.

Serves 16.

Margaret Clark—Birmingham, Alabama

Mayberry flirt Mavis Neff

THE DATING GAME

Andy Taylor flirts with trouble when he tries to make Helen jealous by dating Mavis Neff, played by Elaine Joyce, in "Helen the Authoress" (Episode #213). Elaine was also a regular on *The Don Knotts Show* in the early 1970s, among numerous other television shows.

Part-time work for Floyd

Floyd's English Trifle

A family favorite that's a cut above.

1 thinly sliced jelly roll
½ cup sherry
1 large can fruit cocktail, drained
1 large box flavored gelatin (any flavor)
1 package custard mix (vanilla pudding
   may be substituted)

Whipped cream
Sprinkles
Sliced bananas, optional

Line a deep, glass bowl with jelly roll. Pour sherry over to moisten. Drain fruit cocktail, reserving juice for gelatin. Spread fruit evenly over jelly roll. Make gelatin according to package directions, using juice from fruit in place of cold water. Pour over fruit. Let set in refrigerator. Mix custard according to package directions. Pour over set gelatin. Refrigerate. Spread whipped cream over custard. Decorate with sprinkles. Sliced bananas may be added between custard and whipped cream.

Serves 8.

Sue and Kit McNear—Family of cast member Howard McNear

Mary Scobey's Milk and Cookies

Sink your sweet tooth into this.

1 bag small chocolate chip cookies
Milk as needed

8 ounces nondairy whipped topping

Soak cookies in milk and spread a layer in a glass dish. (A deep dish with several layers is best.) Spread a layer of whipped topping over cookies, continuing to layer cookies and whipped topping, ending with whipped topping on top.
Serves 6 to 8.

Wanda C. Fields—Reidsville, North Carolina

Mr. Schwamp's Frozen Fruit Salad

Hard to top.

1 cup sliced bananas
1 cup crushed pineapple, drained
1 cup miniature marshmallows
6 large maraschino cherries, chopped

¼ cup mayonnaise
8 ounces nondairy whipped topping
½ cup walnuts, chopped finely

Mix all ingredients and pour into a loaf pan. Freeze. When frozen, remove from pan and wrap in aluminum foil. Keep in freezer until ready to use.
Serves 6 to 8.

Mary Lock—Stephens City, Virginia

Philosophical Meanderings Dessert

During our lifetime we travel many roads.

12 ice cream sandwiches
½ cup Kahlua

8 ounces nondairy whipped topping
Slivered almonds

Fit ice cream sandwiches into a 9x13-inch glass dish tightly. Sprinkle Kahlua over. Cover with whipped topping. Cover. Put in the freezer for at least 4 hours (overnight is best). When ready to serve, cut into squares and sprinkle with almonds.
Makes about 2 dozen squares.

Mrs. A. C. Rhodes—Greensboro, North Carolina

Newton's Orange Pineapple Skinner Parfait

You don't even have to be as "ept" as Newton to succeed with this.

1 20-ounce can crushed pineapple
2 tablespoons sugar
1 large or 2 small boxes orange gelatin

2 cups buttermilk
8 ounces nondairy whipped topping
Chopped nuts

Bring pineapple and sugar to a boil. Pour in gelatin and mix. Cool; then add buttermilk and whipped topping. Spoon into parfait glasses and sprinkle nuts on top.
Serves 6 to 8.

Sara Brower—Asheboro, North Carolina

Opie's Blocks

Oh, go ahead—play with your food.

3 3-ounce boxes gelatin, any flavor
3 envelopes unflavored gelatin

4 cups boiling water

Mix gelatins. Pour boiling water into mixture. Stir until dissolved. Pour into two 8x8-inch glass pans and refrigerate until firm. Cut into squares (blocks). Aunt Bee says it's O.K. to eat these with your fingers.
Serves 6 to 8.

Polly and Andy Andrews—Gulf Shores, Alabama

Floyd's Shaving Cream and Cherry Yum-Yum

Not too cherry, no waiting.

1 stick butter or margarine, melted
2 sleeves graham crackers, crushed
12 ounces nondairy whipped topping
½ cup milk

8 ounces cream cheese
½ cup sugar
1 large can cherry pie filling

Mix butter with graham cracker crumbs. Whip whipped topping and milk. Whip cream cheese and sugar. Combine whipped mixtures. In a 2-quart glass dish, place half the crumb mixture, then half the whipped mixture, then all the cherry pie filling, and the rest of the whipped mixture. Top with remaining crumb mixture. Refrigerate.
Serves 10 to 12.

Mrs. Russell Hiatt, Floyd's City Barber Shop—Mount Airy, North Carolina

Baby-Makes-Three Fruit Sherbet

We don't like to brag, but it's good.

3 small ripe bananas
Juice of 3 oranges
Juice of 3 lemons

2 cups sugar
2 cups water

Peel and mash bananas. Add juices. Add sugar and water and stir until sugar is dissolved. Pour into a refrigerator tray and freeze. While freezing, stir every 20 minutes until mushy and the consistency of sherbet. This process takes about 2 hours.
Serves 4.

Stella Hamel—Tulsa, Oklahoma

Web-Footed, Red-Crested Lake Loon Dessert

A leader.

½ pound each purple, blue, and green
    seedless grapes
1 20-ounce can pineapple tidbits
1 11-ounce can mandarin oranges
1 10-ounce jar maraschino cherries

3 apples, unpeeled
Lemon juice
¼ pound walnuts
2 bananas
8 ounces nondairy whipped topping

Combine in a large bowl: halved grapes, removing any small seeds; drained pineapple tidbits; mandarin oranges; and halved cherries. Core and dice unpeeled apples, sprinkling with lemon juice to preserve color. Chop walnuts and slice bananas and mix thoroughly with other ingredients. Serve at once in parfait glasses topped with whipped topping.
Serves 8 to 10.

Shirley Phillips Friel—Angola, Indiana

MAYBERRY TAKE-OUT QUIZ

1. What is the special at the Diner on Fridays?
   Answer: Catfish casserole

2. When Opie played Robin Hood, what food from Aunt Bee did he take to "give to the poor"?
   Answer: Apple pie

3. What did Andy's fortune cookie from Aunt Bee's Canton Palace say?
   Answer: "Try to avoid temptation in the coming week."

STRING TIME

The Country Boys (l-r after Andy Griffith in the photograph on this page: Roland White, Eric White, Clarence White, Billy Ray Lathum, and LeRoy McNees) appeared in two episodes of *The Andy Griffith Show*: "Mayberry on Record" (Episode #19, a scene pictured here) and "Quiet Sam" (Episode #29). Mandolinist Roland White currently performs with the award-winning Nashville Bluegrass Band, and dobroist LeRoy McNees, performs with the California-based Born Again Bluegrass Band.

Andy and the Country Boys put Mayberry on record.

Strawberry Fixer-Upper

*This English dessert is simply the best thing I have ever tasted.
Of course, my sweet wife Jan is from Brighton, England,
so maybe that is a slight advantage.*

1 box yellow or white cake mix
1 6-ounce box vanilla pudding
¼ cup strawberry jam
½ cup sherry, optional
1 16-ounce package frozen strawberry
   halves, thawed, reserving any syrup

1 box ladyfingers
1 cup chilled whipped cream
¼ cup sugar
¼ cup toasted slivered almonds
Fresh strawberries

Bake cake in a 13x9x2-inch pan according to package directions and let cool. Prepare pudding according to package directions. (Do not let it set up prior to use.) Cut cake in half and spread with jam. Cut remaining cake into 8 pieces and split each piece horizontally. Arrange half of the pieces in a 2-quart glass serving bowl. Pour half the sherry on the cake, and then pour half the strawberries and their syrup over the cake. Line bowl with ladyfingers and pour 1 cup of pudding over this. Repeat with remaining cake, sherry, strawberries, and pudding. Cover and chill for at least 4 hours. Beat cream and sugar until stiff. Spread over trifle and sprinkle with almonds and fresh strawberries.

Makes about 2 dozen squares.

LeRoy McNees—Cast member

Country Boys' Fresh Fruit Compote

A certified hit.

1 banana
Several large ripe strawberries
A handful of red or white seedless
   grapes, halved
½ cup chopped fresh walnuts or
   ¼ cup sunflower seeds

1 ripe pear or apple
¼ cup raisins
1 tablespoon orange blossom honey
Juice of ¼ to ½ lemon or lime
   (must be fresh)

Cut fruits and nuts into bite-sized pieces. In a large serving bowl, add fruits and nuts to honey and juice. Mix gently and serve immediately. Eat the compote right away.

Serves 2 or 3.

Roland White—Cast member

Falcon Keeper's Fresh Fruit Trifle

It soars.

Whipped cream
Pineapple cubes
Blueberries
Black raspberry purée
Sponge cake

⅓ cup sugar
¾ cup water
3 tablespoons dark rum
Whipped cream
Fresh fruit

In a glass bowl, arrange in this order: layers of lightly sweetened whipped cream, fresh pineapple cubes, fresh (or frozen) blueberries, black raspberry purée, ¾-inch slices sponge cake lightly soaked in dark rum syrup. Repeat layers. Top trifle with whipped cream and garnish with fresh fruit.

For the dark rum syrup, combine sugar and water in a saucepan. Heat until sugar dissolves. Remove syrup from heat and stir in dark rum.

Serves 6 to 8.

Bernard Fox—Cast member

FAVORITE PUNCH—Malcolm works up a thirst.

Scoop Fife's Cup of Java Sundae

Pickups and splashes.

½ cup strong coffee (can add Kahlua or
  Tia Maria)
¼ cup plus 2 tablespoons firmly packed
  brown sugar

1 teaspoon cinnamon
8½ ounces semisweet chocolate, chopped
3 pints coffee ice cream
¾ cup Heath Bar bits

Combine first 3 ingredients in a heavy saucepan. Simmer until sugar dissolves. Remove from heat and add chocolate. Stir until smooth. Pour sauce over ice cream and sprinkle with toffee bits.

Makes 10 servings.

Nancy Clark—Greensboro, North Carolina

Bee sweet

243

MAYBERRY SON—*Andy and Barney can't believe the gossip Opie has printed in his* Mayberry Sun *newspaper.*

Episode Menu

Here are thumbnail summaries of all 249 episodes of *The Andy Griffith Show* (the first 159 were filmed in black and white and the last 90 are in color). Use this checklist to select an appropriate episode to watch while enjoying a favorite dessert

First Season

1. **The New Housekeeper:** Opie learns to love Aunt Bee when she arrives to care for Andy and him.
2. **The Manhunt:** Andy uses horse sense to help the state police nab an escaped convict.
3. **The Guitar Player:** Andy assists local guitar player Jim Lindsey in joining a band.
4. **Runaway Kid:** Opie befriends a runaway boy and won't tell Andy where the boy is from.
5. **Opie's Charity:** Andy is disappointed that Opie is being stingy with his allowance.
6. **Ellie Comes to Town:** A new pharmacist arrives and won't put up with an elderly hypochondriac.
7. **Irresistible Andy:** Andy gets the wrong idea that Ellie has matrimony in mind.
8. **A Feud is a Feud:** Two farmers won't allow their children to wed in peace due to a long-running feud.
9. **Andy the Matchmaker:** Andy helps build Barney's courage for asking out Miss Rosemary by concocting a bogus case for Barney to solve.
10. **Stranger in Town:** A newcomer to Mayberry somehow knows everything about everybody.
11. **The Christmas Story:** Skinflint Ben Weaver learns the true meaning of Christmas.
12. **Ellie for Council:** Local menfolk are distressed when a woman runs for public office.
13. **Mayberry Goes Hollywood:** A film producer decides to shoot his movie in Mayberry.
14. **The Horse Trader:** Andy shoots himself in the foot when he sells the old town cannon under false pretenses.
15. **Those Gossipin' Men:** A shoe salesman has a banner day when the men of Mayberry get the notion he is a talent scout.

EPISODE MENU

16. **Andy Saves Barney's Morale:** Barney puts half of Mayberry in jail for minor offenses.
17. **Alcohol and Old Lace:** Two elderly sisters find that their flower business grows better with moonshine.
18. **Andy the Marriage Counselor:** Andy brings civility into the marriage of a bickering couple.
19. **Mayberry on Record:** The local musical talent is uncovered by a record producer.
20. **The Beauty Contest:** Andy must select Mayberry's most beautiful woman.
21. **Andy and the Gentleman Crook:** A charming prisoner cons everybody in town except for Andy.
22. **Cyrano Andy:** Thelma Lou uses Andy to make Barney jealous.
23. **Andy and Opie, Housekeepers:** While Aunt Bee is away, Andy and Opie prove to be sloppy housekeepers.
24. **The New Doctor:** Andy believes that Ellie is enamored with the new doctor in town.
25. **A Plaque for Mayberry:** One lucky Mayberrian appears to be descended from a Revolutionary War hero.
26. **The Inspector:** A state official is stunned by how out-of-date Andy's police methods appear to be.
27. **Ellie Saves a Female:** Andy and Barney help Ellie transform a farmer's daughter into a lovely young lady against her father's wishes.
28. **Andy Forecloses:** Andy evicts a young family from one of Ben Weaver's rental houses.
29. **Quiet Sam:** Barney suspects that a shy farmer is hiding something sinister.
30. **Barney Gets His Man:** An escaped con vows to return to Mayberry and even his score with Barney.
31. **The Guitar Player Returns:** Guitar player Jim Lindsey returns to town after leaving Bobby Fleet's Band with a Beat.
32. **Bringing Up Opie:** Opie looks for other places to play when Aunt Bee won't allow him to hang around the courthouse.

Second Season

33. **Barney's Replacement:** Barney is worried when Mayberry gets a lawyer as a second deputy.
34. **Opie and the Bully:** A bully steals Opie's milk money, and Opie must decide whether to fight.
35. **Andy and the Woman Speeder:** A woman speeder butters up everyone in Mayberry except Andy.
36. **Barney on the Rebound:** Barney is tricked into proposing to a pretty newcomer and gets stuck with a lawsuit.
37. **The Perfect Female:** Andy sizes up Thelma Lou's cousin as a mate, but then she shoots him down.
38. **Aunt Bee's Brief Encounter:** Aunt Bee is squired by a handyman who turns out to be a loafer.

246

39. **Mayberry Goes Bankrupt:** Town leaders find out that Mayberry owes thousands of dollars to an elderly man whom the town was trying to evict from his house.

40. **Opie's Hobo Friend:** Opie picks a friendly but lazy drifter as a role model.

41. **Crime-free Mayberry:** The FBI salutes Mayberry's low crime rate, but the agents prove to be crooks.

42. **The Clubmen:** The Esquire Club takes a close look at Andy and Barney as potential members.

43. **The Pickle Story:** Andy, Opie, and Barney try to figure what to do when Aunt Bee makes her horrible-tasting pickles.

44. **Sheriff Barney:** When Barney is offered a job in another town, Andy gives Barney a taste of what it's like being sheriff .

45. **The Farmer Takes a Wife:** A farmer wants Thelma Lou to become his bride.

46. **The Keeper of the Flame:** Opie and his pals begin a secret club and meet in a barn that later catches on fire.

47. **Bailey's Bad Boy:** A spoiled young man is jailed by Andy for reckless driving and vows revenge through his rich father's influence.

48. **The Manicurist:** When Floyd hires a beautiful manicurist, the men don't know what to make of it, and the ladies of Mayberry spit nails.

49. **The Jinx:** Nothing but bad luck follows a seemingly jinxed Mayberrian.

50. **Jailbreak:** Barney lets a crook escape and then he and Andy must track down the con and his accomplice.

51. **A Medal for Opie:** Barney coaches Opie for a foot race.

52. **Barney and the Choir:** Barney seeks a position in the town choir.

53. **Guest of Honor:** A pickpocket is given the key to the city of Mayberry, but he wants more.

54. **The Merchant of Mayberry:** Ben Weaver worries about competition from a meek door-to-door salesman.

55. **Aunt Bee the Warden:** Aunt Bee puts Otis through the grinder at her home prison.

56. **The County Nurse:** A nurse needs Andy's help to give burly farmer Rafe Hollister a shot in the arm.

57. **Andy and Barney in the Big City:** Barney tries to crack a jewel theft in a Raleigh hotel.

58. **Wedding Bells for Aunt Bee:** Aunt Bee takes on a laundryman as a suitor in order to make Andy feel he has more opportunity to find a wife.

59. **Three's a Crowd:** Barney won't give Andy and the county nurse any time alone.

60. **The Bookie Barber:** Floyd hires a barber—not knowing that the man is a bookie needing a front.

61. **Andy on Trial:** A publisher seeks revenge on Andy by having a female reporter uncover his laxness as a lawman.

62. **Cousin Virgil:** Barney's inept cousin pays a visit to Mayberry.

63. **Deputy Otis:** Otis plays deputy when his brother comes to town.

Everybody's ready to go fishing, but Miss Peggy eventually worms her way out of it.

Third Season

64. **Opie's Rival:** Opie is envious of the time his father spends with a nurse and tries to gum up the romance.
65. **Andy and Opie—Bachelors:** Nurse Peggy attends to Andy and Opie while Aunt Bee is out of town, and Andy believes she is after him as a husband.
66. **Mr. McBeevee:** Andy has difficulty believing Opie's tales about an imaginary friend in the woods.
67. **Andy's Rich Girlfriend:** Andy is not comfortable dating Peggy after he finds she is from a wealthy family.
68. **Barney Mends a Broken Heart:** When Andy and Peggy have a quarrel, Barney introduces Andy to a "fun girl" from Mt. Pilot.
69. **Andy and the New Mayor:** Mayor Stoner checks closely on Andy's attention to a prisoner.
70. **The Cow Thief:** A rash of cattle thefts causes the mayor to bring in a state lawman to help Andy and Barney.
71. **Floyd, the Gay Deceiver:** When his lonely hearts club pen pal decides to visit, Floyd frets about having given her the wrong idea about how wealthy he is.
72. **The Mayberry Band:** Andy tricks the mayor into believing the town band really can perform well.
73. **Lawman Barney:** Barney has a tough time getting two roadside salesmen to respond to his law enforcement.
74. **Convicts-at-Large:** A trio of female prison escapees holds Barney and Floyd hostage in a cabin.

The appeal of Mayberry

75. **The Bed Jacket:** Andy uses his beloved fishing pole to reel in the perfect birthday gift for Aunt Bee.

76. **Barney and the Governor:** Barney gives a ticket to the governor, while Otis spikes the courthouse water jug.

77. **Man in a Hurry:** A businessman learns how to appreciate small-town life when his car breaks down on a Sunday.

78. **The Bank Job:** Barney tries to beef up security at the bank by showing how easy it would be to knock it off.

79. **One-Punch Opie:** A new kid in town is a bad influence on the other boys until Opie faces up to him.

80. **High Noon in Mayberry:** Andy worrries whether an ex-convict seeks to even the score, but Barney takes control.

81. **The Loaded Goat:** Andy and Barney deal with a goat that has consumed dynamite.

82. **Class Reunion:** Andy has high hopes that his high school sweetheart will show for the class reunion.

83. **Rafe Hollister Sings:** Rugged farmer Rafe Hollister competes in the Mayberry singing contest.

84. **Opie and the Spoiled Kid:** A pampered boy gives Opie lessons on temper tantrums.

85. **The Great Filling Station Robbery:** Someone is stealing from Wally's garage, and Andy can't believe it's the young man everyone else suspects.

86. **Andy Discovers America:** After a skirmish with the new schoolteacher, Andy tries to get Opie and his pals interested in their history lessons.

87. **Aunt Bee's Medicine Man:** A traveling medicine man enchants Aunt Bee with his smooth talk and elixir.

88. **The Darlings Are Coming:** A mountain family comes to town, and Charlene Darling flips over Andy.

89. **Andy's English Valet:** An Englishman pays off a fine by working at Andy's house.
90. **Barney's First Car:** Barney buys a clunker from an elderly woman crook.
91. **The Rivals:** Barney becomes jealous when Thelma Lou spends some extra time with a lovesick Opie.
92. **A Wife for Andy:** Barney tries to fix Andy up with a wife.
93. **Dogs, Dogs, Dogs:** A pack of dogs trails Opie to the courthouse, and Barney decides they must be returned to the wild.
94. **Mountain Wedding:** Ernest T. Bass wants to court Charlene Darling, even after she has wed Dud Wash.
95. **The Big House:** Two prisoners escape while Barney lectures them about life at "the rock."

Fourth Season

96. **Briscoe Declares for Aunt Bee:** Briscoe Darling woos Aunt Bee, much to her consternation.
97. **Gomer the House Guest:** Gomer moves in with the Taylors after losing his job at Wally's.
98. **The Haunted House:** Andy, Barney, and Gomer explore the Remshaw House.
99. **Ernest T. Bass Joins the Army:** Ernest T. wants to be in the Army so he can get a uniform.
100. **Sermon for Today:** Mayberry gears up for a band concert but everybody becomes exhausted in the process.
101. **Opie the Birdman:** Opie kills a mother bird and must raise her three orphans.
102. **A Black Day for Mayberry:** All of Mayberry gets excited about a secret gold shipment coming through town.
103. **Opie's Ill-Gotten Gain:** Opie receives a straight-A report card but then discovers it was a mistake.
104. **Up in Barney's Room:** Mrs. Mendelbright boots Barney out of his apartment after she catches him cooking in his room.
105. **A Date for Gomer:** Andy and Barney set Gomer up with Thelma Lou's nice cousin, Mary Grace.
106. **Citizen's Arrest:** Gomer charges Barney with making an illegal U-turn and chaos ensues.
107. **Gomer Pyle, U.S.M.C.:** Andy accompanies Gomer to boot camp after the naïve mechanic joins the Marines.
108. **Opie and His Merry Men:** A lazy hobo encourages Opie and his friends to be modern-day Robin Hoods on his behalf.
109. **Barney and the Cave Rescue:** Barney leads a rescue effort after Andy and Helen are trapped in Lost Lovers Cave.
110. **Andy and Opie's Pal:** Andy pays special attention to a fatherless boy, and Opie becomes envious.
111. **Aunt Bee the Crusader:** Aunt Bee and other ladies oppose Andy's having to evict a farmer.

112. **Barney's Sidecar:** Barney purchases a motorcycle with a sidecar for the sheriff's department.
113. **My Fair Ernest T. Bass:** Ernest T. Bass enters the world of polite society.
114. **Prisoner of Love:** A beautiful thief turns the heads of Andy and Barney as she bides her time in jail.
115. **Hot Rod Otis:** Andy and Barney are worried after Otis buys a car.
116. **The Song Festers:** Barney is to be featured vocalist in the town choir until Gomer enters the picture.
117. **The Shoplifters:** Weaver's Department Store is hit with a rash of thefts, which sends Barney into action.
118. **Andy's Vacation:** Andy aims to relax in the hills, but Barney lets a prisoner get away.
119. **Andy Saves Gomer:** Gomer floods Andy with favors after Andy saves his life.
120. **Bargain Day:** Aunt Bee buys a load of beef, only to have her freezer call it quits.
121. **Divorce, Mountain Style:** Charlene Darling leaves Dud and the mountains and comes looking for Andy.
122. **A Deal is a Deal:** Opie and his schoolmates get sick of peddling Miracle Salve but Barney has a solution.
123. **Fun Girls:** Helen and Thelma Lou become jealous when they spy Andy and Barney with the fun girls from Mt. Pilot.
124. **The Return of Malcolm Merriweather:** Malcolm returns to the Taylor house and causes Aunt Bee to believe that Andy and Opie can get along without her.
125. **The Rumor:** Barney jumps to conclusions and has everyone believing that Andy and Helen are eloping.
126. **Barney and Thelma Lou, Phfftt:** After Thelma Lou discovers that Barney takes her for granted, she uses Gomer to make him jealous.
127. **Back to Nature:** Barney and Gomer get lost from Andy and some youngsters during a camping expedition.

Fifth Season

128. **Barney's Bloodhound:** Barney believes a mutt will help Andy and him with their work.
129. **Family Visit:** Relatives come to stay with the Taylors.
130. **Aunt Bee's Romance:** Andy fears Aunt Bee's irritating new boyfriend might win her hand.
131. **Barney's Physical:** Barney is required to gain height and weight to remain a lawman.
132. **Opie Loves Helen:** Opie has a crush on Miss Crump.
133. **The Education of Ernest T. Bass:** Andy and Helen help Ernest T. earn his diploma.
134. **Man in the Middle:** Andy's own romance with Helen becames endangered when he tries to help Barney and Thelma Lou make up.
135. **Barney's Uniform:** Barney won't be caught out of uniform because he's afraid of a tough guy.

136. **Opie's Fortune:** Opie discovers a billfold with fifty dollars in it.
137. **Good-bye, Sheriff Taylor:** Andy decides to take a new job, and Barney becomes sheriff for the day.
138. **The Pageant:** Aunt Bee wins the role of Lady Mayberry in the town play.
139. **The Darling Baby:** The Darlings return to Mayberry searching for a boy to match up with Charlene's baby girl.
140. **Andy and Helen Have Their Day:** Barney keeps interrupting Andy and Helen while they try to enjoy a quiet picnic at the lake.
141. **Otis Sues the County:** When Otis slips and falls at the courthouse, a lawyer talks him into bringing a suit against the county.
142. **Three Wishes for Opie:** Count Istvan Teleky grants Opie wishes that seem to come true.
143. **Barney Fife, Realtor:** Barney moonlights as a real estate salesman and plans to put the Taylors in their dream home.
144. **Goober Takes a Car Apart:** Andy is shocked when Goober assembles a car in the courthouse.
145. **The Rehabilitation of Otis:** Barney's method of treating Otis' drinking prompts Otis to leave town.
146. **The Lucky Letter:** Barney fears a chain letter's jinx as he prepares for the firing range.
147. **Goober and the Art of Love:** Barney teaches Goober how to date Lydia.
148. **Barney Runs for Sheriff:** Barney mounts a campaign against Andy in the race for town sheriff.

"Want to hear me do my sen-tence?"

149. **If I Had a Quarter Million:** Barney uses bundles of dough to trap the crook who lost the money.
150. **TV or Not TV:** Crooks pose as TV producers while planning to rob the Mayberry bank.
151. **Guest in the House:** Helen gets jealous after a lovely family friend spends some time at the Taylor home.
152. **The Case of the Punch in the Nose:** Barney stirs up an old grudge between Floyd and Charlie Foley.
153. **Opie's Newspaper:** Opie's cute little paper is loaded with troublesome town gossip.
154. **Aunt Bee's Invisible Beau:** Aunt Bee wants Andy to believe she is being courted by the butter-and-egg man.
155. **The Arrest of the Fun Girls:** Barney puts the "fun girls" in jail for speeding, and Helen and Thelma Lou are not thrilled.
156. **The Luck of Newton Monroe:** A clumsy traveling salesman tries his hand at several odd jobs for Andy.
157. **Opie Flunks Arithmetic:** Andy bears down on his son after Opie gets a low mark in math.
158. **Opie and the Carnival:** Opie is cheated at the carnival's shooting gallery.
159. **Banjo-Playing Deputy:** Andy tries out a musician as a deputy.

Sixth Season

160. **Aunt Bee, the Swinger:** Aunt Bee and her new beau pick up the pace of their romance.
161. **Opie's Job:** Opie and another kid both seek the same job at the grocery store.
162. **The Bazaar:** Deputy Warren Ferguson nabs Aunt Bee and her friends for running a bingo game.
163. **Andy's Rival:** Andy gets uptight when Helen spends a lot of time working on school business with a man.
164. **Malcolm at the Crossroads:** Ernest T. Bass and Malcolm Merriweather fight for the job as school crossing guard.
165. **Aunt Bee on TV:** Aunt Bee can't quit talking about all the prizes she won on a game show.
166. **Off to Hollywood:** Andy, Aunt Bee, and Opie take a trip to Hollywood.
167. **Taylors in Hollywood:** The Taylors visit the set of *Sheriff Without a Gun*, a film about Andy's career.
168. **Hollywood Party:** Helen becomes jealous when Andy gets a little too close to a Hollywood actress.
169. **A Warning From Warren:** Warren thinks he has extra-sensory perception and makes life rough on Andy and Helen.
170. **A Man's Best Friend:** Opie and his friend trick Goober into believing his dog can talk.
171. **Aunt Bee Takes a Job:** Aunt Bee goes to work at a printing shop, which belongs to counterfeiters.
172. **The Cannon:** Warren uses the town cannon to halt the robbery of the visiting mobile museum.

173. **Girl-Shy:** Warren's sleepwalking surprises Helen.
174. **The Church Organ:** The church needs a new organ but funds are low.
175. **Otis the Artist:** Warren introduces Otis to mosaics as an alternative to drinking.
176. **The Return of Barney Fife:** Barney returns for a class reunion hoping to renew his romance with Thelma Lou.
177. **The Legend of Barney Fife:** Barney and Warren track down a dangerous criminal.
178. **Lost and Found:** Aunt Bee receives an insurance settlement after losing a precious piece of jewelry.
179. **Wyatt Earp Rides Again:** The great-nephew of Wyatt Earp picks a fight with Andy.
180. **Aunt Bee Learns to Drive:** Aunt Bee receives driving lessons from Goober.
181. **Look Paw, I'm Dancing:** Opie is afraid of being embarassed because he doesn't know how to dance.
182. **Eat Your Heart Out:** Goober has a case of unrequited love for a diner waitress.
183. **The Gypsies:** A gypsy family places a curse on Mayberry.
184. **A Baby in the House:** Aunt Bee fears she is losing her touch with babies when a baby girl cries every time Aunt Bee tries to pick her up.
185. **The County Clerk:** Howard Sprague's chance at romance is hampered by his mother.
186. **Goober's Replacement:** Flora is a big hit pumping gas for Wally while Goober is on vacation.
187. **The Foster Lady:** Aunt Bee is selected to represent a furniture polish company in commercials.
188. **The Battle of Mayberry:** Opie discovers the true story of the Battle of Mayberry, which doesn't set well with the town's citizens.
189. **A Singer in Town:** Aunt Bee and Clara write a hit song for a pop singer.

Seventh Season

190. **Opie's Girlfriend:** Opie contends in a battle of the sexes with Helen's niece.
191. **The Barbershop Quartet:** The town's barbershop quartet looks to a chicken thief as a substitute tenor when Howard gets a sore throat.
192. **The Lodge:** Howard is blackballed from joining the town lodge by one person.
193. **The Darling Fortune:** The Darlings believe Helen is meant to become the wife of one of the boys.
194. **Aunt Bee's Crowning Glory:** Aunt Bee wears a wig to impress a visiting preacher.
195. **The Ball Game:** Andy gets in hot water after making a close call at Opie's baseball game.
196. **Goober Makes History:** Goober cultivates a beard along with deep thoughts.
197. **The Senior Play:** Helen directs a controversial senior play which is objectionable to the principal.

198. **Big Fish in a Small Town:** Howard catches Old Sam, the lake's legendary big fish.
199. **Mind Over Matter:** Goober gets a case of hypochondria after being injured in a car accident.
200. **Politics Begins at Home:** Aunt Bee and Howard Sprague both run for the same position on the town council.
201. **A New Doctor in Town:** Mayberrians are reluctant to give their business to a young doctor.
202. **Opie Finds a Baby:** Opie and Arnold secretly care for an infant left on the courthouse steps.
203. **Only a Rose:** Opie accidentally crushes Aunt Bee's prize rose which she had planned to enter in a contest.
204. **Otis the Deputy:** Otis and Howard try to rescue Andy from bank robbers.
205. **Don't Miss a Good Bet:** Mayberrians invest with a stranger who says he knows where a lost treasure is buried.
206. **Dinner at Eight:** Andy is obliged to eat three spaghetti suppers in one night.
207. **Andy's Old Girlfriend:** Helen is jealous when Andy's high school girlfriend moves back to town and joins them on a camping expedition.
208. **The Statue:** The town decides to erect a statue in honor of Seth Taylor before they know all the facts about him.
209. **Aunt Bee's Restaurant:** Aunt Bee opens a Chinese restaurant.
210. **Floyd's Barbershop:** Howard purchases the barbershop property and must raise Floyd's rent.

HAIR APPARENT—
Goober lets his beard do his thinking for him.

255

STRIKING A POSE—Howard Sprague discovers that bowling is right down his alley when he rolls a perfect game for Mayberry's team.

211. **A Visit to Barney:** Andy visits Barney at his new job in Raleigh, and together they bust a robbery ring.
212. **Barney Comes to Mayberry:** An old girlfriend, who is now a movie star, returns to Mayberry the same weekend that Barney does.
213. **Helen, the Authoress:** Helen writes a book for children, and Andy is jealous of her time.
214. **Good-bye Dolly:** Opie tends to a horse, but the animal stops eating.
215. **Opie's Piano Lesson:** Opie is torn between learning to play the piano and quarterbacking the football team.
216. **Howard, the Comedian:** Howard displays his wit on a TV talent show.
217. **Big Brother:** Howard falls for a boy's sister after agreeing to be the boy's Big Brother.
218. **Opie's Most Unforgettable Character:** Opie can't decide whom to write about for an English assignment.
219. **Goober's Contest:** Goober puts on a contest at the filling station, and Floyd appears to be the big cash winner.

Eighth Season

220. **Opie's First Love:** Opie is crushed when his first date cancels in favor of another boy.
221. **Goober the Executive:** Goober buys Wally's garage and deals with the headaches of big business.
222. **Howard's Main Event:** Howard must contend with a bully after he begins dating Millie.
223. **Aunt Bee the Juror:** Aunt Bee is the only member of a jury who believes the defendant to be innocent.
224. **Howard the Bowler:** Howard is on his way to a perfect game, when the electricity fails.

225. **Opie Steps Up in Class:** Opie strikes up a friendship with a rich boy.
226. **Andy's Trip to Raleigh:** Andy weaves a tangled web with Helen after he is surprised to find that his business meeting in Raleigh is with a woman.
227. **A Trip to Mexico:** Contest-winning Aunt Bee takes Clara and Myrtle to Mexico.
228. **The Tape Recorder:** Opie and Arnold learn the location of stolen loot after tape recording a robber's confession in the Mayberry jail.
229. **Opie's Group:** Andy and Aunt Bee resist the idea when Opie joins a rock 'n' roll band.
230. **Aunt Bee and the Lecturer:** A distinguished world traveler falls for Aunt Bee because she resembles his late wife.
231. **Andy's Investment:** Andy operates a laundromat as an investment in Opie's college education.
232. **Suppose Andy Gets Sick:** Goober takes the law into his own hands when Andy gets under the weather.
233. **Howard and Millie:** Howard and Millie decide to wed, then discover how different their interests are.
234. **Aunt Bee's Cousin:** Aunt Bee's cousin is not the successful businessman he pretends to be.
235. **Howard's New Life:** Howard tosses his inhibitions to the wind and moves to a Caribbean island.
236. **Emmett's Brother-in-Law:** Emmett is talked into giving up his fix-it shop for the insurance business.
237. **The Mayberry Chef:** Aunt Bee becomes the star of a cooking show on a Siler City television station.
238. **The Church Benefactors:** A committee must choose between new church robes or foundation repair work on the church.
239. **Opie's Drugstore Job:** Opie accidentally breaks a bottle of expensive perfume while working at the drugstore.
240. **Barney Hosts a Summit Meeting:** Barney guides Russian and American diplomats straight to Andy's house and Aunt Bee's kitchen.
241. **Mayberry R.F.D.:** An Italian family comes to stay at Sam Jones' farmhouse.
242. **Goober Goes to the Auto Show:** Goober tries to impress an old friend in Raleigh.
243. **Aunt Bee's Big Moment:** Aunt Bee decides to take flying lessons.
244. **Helen's Past:** Andy accidentally stumbles across what appears to be a skeleton in Helen's closet.
245. **Emmett's Anniversary:** Emmett considers buying his wife an expensive fur coat for their wedding anniversary.
246. **The Wedding:** Howard changes his home into a bachelor pad after his mom remarries.
247. **Sam for Town Council:** Emmett competes with Sam Jones for the same seat on the city council.
248. **Opie and Mike:** Young Mike develops a case of hero worship over Opie.
249. **A Girl for Goober:** A computer dating service matches Goober with an extremely intelligent woman.

Waiting to hear from friends outside of Mayberry

Watch What You Eat: Slices of Mayberry

Members of *The Andy Griffith Show* Rerun Watchers continue to find inspiration for their chapter names in food-related references from Mayberry. We listed about two dozen of those chapter names in *Aunt Bee's Mayberry Cookbook*, and now there are even more chapters that have chosen names inspired by Mayberry mentions of food and eating:

There's always something cooking in Mayberry. To find out more, write
The Andy Griffith Show Rerun Watchers Club at:

TAGSRWC
9 Music Square South
Suite 146
Nashville, Tennessee 37203-3203

Living the good life

Index

INDEX

INDEX

INDEX

INDEX

269

INDEX

About the National Court Appointed Special Advocate Association

For many of us, Mayberry represents a near-perfect world. It's the kind of place that we would like to call home—a place where our children could grow up carefree while playing with All-American kids like Opie Taylor.

All children deserve a safe, permanent home. Unfortunately, the reality for many youth in America is not so perfect and carefree as Opie's world. Each year, more than 400,000 innocent children become victims of violence, neglect, or other abuse that causes them to have their fates put into the hands of our nation's already overburdened court system.

In 1976, Seattle Judge David W. Soukup recognized that he needed help in making decisions affecting the children whose cases came before his court. Showing a wisdom reminiscent of Mayberry's own Justice of the Peace, Judge Soukup started what would grow to become the National Court Appointed Special Advocate Association, better known as CASA.

Hoping that all kids someday will be able to enjoy a childhood as happy as Opie's, producer Aaron Ruben poses with Ron Howard on the Mayberry set.

"As a judge, I had to make tough decisions," Soukup says. "I had to decide whether to take a child from the only home he's ever known, or leave him someplace where he might possibly be abused. I needed someone who could tell me what was best for that child—from the child's viewpoint. That's what CASA does."

CASA volunteers work on behalf of thousands of children to create an environment that has at least some of the stability and happiness that Opie enjoyed in Mayberry. Appointed by a judge to a case, CASA volunteers conduct thorough research, make a recommendation to the judge on what is best for the child, and stay with the case until a permanent, appropriate resolution is reached. The CASA volunteers become the child's constant watchdog.

The Mayberry connection to the CASA program goes beyond a shared spirit of support for children. Since 1987, *Andy Griffith Show* producer Aaron Ruben has been one of the nearly 40,000 CASA volunteers nationwide. His involvement with CASA is an extension of work he has been doing with children and issues that affect them since 1980.

In a way, too, Aaron has been a part of creating a better world for children throughout his distinguished career in the entertainment business—perhaps most notably through his Mayberry work. It is especially inspiring to see how someone who was instrumental in fostering the wholesomeness of Mayberry is now helping the Mayberry dream come true for the children who need the kind of caring and strength depicted on the show.

"One of the big problems," Aaron points out, "is that most of these children never had a mentor to teach them right from wrong, to help them and nurture them and build their self esteem. Many have gone from home to home, shelter to shelter, and then out on the streets. There's no one they can trust. What we do is provide continuity in their lives."

Aaron offers "Opie the Birdman" as an example of the important mentoring available to Opie but lacking in the lives of many less fortunate kids today. He says, "After Opie kills the birds' mother with his slingshot, Andy tells him, 'You hear that? That's those young birds chirping for their mother that's never coming back. Now, you just listen to that for a while.' Andy does not give Opie a whipping as Opie had fully expected. A whipping would have told Opie that he had done something wrong. But Andy's 'sentencing' Opie to listen to those orphan birds made clear that he had indeed done something wrong. Now, what could he do about it? And so, he becomes 'mother' to the birds, feeding and caring for them until they can be on their own. Thus, Opie brings about his own redemption as he learns a valuable lesson. Andy was the perfect mentor."

And echoing another theme of Mayberry, Aaron says, "The real definition of love is 'being there.' The child can say to himself, 'This is somebody who will always be there for me, to help me and support me.' The whole attitude of Andy and his son—of caring—is so important and is often missing in these children's lives. What CASA offers is somebody to says to these children, 'It's all going to be O.K. There is a future for you. You can do it! You can do it!'"

Through talking with Aaron about his years on *The Andy Griffith Show* and then learning about the work to which he's devoted his time today, one comes away with a deeper understanding of the difficulties faced by many children in our country. Only then, can a person truly appreciate the efforts of thousands of CASA volunteers who are making a difference in those kids' lives.

MENTORING IN MAYBERRY—
Dad's major lesson taught with minor's birds.

Still, as successful as the CASA program is, only about one quarter of the children who need a voice in court now have one. But as Aaron knows firsthand, "One person can make a difference."

If you would like more information about the CASA program in your community (and with more than 600 chapters nationwide, there's likely a group near you), you can call National CASA at 1-800-628-3233 or write: National CASA, 100 West Harrison Street, North Tower, Suite 500, Seattle, WA 98119-4123.

Meanwhile, as you enjoy the Mayberry memories and the many wonderful recipes in this cookbook, you're already helping the CASA cause. A portion of the author royalties from this book is supporting CASA. And a separate donation has been made to CASA in honor of each of the Mayberry actors, writers, and production crew members represented in this book through recipes and/or photographs.

With a little help from CASA, more young lives are having a second chance for a happy future—just like the closing scene in "Opie the Birdman" after Opie has just released the young birds he raised:

OPIE: Cage sure looks awful empty, don't it Pa?
ANDY: Yes, son, it does. But don't the trees seem nice and full.

New meaning for eating like a bird:

OPIE: Pa, pa!
ANDY: Whoa, now. Simmer down there now. You're gonna bust something.
OPIE: Dickie! He's come back. Flew in the cage all by himself.
AUNT BEE: Opie, isn't that wonderful.
ANDY: Yes sir, and I told you he would too. And I bet you that I know why. I bet you that he got out there flying around with some of those wild birds and he saw what kinda poor kinda eating they had. You know, little berries and little seeds, little pieces of roots and stuff like that, and he says to hisself, "I'm going back there to Opie where I can get me some more of that good fried chicken and biscuits and honey and stuff like that." Don't you reckon?
OPIE: I reckon.